For Hummi,
Long Time Dear Friends
and Supporters.
With Fond Regards

GEORGE WORKS!

LAD TO LEADERSHIP

THE MAKING OF A NEW CANADIAN

GEORGE E. DANIELS

George, Tiree, Scotland 1940

1950's McMaster Letter 1954

Broadcast Exec 1983

Flying - COPA for Kids 2016

George and Ruth Daniels and Family - 1988
Front: George, Ruth   Rear: George Andrew, Timothy (Tiff) John, Christopher (Chris) Alexander

Suite 300 - 990 Fort St
Victoria, BC, V8V 3K2
Canada

www.friesenpress.com

First Edition — 2019

Editor: Paul Dulmage

The author has recreated events, locales and conversations from his archives, diaries, published articles and from his eidetic memory. Some names of individuals and places may have been changed, included identifying characteristics and details such as physical properties, occupations or places of residence. No libel is intended.

ISBN
978-1-5255-3773-8 (Hardcover)
978-1-5255-3774-5 (Paperback)
978-1-5255-3775-2 (eBook)

1. Biography & Autobiography, Cultural Heritage

Distributed to the trade by The Ingram Book Company

Foreword by Paul Dulmage

GEORGE WORKS! is a compelling autobiography of a young English immigrant lad who came to Canada and embraced the best of what our country stands for in every facet of his life. He has experienced the wartime horror of The Blitz, personal and professional setbacks, and has responded with what was once called the can-do spirit. Through more than seven decades, he has dedicated himself to his family, his community, his country and his many professions, and in doing so, has been honored by the Canadian and Ontario Governments and many other institutions. His is a life well lived and a story well told.

DEDICATION

I dedicate *George Works!* to my extraordinary, supportive wife Ruth, my three outstanding sons, Andrew, Tiff and Leah, their son Bennett, daughter Darbien, and Christopher. Also, to my siblings and cousins who are part of, and contributed to, my life story.

Themes: Life drivers! Words of wisdom making a major impact on George in his early years, by Peter Drucker, and in his golden years, by Queen Elizabeth and John Glenn.

When asked, in her 90s why she engaged in so many Royal duties, **Elizabeth, the Queen Mother** said: "Work is the rent you pay for life.

John Glenn, 90 years, Astronaut and Senator, when asked by a TV reporter, "To what do you owe your longevity?" replied: "Oh, that's easy; it's all attitude and exercise."

Peter F. Drucker, Management Guru: "Leadership is talent management and building organizations whose cultures embody collaboration, ownership of results and social responsibility."

PROLOGUE
1935

It is the Silver Jubilee of King George V and Queen Mary and celebrated all over the British Empire.

- *Mutiny on The Bounty* with Clark Gable and Charles Laughton wins the Best Picture Academy Award.
- The first radar system to detect aircraft is invented by Sir Robert Watson Watt.
- *Porgy and Bess* opens in New York and *"I've Got Plenty of Nothin'"* and *"It Ain't Necessarily So"* became big hits.
- In Russia, Stalin is starting to purge people who supported Lenin and kills anyone opposed to him, including Army Chiefs of Staff.
- The Great Depression continues.
- Pilot Amelia Earhart becomes a household name.
- In Germany, Hitler and the Nazis repudiate the Versailles Treaty and reintroduce compulsory military service. Furthermore, Hitler enacts laws that make hatred of the Jews legal.
- It's the year that the County of Bedford forms the Air Raid Precautions Department of the Home Office. Later the title becomes Civil Defense.
- Graham Greene's book, *"England Made Me"*, becomes a best seller.
- The Babe Ruth of hockey is Howie Morenz of the Montreal Canadiens.

This is the world that I, George Eaton Daniels, am born into June 23, 1935 in the flat above my parents' Titian Beauty Parlour at 65 Harpur Street, Bedford England. *"You write about yourself to give conclusive evidence that you have lived" --- Anon*

C.C. George Daniels, (Bunty) and children:
George Eaton, Cecil William, Faith (Fay)

- Married Bedford 1934
- Owned hairdressing/beauty salon 65 Harper St. called "Titian"
- George E. born June 23, 1935, Bedford
- Cecil, George and Bunty discontinue business in 1935/36. Cecil George pursues civil engineering, family moves to Elstree
- May 14, 1938 - William Daniels is born in Leyland, Yorkshire.
- 1938/39 - Family moves to the outskirts of Rickmansworth (London suburb) and father CCG starts working for prominent engineering/contractors Robert McAlpine.
- September 1934 - George Eaton has vivid memories of the day WWII was declared. Central London evacuees become billeted at our Rickmansworth house.
- Oct./Nov. 1939 - Cecil George is promoted to engineering superintendent in charge of building a strategic hydro water system near Glasgow. Family moves to Old Kilpatrick.
- Spring of 1940 - The family moves to the Isle of Tiree in the Hebrides of Scotland where Pop Daniels is now in charge of building a Royal Air Force runway and base.
- 1941 - Cecil George enlists in the British Army as a Royal engineer and immediately commissioned as a Second Lieutenant.
- Assigned to General Bernard Montgomery's Staff H.Q. as a First Lieutenant in the 1942 North Africa campaign – always in forefront rebuilding railways, pontoon bridges etc. sabotaged by Germans.
- Wounded at Monte Casino and sent home to recuperate. Returned to war as Military Governor of Bologna in Northern Italy, promoted to Captain (a title which he never used), awarded various medals etc.

1941 - Family moves to Scorton Lancs, near Garstang and the hotel where German Deputy Fuhrer Rudolph Hess was imprisoned.

George E. becomes a Boy Scout and sings in St. Peter's Church of England choir.

July 22, 1942 - Faith (Fay) is born in Preston and father returns home on leave for the event.

1943 - George Eaton sent to Alexander House School in Cheltenham. At the end of the war, school returns to its Broadstairs Kent home.

1946-1947 - Cecil George has difficulty getting UK engineering work, goes by himself to work with Anglo-American Oil Company in Palestine building pipe lines, and just avoids death when King David Hotel is blown up.

Family lives in Whiston outside Liverpool near Bunty's two sisters: Renee (George) Nener (Canon Paul's mother) and Lou (George) Jones. The third sister, Doreen (George, daughter Lindsay) Gibson, lives in Cardiff. Family then moves to Northampton across from Abingdon Park which has been converted to a prisoner-of-war camp.

Early 1947 - Pop Daniels immigrates to Canada and goes to work for the Anglo-American Oil Company in Montreal East.

Dec. 15, 1947 - Bunty and her three children sail from Southampton aboard the RMS Aquitania, the last four-funneled ocean liner and nicknamed "Ship Beautiful", arriving in Halifax Dec. 20,1947. We're now officially landed Canadian immigrants!

It's a two-day train trip to Montreal to join Pop and move into a large rented house in Pointe-aux-Trembles.

And so, our Canadian experiences and adventures begin.

Table of Contents

PART I

In which the author, the son of an Army officer, describes his first 12 years of life as an English schoolboy, experiencing the Blitz, wartime life and post-war preparations to emigrate to Canada.

Part I

English Lad to Canadian Immigrant: Pier 21

It was on September 30, 1938, that British Prime Minister Neville Chamberlain came back from meeting Adolph Hitler in Germany to announce he had achieved, "peace for our time."

In 1939, Winston Churchill continued to warn the British and the rest of the world that Hitler meant war, which began September 1 with the German invasion of Poland. It was also the year my father, Cecil Charles George Daniels, a civil engineer, went to work for one of Britain's prominent engineering contactors, Sir Robert McAlpine.

"This was a company in the forefront of building some of Britain's essential defensive infrastructure."---Canada's Max Aitken, later Lord Beaverbrook.

In late summer of 1939, my father and mother Margaret (Bunty) move our family of four, including 16-month-old brother Bill, to the London suburb of Rickmansworth.

As our moving lorry enters our street, I see large houses with garages. I am told to just stand to one side as Mummy and Daddy work with the men to unload and move in. I cannot stand it. What is behind the garages? They don't see me run off. I am now behind the house. It is smashing. It is a large back yard. I will be able to play lots. Mummy is looking after Bill and Daddy is away at work all the time, so they won't miss me. I am free to roam.

There is a lot of noise at the back of the garden. I now discover that there are workmen and bricklayers building a wall between our new garden and a house behind ours.

I approach with temerity. I notice a ladder on our side. Nobody is using it so I go up gingerly. "Hey lad," is a greeting. I notice tubs with grey goo in them. The men tell me it is concrete mortar. It looks like special sand for mud pies to me. They give me several handfuls and help me back down the ladder to my side of the patch. Ooey, sticky grey hands. Oh what fun. And then, "George where have you been, you look dreadful." Oops. Bath time again.

Several days later we hear loud, wailing noises from far away. I don't know what to make of this sound. Mummy explains that they are Air Raid sirens from the centre of London. And Daddy is away to keep us safe. At four years and two months, the challenges and impact of WWII are starting to enter my life.

Several days later Mummy says we are going to go for a picnic into the woods, which is just down the road. Mummy is pushing brother Bill and the picnic basket in the pram. Mummy spreads out the blanket, gets out the delicious food, and Bill is really good because he is eating everything pushed at him. I wish Daddy were here.

It is now several hours later, setting sun, perfect weather as we stroll home in early September of 1939 to our new home. As we enter our street I see a noisy scene not usual in this quiet neighborhood. In moments we are in the middle of six school buses unloading kids. To me they look like ragamuffins. The children are all running about. Efficient women in uniformed dress with notebooks are trying to keep them in order.

This invasion of humanity is squealing in delight. It is a new adventure for them, amidst relative wealth compared to what they have been used to. Mummy explains that these boys and girls are evacuees from central London, children whose mothers and fathers have agreed with the authorities should not be living in central London, the prime area of attack for Hitler's air force. We are billeting three or four of the evacuees.

I know this is going to be lots of fun. I do not have many friends to play with in Rickmensworth. The new arrivals will be jolly. How wrong I am. Our billets are 8 and 9 years old. I am discovering that they do not want to play with a four-year-old---just my brother. They have taken over my precious scooter and do not let me get a turn at a ride. Now they have broken it. And now I am crying.

Two months later, Father has come home to announce that he is promoted to Superintendent in charge of building a major waterworks plant in Glasgow, Scotland. He will be leaving right away and we are to follow in a week or so.

Mummy now embarks on feverish days of packing for the journey. It's been decided that all the furniture will be put in storage. At our destination, the Daniels family will rent. Essential personal items and clothing are packed in trunks. Shortly we are in the cavernous London Paddington Train Station. It is every boy's delight---a hubbub of new sights and sounds.

Taxis jockeying for curbside positions, newspaper boys blaring headlines, Mummy searching for a porter. She instructs me to stay close because she does not want me to be lost in the crowd. The atmosphere is a mixture of people pushing here and there, barrow boys hawking delightful-smelling pork pies or chestnuts, platform porters with baggage carts piled high aggressively shoving through the crowd to get their customers preferred seats with their luggage stored on the train or in a nearby locker.

The hiss and whistle of train noises are infectious. The trains dominate the station and shunt backwards and forwards. Smoke from the engines drifts up to the Paddington Station cathedral ceiling and descends on passengers like a wet blanket. We are impervious to it. It is like Mr. Jones' smelly farm yard ---another little bit of 'ome. Finally, the train is rumbling off and we are neatly packed into a compartment shared by several others. They do not talk very much.

We arrive in Edinburgh. The train pulls into the landmark Caledonia Station. We are in the middle of the city. Looking up, I can see the big Holyrood Castle perched on what looks like the edge of a cliff.

The Gate of the Year

This poem was written in 1908 by Minnie Louise Haskins, an American lecturer at the London School of Economics, who wrote as a hobby. It was a favourite of Queen Elizabeth, the late Queen Mother, who showed it to her husband King George VI. He included it in his famous Christmas message broadcast in 1939 at the beginning of the Second World War. After the King's death, the Queen Mother had it engraved on bronze plaques on the entrance to the King George VI Memorial Chapel, Windsor, where both are now interred. It was also read at the funeral service of the Queen Mother.

I said to the man who stood at the gate of the year
'Give me a light that I may tread safely into the unknown.'
And he replied, 'Go into the darkness and put your hand into the hand of God.
That shall be to you better than light and safer than a known way!
May that Almighty Hand guide and uphold us all.

So I went forth and finding the Hand of God
Trod gladly into the night
He led me towards the hills
And the breaking of day in the lone east.

So heart be still!
What need our human life to know
If God hath comprehension?
In all the dizzy strife of things
Both high and low,
God hideth his intention.

Edinburgh Scotland: The early 1940 WWII Years

Further to my father meeting us at the Caledonia Railway Station in Edinburgh, we travel 200 miles in Pop's car to Old Kilpatrick, a suburb of Glasgow. My father has found us a unique rental house in the middle of Old Kilpatrick. Our home is a two-bedroom flatiron building in the centre "V" of Station Road and Dumbarton Road junctions.

Our wedge-shaped narrow house is on a special corner located in that part of the road which separates into two streets diverging on each side of our house.

Today, my father is away at work and Mummy tells Bill and me that there is going to be a parade after lunch. Apparently, soldiers are going off to the war.

It's a damp, rainy day. We were going to go outside and join the large crowds lining the streets; however, Mummy decides on a better rain-free view---in our bathroom. Our WC (water closet) is on the pointed corner of our house facing the incoming street; at the exact point that the roads separate around our house (Bill is having his afternoon sleep). Mummy and I take up positions to view the soldiers. I'm standing on the toilet with Mummy holding me as we both expectantly peer out our window. The crowds in front of us have umbrellas to ward off the drizzle. Everyone is expectant. And then out of the mist, I hear the skirl of the bagpipes and the first view of the pipe band. They are advancing towards us. We can hear a buzz in the crowd. Now the pipe band is coming closer, led by a tall, striking man waving a big stick. Mummy explains he is the Regimental Drum Major. She says he's the leader and conductor. The leader's stick is a ceremonial Mace, a massive staff surmounted with a crown.

The music of the pipes is stirring. The tartan-kilted pipers are so colourful in their woolen checkered red, green and black skirts and leather pouches Mummy says are called Sporrans. They are so close; we seem to be in almost the middle of the band.

The thump, thump, thump of the drums and shrilling whine of the pipes is exciting music. And the very colourful Scottish uniforms made the soldiers look oh so grand. I like this stirring scene. Little did I know that this first experience of respect, awe and affection for the Military would stay with me always. This day, standing on a toilet with my mother holding me and watching this spectacular parade I know will be an experience I will remember all my life.

It seems only a few weeks later and my father's firm sends him to the island of Tiree in the Scottish Hebrides.

The Hebrides is a large group of islands in the Irish Sea off the west coast of Scotland. Tiree, my father's new place of work, is one of the small outer islands. Pop has been sent there to be the Chief Engineer for a new airport runway for the Royal Air Force. (I would come to understand later that this location for an RAF base was chosen, like various others in Scotland, as a secure place out of the way from regular Luftwaffe patrols.

Shortly, Mummy tells Bill and me that we will be joining my father on Tiree. Apparently we will be getting on a special big ship from a west-coast Scottish port called Oban, several hundred miles from Old Kilpatrick. Daddy arranges a special company car to take us with piles of luggage and stuff via Loch Lomond and the Ben Cruachan Mountain.

The Oban to Tiree Ferry Adventure (early Spring 1940)

Oban is significant for its Roman Coliseum lookalike on top of the large hills which surround the harbor called McCaig's Folly (a wartime make-work project). Daddy has completed work on the Oban airfield and comes to meet us. We are going by ship to the Isle of Tiree. It is situated in the Outer Hebrides past the famous Isles of Skye and Mull. Daddy has rented a nice house and garden where he is the chief engineer building another important RAF runway for the defense of Britain.

The weather is raw and rainy, the port is bustling with the noise of various traffic; lorries, cars, carts and masses of people jostling their way to either of two large ships. Mummy says they are called ferries. The morning we sail is a typical Scottish mist and foggy day. Damp and chilly to the skin. Mummy is really confined to our cabin with brother Bill while Daddy and I explore the ship in spite of a howling wind and giant waves. These ferries are painted black with red smoke stacks and have the name of an island painted on them, such as the SS Mull or Skye.

I am intrigued by the big door on the back of the ferry. It is open and a ramp lets cars drive into the belly of the ship. People are boarding from a gangway. Daddy is here to meet us. After warm hugs of welcome, my parents arrange tickets and paper for our boarding. I know we are special or so I think because most people are seated or congregate in a large lounge. But we have a small room called a cabin to ourselves.

With toot of whistles, shouts of sailors handling docking lines, the clang-clang-change of engines, our ferry slowly weaves away from the wharf and into rough seas.

All the while Daddy is showing Bill and me this exciting activity from the ship's railing, Mummy, needing a rest, stays in our cabin.

Wide-eyed and thrilled at all the sailors, winches, smoke from the stack and the general hubbub, it was exciting to be on a new adventure. At one moment Daddy and I separated. I found my way up to the bridge.

The Captain invited me into the coziness of the storm-tossed ship that was making many seasick.

The ferry proceeds through the sounds of music to the Port of Tobermory on the north part of the Isle of Mull. In spite of the rainstorm, the seas are quieter in this sheltered sea lane.

By now I have got to know one of the ship's officers who shows me around the ferry. As we leave Tobermory, he takes me to see the Captain in the wheelhouse where they steer the ship. What a view! We are high above the deck and can see miles without any interruptions. The seas are getting rough now. The ferry is pitching and rolling, and I'm enjoying this roller coaster journey. The Captain says we are on our last leg to Tiree and it will only take a few hours.

All of a sudden, I am looking down and seeing my father running up and down the deck. He's wearing his raincoat, no hat and his hair is blowing in the wind. He keeps looking overboard yelling "George, George" – he must think I'm lost overboard. I was laughing sheepishly. The Captain had a bit of a smile too and sounded the ship's whistle, got Daddy's attention, who came up to the bridge and, obviously relieved that I was not overboard, gave me a really good cuff around the ear (known as an English Reprimand) and said, "don't do that again!" Chastised, I felt good that my Daddy loved me and no, I wouldn't run away again. The Captain and I look at each other with smirks on our faces. I start to laugh. The captain says, "no fault", opens the pilothouse door and calls my Daddy.

Scotland: The Isle of Tiree and the Silver Sand Beach story

We arrive at the port town of Scarinish. I am getting used to all the activities surrounding arrivals. A busy wharf, with porters, carts and curious Scottish islanders coming to see our ferry---their three-times-per-week sailing connection to the mainland.

Daddy has found us a nice three-bedroom bungalow with a large vegetable garden on the outskirts of town. It's quite desolate and out of the way really. Will I make some new friends? Daddy says I will; there are neighbours some distance away.

A few days after our arrival, the weather turns warm and sunny. It's Sunday and we are going to go for a seaside picnic. Daddy has found a beautiful white sand beach on a very private cove. Mummy has large picnic hampers of food and drinks. Two large Scottish tartan blankets are spread on the silver sand for our comfort.

No sooner has Mummy opened the picnic basket and started to put out the cucumber sandwiches, sardines and cheese, precious apples, bottled water and a tea thermos than we attract visitors.

Mice! There seemed to be hundreds of them. They all formed a ring about six feet away from us. Daddy got really angry, grabbing sticks that had washed ashore. He proceeded to beat them without success.

Bill and I think they are darling: Mummy is petrified. She says: "Cecil, do something, get rid of them or we go home now". Daddy, using the wood flotsam and old dried seaweed says: "boys, I'm going to make Boy Scouts out of you now. Watch me make a fire whose flames and smoke will scare the mice away." And presto, we had a fire built in a shallow pit of the silver sand and using part of our towel, Daddy wafts the smoke at the mice and they scurry away, Mummy is pleased and Bill and I make sand castles near the water.

After lunch, and with trepidation, we step into the water. I don't know how to swim. The surface of the sea is so calm you see the bottom as through thin glass.

Daddy says Joe---he always calls me this, not George, unless I'm in trouble---I'll take you for a walk on my shoulders. So I get on his shoulders with delight. He then walks about 10 paces into the sea. I don't know how deep it is because it's so smooth and clear. Suddenly, grabbing me by the waist, Daddy throws me into the water about four feet from him. Shock, panic and fear envelope me as I splutter and spit, crying and yelling. I'm trying to paddle without success. I can hear Mummy screaming, "Cecil, what have you done to George, get him out of there now. Rescue him!"

My father does so, bringing me ashore and to my hysterical mother he says, "Bunt, the boy has to learn to swim some time". For the next year or so, I will be terrified of the seaside.

My new Tiree friends and I discover a Scottish Hebrides secret. During the few short months of our stay, a large ocean freighter with 50,000 cases of Scottish whisky destined for the United States founders off the Tiree coast and the islanders and others immediately plunder its cargo. The challenge is where to store it all.

One day, a friend and I are in the MacDonald's scullery, planning to scoop the cream off the top of the butter churn for our usual treat. Just as we get our hands in the churn, a voice from the heavens says, "Hoot boys, get yer hands out of there! Be off the lot of ye!". The churns hid bottles of whisky. Then, a day or so later, helping my mother dig up potatoes in our garden, we discovered whisky bottles buried amongst the spuds.

Well, our Tiree stay soon comes to an end as my father is called back to rejoin to Montgomery's Eighth Army. We return to the mainland at the Port of Oban. Little do I know that I won't be back in Oban for another 60 years!

Scorton, Lancashire 1941-44: Beans on Toast, Bangers and Fish and Chips

We have moved from Tiree to the English Midlands. Daddy and Mummy have found an "out-of-the-way-from-war" quaint little village called Scorton. Its nearest town is Garstang, midway between Preston and Lancaster, not too far from Mummy's family, our aunts and cousins in and around Liverpool. However Liverpool is just close enough to be a major port and hub for the war effort, so we in Scorton are certainly in range of "Jerry", one of the names given to Hitler's Luftwaffe.

Our Tudor house is called Wyersdale, several miles out of Scorton, and up a hill amidst a beautiful orchard of crab apples. Daddy likes it because he can use his bunduke, a 12-gauge shotgun which he uses to bag pheasants at the edge of the garden. Mummy really likes these fowl to make delicious meals. Daddy has an old Austin car to do errands in the village and drive me to school.

All this relatively easy living comes to an end when Daddy enrolls in General Montgomery's Eighth Army Royal Engineers. The old Austin is now parked in the garage, the bunduke put away and we get our last glimpse of Daddy in his new snazzy uniform with one pip as a second lieutenant as he goes off to war.

Recently we have a new addition to the family: Nola, a black and white Cocker Spaniel puppy. She's cute and cuddly and is becoming a real friend.

Mummy, Bill and I with Nola to guard us, we're now on our own to fend as best we can in wartime Lancashire. The reminders of war are everywhere. The Beeb, as the British Broadcasting Corporation Radio is called, has frequent wartime bulletins.

"This is London. It's 12 noon Greenwich Mean Time, Raymond Glendenning reporting. The Prime Minister, Winston Churchill, addresses the nation on BBC One this evening at six o'clock. It is expected he will deliver news on how the RAF is fighting against the Luftwaffe raids."

We are glad we have the radio. Many people don't and others rent radios and share special broadcasts with friends and neighbours. The Beeb has many programs. I especially like *"Dick Barton, Special Agent."* His adventures are exciting; he always gets out of scrapes and wins the war. I can see it in my mind's eye as the radio loudspeaker blares with "the noise of advancing giant ants onto Dick Barton's desert camp. Will he escape in time to rescue his trapped friend behind enemy lines? Stay tuned until next week's episode."

But wait, it's time for supper and Mummy has prepared beans and toast! Mummy says Mr. Gaskill the butcher and grocer did not have any meat this week due to rationing. Apparently, he has listed us for some sausages next week. Wartime rationing is in full force so an alternate to beans and toast is sardines (tins labeled 'Fish She is Very Small').

Another of Mummy's scrumptious recipes is bangers and mash, which is sausages and mashed potatoes. And we always have a red and green vegetable scrounged from the neighbours' gardens. At Wyersdale, we are spoiled because of the crabapple trees, so Mummy has made bottled preserve jam and other fruit which are also converted sometimes into pies but only when she can get the suet for the flour to make pastry. When the sausages do arrive, our bangers and mash are smashing!

It's Friday and next to Gaskill's is a Fish and Chip shop. They are not always open now due to wartime shortages. This week however, to look after the Scorton Catholics who can only eat fish on Fridays, they have been able to get halibut, plaice and some cod. We get halibut deep fried with chips, carefully placed on a small piece of wax paper and then sprinkled with just the right amount of malt vinegar and salt, all wrapped in newspaper to take home. The aroma is mouthwatering: the feast is outstanding.

Austerity Living and War on the Home Front

Wyersdale proves to be too far away from Scorton. Mummy, with no car to drive, no buses and only a bicycle with a shopping basket, finds it hard to peddle our hill and look after Bill and me, so we move into Scorton. Our Sundial Cottage house has a whitewashed terrace on the main street opposite Mr. Brown's farm. Mummy has eyes on obtaining (by passing our ration book restrictions) milk and eggs and maybe the odd hen from the farm.

In addition, there is a large narrow garden. It has a vegetable garden and rabbit hutch and runway. The rabbit pen is important so the rabbits don't get away and in turn are not scared by our dog Nola. Some 'brare rabbits' become delicious baked pies, some of the only meat we get.

We have got to know some new-found friends; Mrs. Short who has a car, Mrs. Moss and her son Jeff who is in the RAF and Mr. Jackson, the Vicar of St Peter's, our Church of England Scorton Village Anchor and School.

Our school is one large room with two small offices. We boys and girls have uniforms as best we can. There are many bits of clothing that are handed around and repaired with elbow patches, cuffs re-sewn and gaping buttonless flies on boys' pants. Mummy says we have to learn to live with what we have and be frugal. We all have our gasmask box which holds the luncheon sandwiches, sandwich spread and an apple.

Many a lecture we also have from the fire wardens and the Home Guard. We are shown pictures of German airplanes – Focke-Wulf 190s, Stukas, Heinkels, Messerschmitts, English Spitfires and Hurricanes - and learn to differentiate by sight and sound. We are to be on the alert and report everything. The Home Guards show us bullets, grenades and mortars and admonish us not to touch them. We are not to go into downed aircraft as it's dangerous because all of the things could blow up as they are carrying explosives. Mortars might be in deep puddles because we get a lot of rain in Scorton.

So Norm Farrar, my friend and I, go looking for mortars and other adventures. One day, we see a farmer's haystack that had a special pathway. We managed to push open (it's a disguised barn) a straw door and wow, inside there are pieces and piles of wood marked "Mosquito" with a special rack of wheels. We learn they are to help build and repair the RAF Mosquito reconnaissance and bomber planes. I would later learn it was plywood from

Canada and much of it manufactured in Kaufman's Furniture Factory in Collingwood. Of course we looked for spent bullets, ammunition and other treasures, just what boys do!

We join Mr. Jackson's Boy Scout troop and have weekly meetings. We learn the Scout Motto and are told it's important in all we do. Our Scout troop is divided into patrols of six boys. We aspire to be patrol leaders but I am too young, so we go camping and help the air-raid wardens. Go around after dark and learn how the black-out is important. No light is to be showing behind any curtain so as to not alert the Hun. If there is, the warden knocks on the door, severely scolds the owner and closes the curtains properly.

Every used tin and piece of scrap metal is part of our Scout weekly scavenger hunt. It's all collected and piled up ready to be melted down for guns and ammunition for the war effort. We are proud to do our part.

A precious piece of my Scout kit is the three-in-one self-contained metal mess kit. It is a square pan 3" to 4" deep with a handle that works for cooking over a campfire with a small cup, knife, fork and spoon. When we add a torch (flashlight) and multi-bladed Scout knife, we can camp anywhere.

John Sargaent, our troop leader (he has not been called up to the Army yet but is in the Home Guard), catches one of the boys stealing a mess kit. The punishment is not to be forgotten. Stripped down to his underwear and tied down on his back "spreadeagle style" so he could not move. Treacle (syrup) is poured over his chest up to his neck (not his face) and his legs and feet. He is under the shade of a large tree. Troop leader John takes us on a one-hour hike. When we come back, there are flies all over the thief's body, eating the treacle, with the culprit in tears begging for forgiveness. We all vowed we would never steal. Scouts teaches some important lessons.

I am growing up. Mummy is concerned about me speaking with a Lancashire accent. She doubles as a teacher and keeps saying elocution is important. A-E-I-O-U must be said over and over. Table manners are being drilled into me as young Bill watches:

"Eat your porridge at breakfast. Take the orange extract and cod liver oil. Hold your knife and fork properly. Be obedient. Respect your elders. Speak when you are spoken to. Always eat your vegetables (often carrots, cabbage, chard etc." But I still learn how to speak Lancashire: "Ee by gum' and all".

"Albert and the Lion" becomes one of my favourite Lancashire poems. *"There's a famous seaside place called Blackpool, that's noted for fresh'ar and fun" --- recited by George Formby and Arthur Askey.*

I learn it and enjoy performing it in a Lancashire accent. We are entertained on the Beeb by Gracie Fields and her Lancashire accent and Vera Lynn with songs that won the war. Richard Dimbleby reporting on football and the Australian tests. Arthur Askey and George Formby, the comedian. Singers Spike Lee *"in Der Fuhrer's Face"* and Scotland's Jimmy Edwards who recounts that when a visitor kept his hand on the door bell buzzer for nearly two minutes, Jimmy opens the door very agitated and says: "Hoot mon, don't you know a battery costs sixpence?".

At home, we eat the usual sparse fare plus drippings on toast, bubble and squeak, fried leftover vegetables and apple pieces, toad in the hole (sausages wrapped in pastry) lousy-tasting brisket and tripe from the butcher, all with lashings of HP sauce to disguise the taste. Stale bread makes delicious bread and milk pudding for snack time, and a "cuppa tea" is the antidote for everything.

In the summer and at harvest time, we Boy Scouts help Mr. Brown from time to time on his farm. Cleaning the barn and mucking the cows and chickens earns precious rewards that Mummy and Bill really like; dairy cream, a few fresh eggs, spuds, green vegetables and carrots will go a long way in our larder at the end of haying.

It's time to load the two silos. Several boys at a time are inside with pails of farm-grade treacle. As the newly-cut hay is pushed by conveyer into the top of the silo, the grass builds up. Our job is to tromp down and every several feet, pour the treacle over the hay. The silage then becomes a sweet special food of the cattle in the coming winter. Our reward is a milk bottle full of this treacle to take home. All the village housewives, including Mummy, love this treat. It is subsequently used for cooking, watered down for table use on porridge, pancakes and French toast. We go anywhere; barnyard manure to hay mow, clogs on our feet. We are farmyard chore boys and we love it!

Eight to Nine Years Old: War's Effects, Impressions and Experiences that will last a Lifetime

Every day at home, I am reminded about the war; BBC Radio, walking to school, join-the-war-effort posters, in the shops, scarcity of goods and rationing, at school, air-raid warning practice with gas masks and in Church praying for the Armed Forces.

The sounds of war: air-raid precautions and sirens and the All Clear penetrate with alarming effect. Barrage balloons dot the sky. Military convoys in camouflaged lorries drive our back-country roads to their military outposts, gun emplacements and sand bagged pillboxes and traffic control gates. Unexpected sounds with a roar of soaring majesty and screams of overhead aircraft all invade our senses. And, of course, our radio:

*"Bong–Bong–Bong–Bong–Bong–Bong: the sound of Big Ben. This is London and the BBC news at 6 o'clock. Today the Prime Minister Winston Churchill announced in the House that Their Majesties the King and Queen were unhurt in last night's London bombing raid. Buckingham Palace took a direct hit and miraculously King George and family were not hurt." f*ollowed by a band playing our National Anthem, "God Save The King."

The King and Queen are our country's role models. We don't want to see them get hurt, and of course our troops inspire us also. Our Vicar Mr. Jackson, who is Scoutmaster and teacher, explains to us the various uniforms being worn by Civil Defence volunteer forces, police and the Armed Forces. Some of our troops are highly enough to have a Scout uniform – we who don't try to look clean and pressed – we often resemble ragamuffins compared to the spit and polish, Sam Browne belts, Navy and Air Force braids we see on many of our troops. They make us proud, and like them, we have to act brave and we admire them.

Recently a telegram arrives: Daddy is finally coming home on leave. A few days later, a late-night surprise with loud banging on the door, Nola barking and we're awake. What joy, it's Daddy, hugs and kisses all around and Mummy puts on the kettle. Due to wartime secrecy, he says he's not allowed to tell us much.

Boy, does he look spiffy in his officer's uniform, although his boots look scuffed and dusty. Apparently he got a train to Preston. It arrived too late to catch the Garstang bus and there being no other transport, he walked all the way home, 16 long miles, what a soldier, what a Dad. He's got presents too, a scarf for Mummy and sweets for Bill and me.

Daddy's home only for a few days. Apparently, we are going to be moving to Mrs. Moss' thatched cottage at the other end of the Scorton main street. It's a furnished house with a large garden and three bedrooms. Jeff Moss is also home on leave from the RAF. He helps all of us move into their house. Daddy says Mummy needs a rest from the household hubbub of us boys, Nola and all the activity, so he plans to take us on an overnight camping trip. Scouts has taught me lots, and we borrowed a small tent, enough for two boys, a Dad and Nola. The hills around Nicky Nook, the entrance to the Trough of Bolan is our campground.

What fun and scary too! Eating our sandwiches for lunch, bangers on sticks over a campfire, Daddy's stories and the starlit sky---it's amazing. I ask Daddy if a grandfather can be called "grandpop", may we call him Pop and he says yes. So from now on, he will be Pop.

On the way home down the country hedgerows we are carrying our kit, when we hear the unmistakable noise of an aircraft. It's coming our way, it's very low and the engine is screaming like a banshee. All of a sudden Pop yells, dropping everything into the ditch and he bundles Bill and I into the roadside gully, spreading his large army coat on top of us and covering us with his body.

We are all shaking as the diving Luftwaffe Focke-Wulf opens fire with a rat a tat tat, rat a tat tat right on the road where we had been walking moments before. Pop says we are all right, stay motionless and quiet. After what seems forever, the airplane does not return. We shout "Hurray – Pop saved us! Mummy will be proud."

What chatter on arriving home. Mummy says, "Cecil, how dare you put our boys in harm's way?" The village is a-buzz with the story. RAF man Jeff Moss explains the Beeb has reported enemy single-reconnaissance planes have been spotted in the Midlands and Jerry is also bombing the Liverpool docks. The Blitz is here, an indelible experience.

The Moss Cottage, Garstang, Cinema and a New Sister

We've moved into the Moss cottage. Wow, it has lots of space and an extra bedroom compared to Sundial Cottage. It's across the road from a big barn painted black with a guarded and sandbagged gate. We wonder what wartime stuff might be inside.

Our Daddy, now Pop to Bill and me, is in Montgomery's Eighth Army. Pop says he will soon have to go away again to fight Hitler and be sure to look after Mummy, you're getting to be big boys now. We don't know when he is going or when we will see him again.

Jeff Moss says he works on Spitfires and Hurricanes. His job is to keep them in the air. And as usual when talking to soldiers or most in uniforms, they cannot tell you anything because as the British war effort posters say:

"Careless talk costs lives / Keep Mum she's not so dumb". The last part – a picture of a smashing lady surrounded by interested men – suggests she might be a spy among us.

Jeff becomes our pal. He has fascinating stories about goblins, fairies and Rumpelstiltskin. He explains how we can help Mummy by cultivating the vegetable garden as the poster in the Post Office says: *"Dig for Victory".* We are growing potatoes, carrots, chard and peas. Our wooden-soled clogs help push the spade into the soil. We know how to till and dig for victory.

A ball of thin twine, two cans and several notched poles become our new back garden telephone line. Jeff Moss shows us how to string the twine from the back of the house to the end of the garden. It's several hundred feet. Punching a small hole into the bottom of the open can, we thread the twine into the can and tie a knot so that when pulled taut the string will not pull away from the can. We did this for both ends of our new "length of the garden" telephone line. The line is supported and threaded through four poles. We've previously made ½" holes at the top of the poles.

Jeff shows Billie and me how to keep the twine taut and with one person talking into a can at one end, the boy on the other end puts his can to his ear and can hear his brother speaking into the can from the other end. We have the Daniels' boys' telephone line. We become popular with our friends as they came over to play war. The can microphone/ear listening tin at the house end of the line becomes England; several hundred feet away at the end of the garden is our frontline fort with its telephone tin is our listening outpost from where we are going to repel Hitler and his Jerries. We imagine we're in the forces now. The lads think we're brilliant.

Scorton School next to St. Peter's Church arranges class outings from time to time. Wednesday afternoons are usually sports days. Always at our village Common we play football or cricket depending on the time of year and the girls get involved with roundabouts, running etc. One Wednesday, the teacher and Mr. Jackson arrange an outing to Garstang. We are going to the Cinema and see a war display put on by the Home Guard. Inspite of petrol being scarce and rationed, enough cars are arranged to cram several dozens of us into them for the eight-mile trip.

The whitewashed pub on the junction of the A6 motorway is the wartime prison of Rudolph Hess, Hitler's deputy, who had parachuted into Scotland several years before with the idea of stopping hostilities. The pub has apparently been converted into his cell and has constant searchlights aimed at it throughout the night in case Jerry wants to come and bomb him. They never do. In the Garstang square, we are paraded around displays of anti-aircraft guns, searchlights, tanks, and posters, many telling us what to be alert to:

Hitler will send no warning – so always carry your gas mask.

Beat Firebomb Fritz, Britain's Fire Guard is Britain's defense.

In the middle of all this, cordoned off and guarded by several khaki uniformed Home Guards with a similar number of women in fire warden uniforms with truncheons, is a German airplane. What a sight. Having been shot down, it shows a damaged windshield and bullet holes in its crumpled fuselage. One of the wings was only partially attached and we were told this Focke-Wulf 190 had been downed in a raid over our part of the country. How scary. We are keenly interested and excited. How do pilots fly these things? We've been warned in school and everywhere not to go near or in a downed aircraft as they may be hazardous.

Boy will be boys, so when the guards aren't looking, Norm Farrar and I duck under the cordon, scramble up and over the broken wing and pretend to fly in the cockpit with the airplane's control stick (we know it's called a joy stick). Wow, what a thrill and then the thundering voice of a Home Guard officer: "Hey you urchins, get off there, common scarpers, you louts, you're goin' to get a cuff around the 'ear 'ol".

We scamper down and hide among the rest of the boys and girls who are giving us subdued cheers. Mr. Jackson is scolding all of us and threatening "lines" at home. We sheepishly sidle off. Secretly we feel exhilarated to have been in a real plane. We're up close to the war.

The Perils of Pauline is at the cinema and we all enjoy the theatre after our airplane adventure. The movie is equally exciting as Pauline, tied to the railway tracks, avoids death at the last minute as the hero switches the rails in another direction and the rapidly-advancing train veers off to one side and Pauline escapes.

Cinema intermission has us singing and following the bouncing ball: *'Bless 'em all, bless 'em all, the long and the short and the tall'* is George Formby's rousing song in support of the troops. Pathe Movietone News shows the ravages of the Blitz, with lots of marching soldiers and the typical English airfield scrambling Spitfires to fight the Luftwaffe.

It's been a moving day and we're touched by all we've experienced this Wednesday.

The Early Years at Scorton: Boys will be Boys

Scorton is situated halfway between Lancaster and Preston, and nearby Garstang. We are in Lancashire. I have been told that this is where we are going to spend the war out of harm's way. We have moved here from the island of Tiree. It is 1941. The Church of England, Saint Peter's, is very much part of the Scorton community. The Rev. Mr. Jackson is welcoming me. He suggests to me that being a choir boy might be just the ticket.

I am impressed with all the trappings and paraphernalia of cassocks and surplices. I'm now part of a group. Singing hymns is marvelous. *"Onward Christian Soldiers"* gives me a feeling that I am now helping Pop in his fight with Hitler.

We choirboys even get rewarded; we are allowed into the little room where the bellows are like a giant leather envelope. They have two great big paddle-type handles. Two choir boys are chosen every second or third week to pump the bellows; one lad on one handle, the other on the second one.

Entrance to this musical organ support system is through a three-and-a-half square foot opening behind the choir stalls. Reverend Mr. Jackson can look directly through the small opening but the choir master cannot. Adults are unable to navigate the narrow passageway.

Like most old Churches, some things get run down. The leather bellows is no exception. One corner has six- to eight-inch holes in it, so to maintain the air pressure, the hole is stuffed with a large rag. Boys will be boys. So as a prank, waiting for the organist's high note on *"Hark the Herald Angels Sing"* we quickly pull out the rag, and with delights of glee hear the organ collapse with a large ploof sound. Actually the best release of gas, (fart) you've ever heard. Rev. Jackson went livid red, couldn't reach us and had to restart the service. But we did get our comeuppance later.

Grub, Loverly Grub:
The Yanks are Coming, the Yanks are Coming

"Bless 'em all, the long and the short and the tall, you'll get no promotion on this side t'ocean." (Popular wartime song)

It is mid-December 1943 and Mummy says Mr. Churchill, as reported on the Beeb, states that in general, things on the home front are improving. Maybe they are, but from Heligoland, John o' Groats to Land's End, the BBC reports vicious storms. Rain, hail, sleet and snow pound down on us without letup. Often drenched to the skin, our Macs and wellies are soaked right through. The clogs on our sock-covered feet see us slipping and sliding on the icy walkways and they leak, too. Thank goodness Mrs. Moss' cottage has a large fireplace and we have, in spite of shortages, sufficient wood to dry out sopping clothes. We huddle and keep warm.

Christmas is coming and Jeff Moss tells us that he should be on leave from his RAF Squadron in time to see Father Christmas with us, as Mummy has invited him to join us for a special dinner.

On the Garstang road, Mummy has arranged with Mr. Braithwaite to get one of his ducks for Christmas dinner and I'm to go and pick it up after farm chores at 6 pm.

With Nola for company, I set off in a wild, cold and wind-driven snow-storm. It is nearly dark. The snowbanks on the side of the roads are very high.

Nola just loves the snow which she doesn't see too often. She tries to bite the snow and chase it and generally does not pay attention to anything else.

Walking in now ankle-deep snow, with the occasional lorry going by with hooded (for wartime) headlamps is a slog. I'm getting puffed and a bit scared of the dark road that seems kind of spooky with the snow piled high on the hedgerows making a sort of tunnel. I'm nervous and cannot push on fast enough to get to the farm two or three miles away.

Finally, I'm at the Braithwaites. Mrs. tells me to go to the back of the farm house where I will find Mr. preparing hens and ducks. I'm very gruffly greeted by an unshaven, farmyard-dirty Mr. Braithwaite. He is sitting on a small stool in front of a large laundry tub of water. Feathers, lots of feathers are strewn around a sawdust-covered floor.

"You the Daniels boy." I nod somewhat awed and apprehensive. He yells at me, "you'll have to wait, I haven't enough watter" (emphasis on hard Lancashire water). Nola and I hang around. Finally he has our duck. It's been slaughtered and hung earlier. His strong gnarled hands rapidly and with forceful skill pull the feathers out of most of the duck's skin. This special butchering is a very interesting sight. I'm realizing what it takes to prepare our Christmas duck. This duck is very special; it's more food than we have seen in a long time.

Getting ready for Christmas is very exciting. We are always hearing stories from Jeff about the dashing red knight and bugle so we are tickled when we get a special Christmas card from Father Christmas with colourful drawings of the red knight and bugle.

Mummy cooks our Christmas duck. It's perfectly roasted; lots of stuffing, mashed spuds, delicious gravy, carrots and Brussels sprouts, mouth-watering. Christmas pudding too. And then as promised, there's a knock on the cottage window and there is Father Christmas in his bright red suit. A rap on the door with a jolly HO-HO-HO! We rush to welcome him. He's got a bag for toys and a long white beard. Father Christmas is jolly, Billy is amazed, Fay is gurgling and Mummy impressed. And all of a sudden, I realize it's Jeff Moss.

The myth of Father Christmas is revealed. I gasp, Mummy detects I know, takes me aside and with a little smile says, "Now we have our little secret. Don't tell, don't spoil it for Bill".

RAF Pilot Officer Geoff Moss
(a.k.a. Father Christmas)
Christmas Present, Scorton 1943

from Geoff
to George.
With Happy Xmas Wishes
1943.

HOW TO DRAW
'PLANES

By

FRANK A. A. WOOTTON

THE STUDIO: LONDON & NEW YORK

INTRODUCTION

Aircraft today are very much in the front line and I think that a good many of you will be familiar with the best known types. To be able to distinguish between these types is to appreciate the design of them and in some cases to recognise the subtle differences between one design and another.

I'm doing errands one day for Mummy who is nursing baby sister Fay and keeping an eye on Billy. I've been over to Mr. Brown's farm for some fresh eggs. My next stop is Gaskill's grocery for various items including sugar which is scarce and rationed like many items. I arrive to hear two women talking about making apple pies. They are discussing how to avoid the raw apples turning brown after being peeled when they are exposed to air while the pastry for the pie is being prepared before all is assembled for the oven.

The ladies say that apples should be peeled under water in a large bowl and left under water until ready to put in the pastry shell before putting it in the oven and this way the raw apples will not turn brown. I'm all ears regarding this recipe. When I get home and tell Mummy, she listens to the placing apples under water story with keen interest. She says I've done a good job and she's going to use the idea in the future.

Rice pudding is one of our favourites. Billy and I are now able to persuade Mummy to cook some of her mealtime ideas. Especially that now, early 1944, some foodstuffs are more readily available than they have been; Welsh rarebit, which is sliced tomatoes on toast grilled with Gaskill's cheddar cheese melted on top, green vegetables on the side is a step up from austerity beans on toast.

A rice pudding would be super. Mummy is feeding Fay and not feeling well and she instructs me how to make a rice pudding. Get out a Bakelite dish, rice, milk and if we have them (it's wartime) raisins. Put rice about an inch deep in the dish, cover with milk, sprinkle a few raisins, put in the oven to bake on slow/low heat. Watch out for my hands and using a towel, remove dish about halfway through and sprinkle the developing hard surface on the pudding with a bit of butter and if we have it, a pinch of nutmeg. Out of the oven hot, it's scrumptious; the cold leftover "pud" is delicious. I'm now a rice pudding chef. We'll have it again.

Mr. Jackson's Scoutmaster duties with troop leader John result in adventurous hikes into the Nicky Nook Hills with stops for campfires. We are learning how to cook over a campfire. Warmed Ovaltine in our tin pans, bangers and bannock on a stick; the Scouting trail is nurtured by food. The Yanks are coming and we've been learning their songs. The Beeb has news of the Americans coming to help us fight Jerry and now they are here.

They are a jolly lot. They drive around in new vehicles we've never seen called Jeeps. The Yank soldier mufti (clothing) is not as spit and polish dress as we are used to seeing on our Brit servicemen. They have jaunty hats and often baggy pants with loose jackets and always seem cheery. They are stationed at a nearby camp for training.

The Yankees also have more, food, sweets and pop than we have ever seen. Apparently, they have a special canteen called a PX where all these extras; cigarettes in funny paper packages, compared to our Player's and Capstans in boxes, and Mummy and her friends hear about nylon stockings these Americans might have. They want some if possible. These soldiers, Mummy says, are brash, forward and a refreshing change.

One of our buildings in the village is a barn and doubles as an entertainment dance hall for weekend do's. The Yanks, not shy, invite everyone. Scorton's young girls and women are gaga (we boys smirk) not knowing how to handle all this.

But it did not take us long to catch on. Mr. Gaskill would happily take beer bottle returns at his grocery at a half penny a bottle. We are rich and the Yanks let us take the bottles. Wow. They also have those sweets: packages of biscuits and little cakes, sweets from Cadbury and America, and Wrigley's gum. Gum we'd never heard of. Soon it became very desirable and we learned how to cadge it off them regularly.

"Got any gum chum?" in our Lancashire accent usually resulted in a package that could last up to a week. War had never been this good.

Smoking is a very adult thing. It's shown on posters and at the cinema and the Yanks make it even more popular. The adults tell us it's not for us, so we learn how to smoke in secret with cinnamon sticks we buy from Gaskill's (Mr. Gaskill does not know why we're buying it with the bottle return money). In later years, I would realize that this bottle money for cinnamon purchase was my first sales experience.

Mussolini's Fascist Youth, like Hitler's as shown at the cinema, is their version of *"Military Boy Scouts"*. Daddy, now a Second Lieutenant, has been wounded in Italy, and is sent home on leave for recuperation. Secrecy is the watchword so we do not know it, but he got shot at Monte Casino, the huge abbey on a hilltop in southern Italy. Daddy brings home two Mussolini youth rifles for Billy and me. They are very similar to a scaled-down version of a Lee-Enfield rifle.

Yes, we do know this widely-used British Army rifle as we see it all the time used by the Army by RAF guards at the various pillbox stations. These rifles have a light-coloured wooden stock with a retractable blunted bayonet. Dummy wooden bullets are loaded into a real bolt-action firing breach. They also have a carrying strap. Billy and I can now parade around looking like real solders. Norm Farrar and the rest of the boys are envious. Daddy says we can only parade with these rifles in our back yard, in case they are seen by someone who thinks they are real.

We now stage our own war games. The backyard telephone line becomes a "vital Signal Corps" link. We lads break up into opposing forces; one group by the cottage with me as the rifleman and Norm Farrar and Billy with his Mussolini rifle at the end of the garden fort. "Pow, pow!" we yell. "Gotcha!" we say over the tin-can telephone. We are really having fun. Our back yard is a popular playground.

One day I hear a piercing scream from Billy at his end of the garden dugout. His rifle is thrown away and he comes running for Mummy sobbing, crying and holding his right cheek. It's really bleeding between his fingers. What happened? Sighting his rifle in the standard prone position, he has pulled the bolt action back to the ready fire position. He has rested his cheek so that the fleshy part got trapped in the breech, and when he pulled the trigger, it severely and painfully pinched his cheek between the bolt and the breech What a crisis, what a mess! Mummy is desperately trying to stop Billy's bleeding with a soaked alcohol cloth that obviously stings and gets Billy crying all the more. Eventually the bleeding stops, bandages are applied and Billy looks like he has a giant toothache. When the bandages do come off, Billy has a scab and when it goes, he's left with a large shilling-size crescent moon-shaped scar on his right cheek. Now he has a badge of courage, a scarred face to brag about with the lads. A scar that is unique, and his life mark to this day.

Bebe Daniels and Ben Lyon headline new afternoon programs on the BBC and when we come home from school, we find Mummy enjoying to these broadcasts. She says the information, recipes and general family chatter are a welcome break from the wartime news. They also have a Birthday Wishes feature where they dedicate a song and wish Happy Birthday to their listeners Mummy has sent in Billy's name, mine and Fay's to be broadcast. The Beeb even sends a card to us saying which days Bebe Daniels and Ben will mention our birthdays, so imagine the excited anticipation when we all crowd around the radio and hear our own names;

"Now, special birthday wishes going out to another Daniels family (no relation to me) in Scorton, Lancashire, two brothers Billy, May 14 and George, June 23 and their sister Fay are in our spotlight today and their mother Bunty has requested we play The White Cliffs of Dover by Vera Lynn, so to all the Daniels, Happy Birthday from us to you". Wow, we are on the wireless from London, we are all smiles and do we feel chuffed! (excited).

Our Church of England is St. Peter's on the hill above Scorton and is an important part of my weekly routine. Mr. Jackson, our Vicar, is also the Scoutmaster and he puts us through our "we promise to do our duty" pledge by collecting scrap tins and items for the war effort. Daily good deeds help on yard cleanups at homes where the man of the house is not there because he's away in the army, like our Daddy. I'm a choirboy who gets into some mischief as I told you with the bellows story.

Mr. Jackson also has his Sunday school twice per week after school. Not on Sunday, as we're too busy then helping with the service. One Sunday school lesson was all about being "one of God's children". I didn't know it but would find out later that it was from 1 John 3:1.

"Are *you* one of God's children?" Mr. Jackson asks, explaining that to be so, you must be baptized. When I get home, I ask Mummy if I am one of God's children. Of course you are, she says. So I immediately ask (knowing it's babies who get baptized) when was I baptized? "Well, you weren't, what with all the moves, the war and everything we never got around to it," says Mummy.

I feel hurt. Mummy, can I get baptized *now*. After a few moments she says, well, Fay is old enough now I will talk to Mr. Jackson. So it was all arranged; we three kids are going to get baptized together; Fay 18 months, Bill, six and me, nearly nine. It turns out to be a lovely christening with some of the people from the village and cake as well. Now, I'll really be able to look Vicar in the eye.

Billy and I, with all the nappies Fay needs and everything else to do, are now becoming quite a handful for Mummy. She tells me that in writing to Daddy they feel it a good idea that I go to Boarding School. It will get me out of some loutish Lancashire-accented boy's behaviour and improve my schooling, because my Scorton school is good for stories and making model airplanes of Plasticine and other wartime things, but my arithmetic is not too good and my writing needs improving, says Mummy. After various letters to schools who might have me, one is selected in Cheltenham.

We are now in October 1944. Auntie Dor, Mummy's youngest sister, comes to stay with us for a few days. Dor apparently has left her baby Lindsay with another sister in Liverpool to come and mind Billy and Fay while Mummy takes me to my new school. How exciting; we are going from Preston on the famous London, Midland and Scottish Railway. It's the second or third time on one of England's super trains and being more grown up, I'm enjoying it. We are on our way to Cheltenham.

Public School (The Brit Stiff Upper Lip) and the Making of Young Gentlemen at Alexander House School, Cheltenham, Gloucestershire

The clackety-clack of the steel wheels on the railway carriage seems to build excitement as we travel the LMS from Preston to Cheltenham and Alexander House School.

Mummy says this school will be the making of me. Apparently, there will be strict discipline and lots of new friends with sports and games I have not experienced at Scorton School. Mummy explains that this will quickly improve my scholastic work. I'm not so sure. Frankly, I'm enjoying the anticipation of soccer, rugger and cricket but quite nervous about my sums as I'm really no good at long division.

On arrival at the Cheltenham train station, we get a porter to help with my trunk and other kit required for a public school. A short taxi ride and we are at Alexander House School.

The school is situated in a very nice gentrified area of Cheltenham. The long driveway runs through several large playing fields used for football and cricket and sweeps up to a very impressive red brick four-story main building with spiral turrets (I would later think this magnificent piece of architecture is right out of *Wuthering Heights*).

Mummy explains that Alexander House School, although not an Eton or Harrow, will be more like Rugby (of *Tom Brown's School Days* fame) or Gourdonston, a school offering formative education for tomorrow's leaders.

We are welcomed by a housemaster. He says Mr. Green, the headmaster, is expecting Master George. I now feel nervous. My recent feelings of pent-up excitement vanish. ("Mummy, don't forget to tell him that I don't know long division"). Nine-year-olds are supposed to know their basic sums. I'm awkward, shy and a bit scared. After all, I'm just a North Country Lancashire village lad about to be among some of the toffs' children.

Mr. Green is very welcoming. It's afternoon tea time and so we enjoy a "cuppa and cake" while he explains what is in store for my settling in. Mr. Young will be my housemaster. I will be under his guidance. My house will be above the large coach house. The dormitory has 18 boys from eight to 14 and I will do some basic tests so they can put me in the best "form" (class) for my ability. Yes, he knows of my concern about my sums and long division and says not to be concerned.

Mr. Young is called and we meet what turns out to be my best mentor and friend, who says the boys call him Doo Da. Doo Da promises Mummy that he will look after me. It's now late afternoon and Mummy gives me a big hug and be a good boy, kiss goodbye and says that I'll see her in six weeks for the Christmas holidays.

Mr. Young says it's now time for dinner and to meet some of the boys and other teachers. We are off to the large dining room called the Refectory. There is a head table for the teachers and Mr. Green is at the centre. After finding our seating we all stand for grace. Mr. Green says the Church of England prayer; *"For what we are about to receive may the Lord make us truly thankful. Amen".* I would find that this blessing is standard procedure for all meals and sometimes augmented with a hymn. The church traditions are part of the Alexander House School curriculum.

Mummy had said that the school will know how to feed hungry boys and there are over 150 of us sitting down for the evening meal. Lots of stew, mash and cabbage with a slab of cake for dessert, washed down with a glass of milk. It tastes fab and I'm impressed.

After dinner, all students then return to the classroom for a one-to-one and a half-hour supervised study period. Having not done my evaluation tests scheduled for tomorrow, Mr. Young takes me to his classroom. I note there is no teaching: rather a list of topics to be studied. The students use course books and notebooks to read and write their comments about the subjects assigned.

It's now about 9 pm and time to be introduced to my house and dormitory above the coach house. Doo Da escorts me across the yard on a very dark November night to the doorway entrance to the second-floor door. There is an older student Prefect there to welcome me and to take over from Doo Da. My trunk and kit have been delivered and my bed assigned.

The moment Mr. Young leaves, this chap switches from his welcoming smile to a leering grin. He tells me to, "beware the ghosts of crawly growls" as I go up the stairs. He lingers. I take the stairs slowly one at a time. All alert, my heart pounding and not knowing what to expect. I feel scared but as Mummy said, be a big boy, so I get to the top of the stairs all in one piece and relieved. But I'm all by myself and gingerly open the door to the dorm.

A whole lot of yelling, "here's Daniels, let's get him," and immediately four boys grab me, fling me on a bed and strip me of my pants. They stand me up, two chaps on either side and me with a bare bottom and parts hanging out.

They explained to the Prefect I'd seen downstairs that the house initiation is to run the gauntlet. Their dorm gauntlet is each boy standing at the end of his bed with his belt and I have to walk fast down the centre aisle, between the beds as each boy gives me a swift smack on my bare bottom with his belt. Eighteen boys about to beat my bare bottom and there is no escape. The goal is to get the end of the aisle. No screams, no crying allowed or you're a sissy. I say to myself, be tough like Pop in the Army, get it over with and Doo Da's not around to see what's going on.

I walk fast. Some of the belt strikes are not hard, others really sting. I bite my lip, hold back the possible sobs, and eureka, arrive at the end of the aisle, less the worse for wear and more strengthened for this experience. Then, all the boys cheer, say welcome, give me a cold flannel to wipe my stinging bottom and give me my pants back.

I'm now an official member of the house and take to my bed; it's on the lower bunk of a double and I quickly change into my pajamas, get under the covers and thank God that I've survived my first day at Alexander House School.

The following morning, we are awakened at 7 am by Mr. Young. "Come on boys, wakey wakey, into the bathroom now, inspection's in fifteen minutes."

Reluctantly my bleary-eyed house mates and I stumble into the loo with our flannel and towels. Do the necessary and start to wash. One chap tells me to be thorough as Doo Da really checks us over. Carbolic soap and a scrubbing brush are the kit. Precisely fifteen minutes and Mr. Young says, "Line up boys, pajama bottoms on only, let's see how well you've done". He proceeds to ask for hands out stretched and looking for dirty finger nails and uncombed hair and as he says, "wax in the ear'ole", "how are you going to learn anything if your ear'ole is bunged up." He sends two boys back to the bathroom for more carbolic and brushing needed. I'm safe and clean. Scorton training worked.

Then it's off to the Refectory for breakfast. Watery, synthetic, rationed orange juice, heaping bowls of porridge, sugar (what luxury), milk and Lyles on toast and tea. Smashing, I'd say.

Then we are off to classes. My tests are English grammar, some history and geography and arithmetic and of course, long division questions conducted in the morning by a stern Mr. Brown.

After exams, Doo Da appears and says he's going to introduce me and show me the rest of the school. Our first stop is the large kitchen. I meet Chef and his assistant Mrs. Smithers who is also the school nurse. She says, "Now George, if you ever feel poorly or have cuts and scrapes, be sure I'm here to get you better."

Then it's on to various classrooms, Nurse's small surgery, past headmaster Green's study which I've seen and the outdoors to the large playing field. It's all set up for football and rugger. One large pitch and a smaller one. Doo Da explains in the spring, it's converted to a cricket pitch. Apparently, every Wednesday, Saturday and Sunday afternoons are sports times for athletics; running, football etc.

I'm reminded that the war is still on. At the back of the field there are several sandbagged Quonset hut air-raid shelters. Warning sirens can apparently be heard from midtown Cheltenham and once per week there will be precautionary evacuation drills Back in the main building, I'm shown the tuck shop. It's near Mr. Green's office. Doo Da explains it will be open, supervised by Nurse three days per week after lessons from 4-5 pm. I'm told parents have left money with the school so we get six pence per week pocket money. We can spend it on whatever we like. I note that the tuck shop has Cadbury sweets (chocolate bars), comics and batteries for a torch (flashlight) plus other small sundries. I'm told to save my pennies, beware others taking my tuck and spend wisely. I feel I'm rather rich as we never had anything like this in Scorton. Six pence can buy me a Cadbury and a comic; smashing.

Supervised studies after supper Monday through Friday evenings are interrupted once per week when we must write letters to our parents. The teachers coach us on some things to say such as our activities, new friends and in general how we are getting along and to thank them for the "CARE parcels" many of us get from time to time.

Mummy sent me an extra sweater she has just finished knitting with a sweet. I ask her to send me a model airplane kit of a Spitfire. We see the real airplanes flying over regularly from the nearby Gloucester RAF base. They sound and look marvelous and I want to make one for me. I'm also writing to tell her, Billy and Fay about our Saturday walks/hikes. It's like a parade. We school boys, two side by side, dressed in our public best, school caps on, teachers; front, back and middle take us into Cheltenham.

Today we saw a big billboard: James Mason in *"The Last Man"* and Doo Da remarks that Mr. Green is getting a cinema film for us soon, a cowboy film for a treat and it will be shown in the Refectory. One of our special sites is the Cheltenham racetrack. We are told that this steeplechase horse circuit is famous. It has been closed during most of the war and expected to reopen soon. It looks grand.

November and December pass quickly and it is now time to go home to Scorton for Christmas. Mr. Green and Doo Da have arranged that I will travel by LMS train by myself under the train conductor's care so I find myself in my Alexander House School dress-up togs with a large label/placard around my neck. It says, "Help Student To Preston". The conductor is a fatherly gentleman. "C'mon son, we're going to look after ya all the way 'ome," he says. He puts me in one of the best compartments where he can keep an eye on me. I feel very safe and am enjoying the train ride.

Mummy is very loving and welcoming when I get to Preston. She says I look very good in my posh clothes. We're going to take the bus to Garstang where we are then going to be picked up by Mrs. Short in her car for the trip home. It's another Lancashire Christmas. I wonder if Father Christmas or Pop might arrive to surprise us.

It is going to be a white 1944 Christmas. It has been snowing for a few days and everywhere looks magical. Mummy and Billy have set up a small Christmas tree and Fay loves it too. My chums, led by Norm Farrar, are pleased to see me, and are alternately jealous and tease me about being at a school for toffs – they say I now speak funny – I've sort of dropped the "eeh ba gum" Lancashire accent. Gaskill's grocers have a Christmas wreath in the window and St. Peter's has holly bough decorations. I'm asked to again join the boys' choir for Christmas services and carols. Rev. Jackson is pleased to hear about my Alexander House School regimen.

We Wish You a Merry Christmas and *Good King Wenceslas* are some of stirring and jolly carols being sung by the Scorton men and women warden group as they go door to door on Christmas Eve. *God Rest Ye Merry, Gentlemen* gets them an appreciative tip from Mummy at our Moss Cottage door.

We also huddle around the wireless for news and Christmas programming. The Beeb quotes Prime Minister Winston Churchill:

"General Eisenhower and General Montgomery's Eighth Army (now we know where Pop is) are fighting Hitler and Mussolini's retreating Army up the boot of Italy – on our Allies push up for victory over the Hun." We pray for Pop's safety and for Jeff Moss in the RAF.

Father Christmas does arrive in time for Christmas morning. Small presents all around with a surprise for me; a crystal set. I had asked for a crystal set in one of my letters home from school, explaining that most of the boys have one of these inexpensive small amateur radios with an ear piece. I felt left out by not having one and now Father Christmas had filled this need. I gave Mummy a really big hug for arranging this for me. How she has manipulated the ration book and negotiated with Mr. Gaskill we don't know but Mummy cooks a scrumptious ham for Christmas dinner with all the trimmings. It's a grand time and we wish Pop were here.

Now it's time to go back to boarding school. Mummy retraces our journey to Garstang (with Mrs. Short driving) and bus to Preston and the London Midlands and Scottish train to Cheltenham. I'm a big boy and experienced traveler now and get on the train myself to be escorted the whole way by another friendly conductor to Cheltenham.

Back at school. It's now January 1945 and I'm quickly into the schedule. Up early with post bathroom washing inspection and Doo Da sounding like Mummy: "Remember, cleanliness is next to godliness and a public schoolboy's first responsibility". No slovenly appearance allowed.

The pre-Christmas test results are out and I have not done very well. Mr. Brown says, "more study time Daniels, you've got to get down on the books, we need to get you up to snuff". I'm chastised and now marked for attention; I'm watched and coached constantly at study time.

I cannot wait to set up my new crystal set. It's mounted on a small eight-inch long by three-inch wide board. The crystal is the size of your small fingernail and about three-eighth inches thick attached to one end of the board. A wire for the earpiece receiver protrudes from the base of the crystal. On the other end of the crystal board is the three-foot antenna wire. At this opposite end and as part of the antenna mechanism is a hinged stylus pin like one on a record player. By moving the pin onto different points on the crystal and listening to the earpiece (earphone) I am able to receive various radio signals. The other boys who have a set teach me to attach the antenna wire to the metal bed springs below my mattress. The 3 ½ x 6-foot metal mesh of the bed springs is an ideal antenna. It really helps bring in the signals What fun; I can hear the BBC overseas wireless broadcast from various countries including as far away as Australia. Apparently, this is a result of wavering atmospherics. But I really feel I'm in an airplane cockpit now. I can listen in to RAF fighter planes – Spits and Hurricanes and a Yank Mustang.

I can even hear, *"This is Berlin, Lord Haw Haw calling you British --- Hitler is on the march, you will be defeated."* What a laugh, I know differently. We believe Prime Minister Churchill as he reports on our advancing armies, our winning Royal Navy and the Battle of Britain won by the outnumbered RAF.

My model Spitfire made with balsa wood, glue and paper fabric wings and fuselage is a hit with my roommates. I've carefully painted it in camouflage and RAF decals. The propeller works an imaginary engine. Knowing I can get another airplane kit, I trade the Spit to one of the boys for two weeks of tuck. Just imagine, I'm going to have extra sweets and comics in return for making a Spitfire fighter plane. I feel chuffed with my swapping skills and a lot of boys are envious. So, I am in the business of swapping.

I write Mummy to send me another model airplane kit with her next parcel of goodies. A few weeks later a kit arrives. It's a Hawker Hurricane and I busily get to work assembling it in my spare time. Eventually it's made and looks really good.

Again, I swap it to one of the lads for three weeks of tuck this time. In the beginning the fellow who now has the model airplane is happy and gives me his tuck, as agreed. Little did I know that he also wrote home to complain that he doesn't have tuck and sweets any more, saying that they've been taken by that Daniels boy. I later learn he didn't say he'd swapped sweets for a model airplane. Apparently his parents got upset and complained to Mr. Green.

I am called on the carpet (actually Mr. Green's office). He tells me about the complaint and scolds me for swapping my planes for tuck and says it's not fair, against the rules and not to do it again. I'm relieved I did not get caned, often the punishment for doing something bad in the eyes of the staff. Sheepishly I realize that I got away with some good extra tuck and comics.

Winter turns to spring and Mummy comes to see me for the long Easter weekend. She tells me that Billy and Fay are fine and that our family is going to be moving to Northampton, while I'm here at public school. She describes Northampton as being a better town to help raise my brother and sister and has more schools and shops. Grandmother Burton, Pop's mother whom I hardly know, also lives nearby. The new house will be near a big park and a good location for Pop to find work when he gets out of the Army and the war is eventually over.

So, this is another thing to look forward to. The Beeb reports on the wireless that the Allies have penetrated Germany. Horrible conditions and terrible prisoner-of-war and civilian concentration camps are found. Hitler's armies have inflicted awful deeds on the Allied soldiers and airman. We hear that Movietone and Pathe News at the Cheltenham cinema show revolting films of mangled dead people. Later we would see these atrocities' films ourselves, resulting in nightmares and revulsion of war.

All of this comes home when one of the school's former teachers who had been called into the RAF returns, after having been rescued and released from the infamous Bergen-Belsen, a German concentration camp. He is Mr. Jeffrys and is in the personal care of Nurse and in a wheelchair. He is skin and bones and looks like a beanpole with sunken eyes and white pallid skin, protruding veins and yellow nails. He looks ghastly. That's what prisoner-of-war starvation looks like. Mr. Jeffrys talks with a raspy voice and forced smile and can only eat morsels of sandwich food and cuppa teas. His stomach cannot take too much. Nurse says it will take three to four months to nurse him back to some semblance of a human being. The ravages of war are indelibly imprinted in my mind, as I would come to know for the rest of my life.

Alexander House School: VE Day May 7, 1945,
Northampton and the move to Broadstairs
Conduct, Rules, Misbehavior and Consequences:
Lines, Coventry, Gated or Six of the Best

I got in a fight today with Rogers. He kept teasing me for no reason. Actually, the tubby, snotty ruffian had been persistently bothering me for some time. All for no apparent reason. Was it jealousy because of my being able to get (negotiate) extra tuck from my model airplane trades?

It all started in class. Seated in the desk behind me, Rogers could alternately pull my hair, rap me on the shoulder with his ruler and otherwise pester me when teacher is not looking. So in frustration I turned around and flung my fist out and whacked him a good one in retaliation on the cheek just as Mr. Brown turned around from the blackboard. "Daniels," he barked "stop that right now."

"But sir," I said, "Rogers has been hitting me and aggravating me."

"Not that I've noticed," teacher said, "Now get back to school work."

So we are quiet for a few minutes. Mr. Brown is back at the board and "pow", Rogers smacks me with his ruler on my neck, no doubt thinking he got away with it, so I instinctively yell. Teacher turns around and says," Daniels – cut it out," and I immediately answer back, "but sir, it's not my fault; Rogers hit me again." "Daniels, do not answer me back," said Mr. Brown.

"But sir," I said, "Rogers keeps hitting me." "Don't be insubordinate with me young man. This kind of classroom behaviour is not allowed, so: Daniels, 500 lines by this time tomorrow saying "I will not be insubordinate" and Rogers, 500 lines by this time tomorrow saying "I will not rough-house in classes. And boys, the time to write these lines on foolscap-lined paper will be tacked on to your evening study time, observed by Mr. Young."

I am really seething at Rogers for getting me into this punishment. It wasn't my fault. Yes, I had answered back to our teacher and I think he deliberately used the word insubordinate because it is 14 letters long and more cumbersome to write.

"And Daniels," Mr. Brown said, "you will look up 'insubordinate' in the dictionary to really understand our Alexander House rules. I did: *"Not obedient to the orders of superiors,"* said the Oxford Universal Dictionary When class was over and we were outside, I confronted Rogers.

"See what a fine lot of trouble you got me into you hooligan," I said. Rogers, taunting, said, "so what are you going to do about it?" The other chaps, seeing this argument, urged me on; "Hit him! Hit him!", so with their encouragement (they know as I do he enjoys being a bully), I gave him a big shove with both arms and he in retaliation swung at me with his fist.

I rush in for a big clinch. Lots of muffled blows, our nice school jackets getting in the way. He stuck me around the ear. Boy it hurt, so I tried his nose and talk about smashing. I did connect and now it's bleeding. He's really mad, grabs me and we go tussling to the ground. Trying to swing to and fro like wild rugger players when all of a sudden a yell – Doo Da – the next thing I know Mr. Young is pulling us apart and is really mad.

"Look at you young urchins," he says. "I don't care what this is all about. Rogers you go see Nurse to fix your bloody nose and then I'll see both of you in my study in half an hour to decide what corporal punishment you both deserve."

I'm thinking how unfair all because of Rogers' bullying antics. What's going to happen? Will it be lines, being gated or six of the best?

So now we are in Mr. Young's study. We've cleaned ourselves to look presentable and I'm nervous about what Doo Da is going to do.

We get a lecture that good behaviour is expected, roughhouse fighting is not acceptable. "We have to learn to be gentlemen," he says. Apparently he talked to Mr. Brown about the classroom insubordination and he knows about our 500 lines. He says he really should march us down to Mr. Green's office to get the cane to give us at least three of the best on each outstretched palm of the hand. (Public school traditional first-class punishment (caning), well you really have to be a scoundrel to deserve this.

Instead, he decides we are going to be "gated" or restricted to our dorm all Wednesday afternoon and will be excused the fun of athletics and football with all that jolly activity. We are to hand in our crystal sets for the rest of the week so we don't get the thrill of the wireless, and in addition, the 500 lines for Mr. Brown is increased to 600 lines by tomorrow. He says he hopes we have learned a lesson and that we got off lightly.

I've certainly learned several things. Beware of bullies and justice in the classroom and school is not always fair. And I've also learned from some of the other boys how you can cut your writing lines down to nearly half the time you thought it might. So, using good schoolboy ingenuity, this is what I do. Write 600 lines of: *"I will not be insubordinate"* using three newly-sharpened H-type lead pencils, so the script is dark from the wide easy-to-write soft lead in the pencil. I stack them together. One pencil on top of the other, on a precise sloped angle, held together with a rubber band. The angle is such that the three pencils fit comfortably in my right hand.

I have only to place the first or top pencil on the first line of the foolscap paper. When I start to write, paying attention to the first or top pencil, the bottom two are lined up with the two lines below and I'm able to write three lines at a time, all looking the same. Every once in a while, I have to readjust the angle, as the lead in each pencil is used up, the elastic band is made snug in my writing hand.

Done, turned in to Mr. Brown. "Now Daniels, I hope you've learned not to be insubordinate. Do you realize in some armies you can be shot for insubordination?" Lesson is learned: act and play by the rules.

On the Seventh Day: Sunday in the Pews with the Vicar

This Sunday morning, like all of them, is a treat. We are allowed to sleep in for an extra half hour before the carbolic soap and scrubbing ourselves in the bathroom then the Doo Da parade for cleanliness inspection.

I'm awake anyway at the usual time. So, a quick trip to the loo and back to bed to snuggle down with the crystal set under the bedcovers (my little cave) to try to hear the BBC or the RAF.

"This is London. RAF and American raids over Dusseldorf precede General Eisenhower's Allied troops penetrating to the heart of Hitler's Germany. On the

Eastern Front, our correspondents report Russian General Zhukov is steadily pushing towards Berlin."

I wonder where Daddy is. Is he fighting in Germany? I hope he is safe.

Mr. Young marshals us through ablutions and it's down to Sunday breakfast. Mr. Green presides as our stand-in Vicar. Our hymn today is, *'The Church's One Foundation,'* followed by Grace. Now we can all sit down to the usual synthetic orange drink and cod liver oil, followed by porridge and treacle with one glass of rationed milk. Still hungry, I cadge another pupil's leftover porridge and dry toast.

Mid-morning, we are all going to have a supervised walk into Cheltenham. This Sunday, it's to visit the Church of England where a large number of pews have been reserved for us. Mr. Green is invited by the Rector to deliver the sermon (we try to stay awake), fidget and generally hear that Christ said love one another, which is hard to do when the boy next to me is trying to pinch my bottom to elicit a noise that would get me a reprimand. Schoolboys can be brats. One of the Prefects reads the lesson and we take pride in him being at the lectern. Little did I know that I would be reading a lesson several years from now in a faraway former military church.

Back at school. Lunch is bubble-and-squeak with bread pudding, fortified with cups of weak tea and milk; no sugar due to rationing, just coal-tasting sweetener. But the tuck shop will be open this afternoon so a Cadbury sweet will be a pick-me-up.

Our afternoon is free. We go to the playing fields for pick-up games of football and for general tomfoolery; tag, and cricket batting practice or rounders (the English version of baseball). Lots of yelling, shoving and the odd game of marbles and lots of fun.

Our Sunday evening meal is going to be special. Mr. Green will lead us to spiritual awareness of Christianity no matter how bored or indifferent some of the lads are. Mr. Green's mini-sermon reminds us that there is a war on and we should be proud of our solders, airmen and sailors, so we are going to sing the rousing hymn: *"Eternal Father, Strong to Save."*

I'm particularly stirred by our strong voices singing *"for those in peril on the sea."* This is followed by another emotional hymn in support of our troops. *"Onward Christian soldiers marching as to war."*

Mr. Green says the Latin version of our usual grace:

Benedíc nos Dómine et haec Túa dóna quae de Túa largitáte súmus sumptúri. Per Chrístum Dóminum nóstrum. Ámen. (Bless us, O Lord, and these Thy gifts, which we are about to receive from Thy bounty, through Christ our Lord. Amen.)

Our chef has worked hard, even with rationing limits, to produce a special meal for this Sunday. She has scoured the market for fresh vegetables so we're going to have a good red and green; carrots and Brussels sprouts, my favourites. The main meal will be fried Argentina beef. It actually is tinned Hereford corned beef. I like it cold or hot and HP sauce helps with fried drippings and bread. We boys wonder that with all sunken Atlantic convoys, how do tins of Argentina's bully beef as we call it, get to England. What kind of trans-Atlantic ships get through the German U-boats so we can enjoy our suppers? The main is followed by rice pudding with a few raisins. It has that condensed (tinned) milk flavour to it. Delish!

Now Vicar Green is completing our loaves and fishes with his favourite closing hymn *"Abide With Me"* for we often-recalcitrant boys who need some spiritual uplifting. We sing resolutely.

Victory and Triumph: Alexander House Schoolboys Celebrate

The BBC blares the news: *"Raymond Glendenning reporting. Today, General Eisenhower, Supreme Allied Commander, announced alongside Field Marshall Bernard Montgomery that Berlin has been taken. The Allies have joined with Russian General Zhukov's troops and Hitler's forces have been defeated."* The news reports reveal extreme damage to the Hun and his country and Hitler is reportedly dead. It is not known how he died. Tomorrow, German Admiral Karl Doenitz, Hitler's appointed deputy, will sign the official surrender on May 7, 1945.

It's now May 7 and England and the world are calling it VE Day – Victory in Europe Day. Doo Da and Mr. Young who were in World War I are very moved and tell us we should be very pleased that World War II is nearly over. He points out that it's not over yet. The Japanese are still fighting the Americans in the Pacific. We don't know yet what sacrifice it will take to bring them to their knees.

Mr. Green announces that we are having the day off. Special prayers of thanks, the Twenty-Third Psalm and the Lord's Prayer are said at breakfast.

When the meal is over we all stand patriotically and sing *"God save our gracious King, Long live our noble King."*

Every radio in the school is turned on to hear Prime Minister Winston Churchill's address to the world:

"Today, we may allow ourselves a brief period of rejoicing; but let us not forget for a moment the toil and efforts that lie ahead. Japan with all her treachery and greed, remains unsubdued. We must now devote all our strength and resources to the completion of our task, both at home and abroad. Advance Britannia."

We boys are now all running around playing pretend WWII and "Gotcha Hitler." All the teachers and maintenance staff are cleaning out every bit of burnable rubbish for a huge bonfire being built in the middle of the playing field. Old fences, doors, crates and prunings are used. Some wag comes up with the idea to burn Hitler. This is loudly approved. Some hours later, we have a Woolworth mannequin. I don't know how it's been obtained. An old Army coat, large picture of Hitler from the newspaper and glued to the face of the mannequin and a jaunty Nazi style hat is placed on the new Hitler dummy. The Hitler statue is strapped to a tall (spare) rugby goal post and placed in the middle of the growing bonfire construction.

Several hours later, everyone admires the handiwork of the teachers, staff and pupils in the giant pyramid, topped off by our hated enemy Hitler, who had made life miserable, caused catastrophic strife and attempted to break our Britain. We're about to get our own back, or so we all thought and felt.

Seven o'clock after dinner and we are all assembled on the playing field, dusk is starting to turn to night; ideal bonfire times.

It has been quite a day. The tuck shop is open and we all get a free sweet and an apple. The weather and God cooperated. No rain or mist---ideal for outdoor fun. At supper, we are treated to a dessert of a creamy and delicious Wall's ice cream bar. Wow, we've not seen one of these in months. And we're told Mr. Green has arranged for fireworks with the bonfire. VE Day, and victory over Hitler is certainly being celebrated Alexander House Public School style.

Now as it gets dark we are all singing camp songs – *'The Good Old Duke of York, he had 10,000 men, he marched them up to the top of the hill and he marched them down again.'* And more from the Beeb and the Vaudeville halls:

'Bless 'em all, the long and the short and the tall,' for our solders and air force; *'Kiss Me Goodnight, Sergeant-major.'* We are jolly and having a gay time.

All of a sudden, there's an explosive swooshing sound and with a ka-thump, a rocket firework brightens the night sky with a mushroom cloud of twinkling blue, white and red colours. There are more, one after another.

We all are seated on the ground, theatre style, row on row, with Mr. Jeffrys, our concentration camp survivor, in a wheelchair at the front with Doo Da, who is our World War I veteran and Mr. Green and the staff.

The fireworks form a sparkling rainbow cloud canopy of gunpowder smoke and energy that gives us all goose bumps and thrilling exhilaration. This is far better than the Guy Fawkes' Day Gunpowder Plot, the November fireworks display that is our annual celebration of Guy Fawkes' attempt to blow up the Parliament Buildings in November 1695 in the time of Oliver Cromwell.

Now it's time to light the bonfire and burn Hitler. Mr. Jeffrys' long flaming torch sets alight the few newspapers and kindling to get it started. Fairly soon the flames spread. Slowly at first, then a kaleidoscope of colours, orange and red enhanced by the snap and crackling of burning kindling. The slight breeze fans the flames that creep sideways and upwards. The smell of the burning wood is pungent. We are all anticipating the fire climbing the pyramid of wood, brush and dustbin refuse to reach the Hitler effigy at the peak of the bonfire. I'm reminded of Joan of Arc, but evil Hitler is no martyr to me and the others.

What a show as the night sky lights up! Our faces are gleaming in the reflected light and our ears pierced with the noisy inferno. What a spectacle! After what seems an eternity, the flames start licking at Hitler's tunic. A rousing cheer goes up from all of us. Our youthful exuberance and our school comradeship are reflected in our enthusiasm and wartime patriotism, even if just a small amount in the larger scheme of the war effort.

Hitler is now engulfed in flame: his mannequin topples into the bonfire's cauldron and then another rousing cheer erupts. Someone calls for three cheers for Mr. Green; Hip, Hip Hooray, Hip, Hip Hooray, Hip, Hip Hooray, then we all stand and sing; *"God save the King"*.

VE Day and the celebration will be forever part of our precious memories!

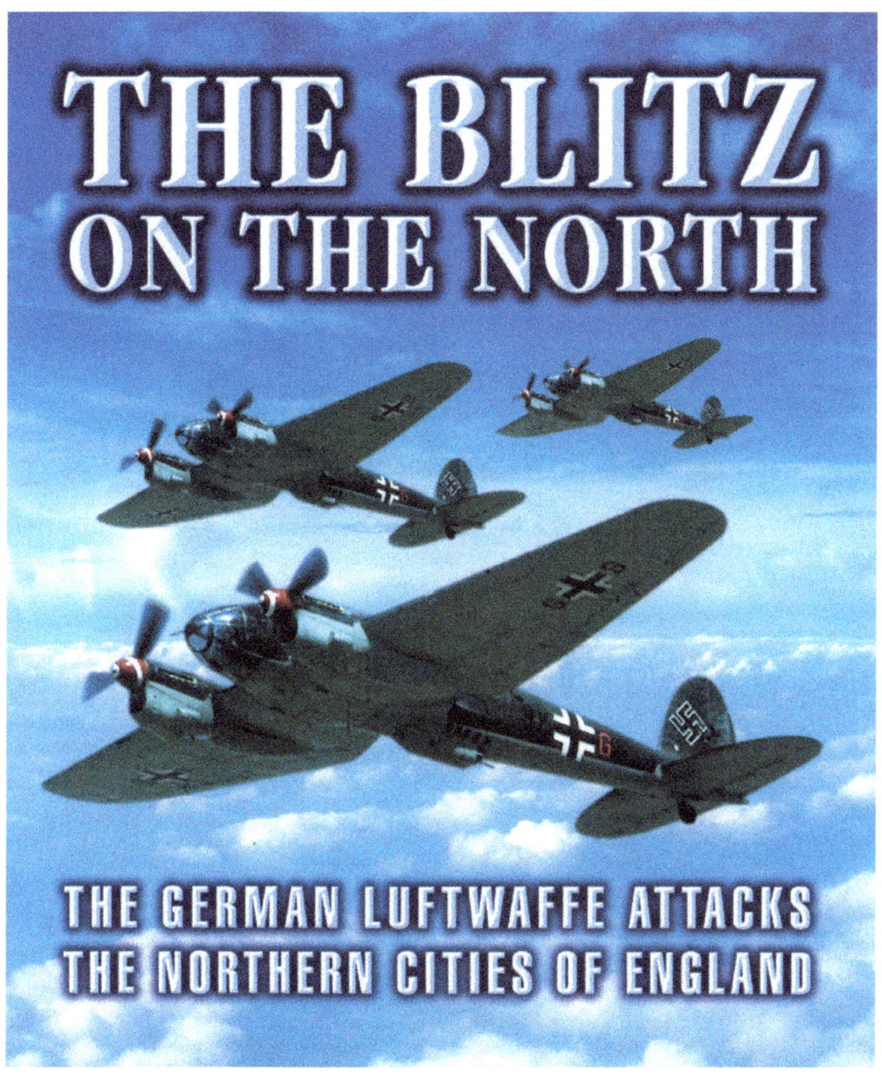

During Britains "darkest hours", the German Luftwaffe and flying bombs caused devastation and chaos across the North of England and parts of Scotland. With the fall of France and Norway, Hitler had a convenent launch pad to turn Britain into a "garden of ruin". Industrial areas and factories producing war materials were targeted by the bombers but nothing it would seem could dampen the peoples spirits or the munitions workers determination to keep Britain armed.

THE SCOUT PROMISE

"ON MY HONOUR, I PROMISE THAT I WILL DO MY BEST—

TO DO MY DUTY TO GOD, AND THE KING,

TO HELP OTHER PEOPLE AT ALL TIMES,

TO OBEY THE SCOUT LAW."

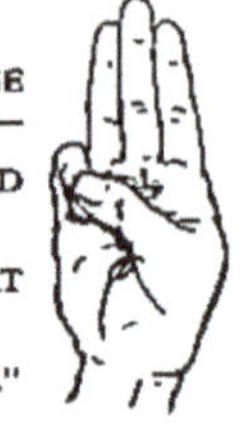

George does his bit as a member of Scorton's Scout Troop.

Geoff Moss is in the RAF. We learn about the Spitfire Mark 1, with Mitchell's famous, instantly recognizable elliptical wings.

A shot down Luftwaffe Folke Wolf 190 with fuselage and cockpit intact. Similar to the one George pretends to fly in Garstang Square

Our Role Models in WWII

"Winnie" at his best – Rallying Britain.

King George V1 and Queen Elizabeth tour bombed districts in northwest London following Luftwaffe air raids, September 28, 1940

December 1st, 1940 – the Battle of Britain may be over, but the Blitz continues. Here a British family huddle in their corrugated iron Anderson shelter – a cheap but effective method of protecting civilians from aerial bombardment. The shelters were usually covered with earth

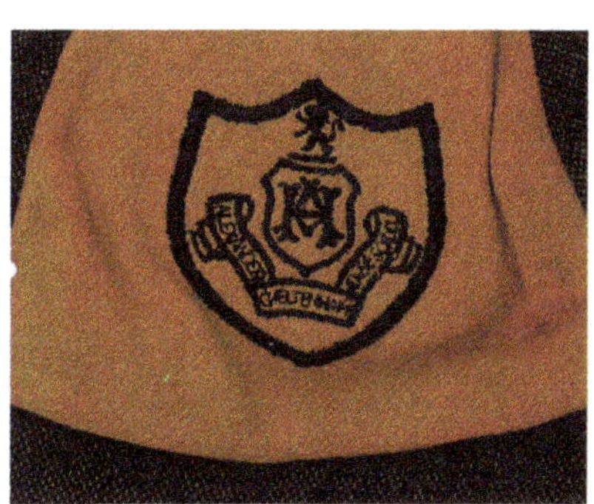

Alexander Cheltenham School cap with crest.

Air raid alert. Classroom gas mask drill for all students.

Prime Minister Winston Churchill, our wartime leader

V.E. Day Special Edition

- Bless 'em all
- We must all stick together
- We'll meet again
- In the mood

Source
The National Trust

The essential war time ration book. Required by all, and more valuable than a passport.

- Bangers and mash
- Toad in the hole
- Boiled beef and carrots
- Fish and chips
- Scotch eggs
- Jam roly-poly
- Pub lunch
- English teas

HISTORY

OF

CIVIL DEFENCE

1935—1945

❖

"A tribute to the patriotism and self-sacrifice of the citizens of Bedfordshire"

DAYLIGHT RAID ON BEDFORD

Photograph by "The Bedfordshire Times"

DAMAGE TO THE GROSVENOR HOTEL, ASHBURNHAM ROAD, ON 23RD JULY, 1942

London school children carry gas masks and baggage as they are evacuated by train to Devon at the start of the war.

On the white sand beach of Tiree, early 1941. Pop, Billy, 2 years, George, 4 ½ years, Mommy and Nola our cocker spaniel.

Scorton Circular Walk in Scorton Village, 2 Miles north of Garstang (Junction of A6 and M6.) ***Lancashire. Wiresdale, School*** *at St. Peters.*

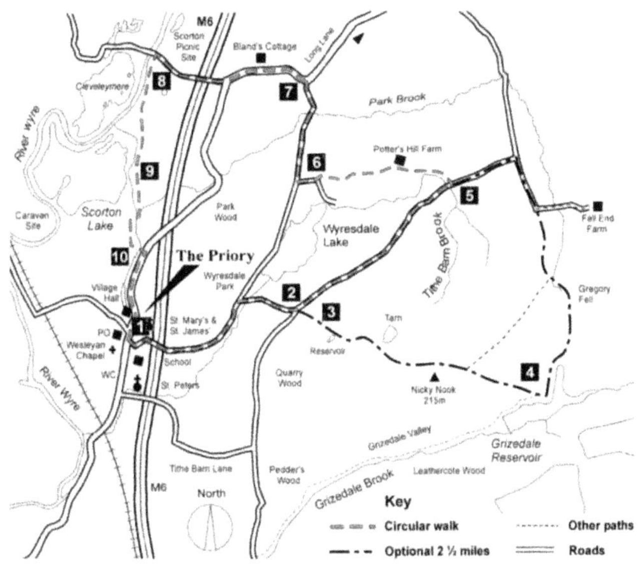

Gateway to the Trough of Boland, one of Queen Elizabeth II's favourite English landmarks.

The Daniels' first Scorton Home
Wyresddale Cottage, 1941.

St. Peters Church, Scorton.

George's St. Peter's School

Nicky Nook

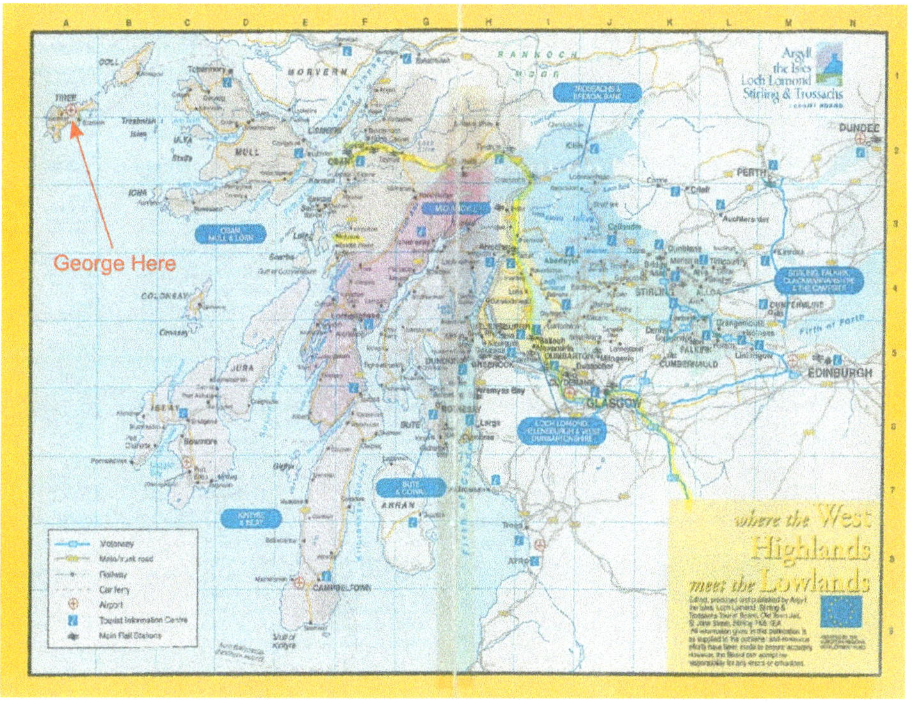

VJ Day: Italian and German prisoners and Family Relocation

I had received Mummy's letter shortly after VE Day. She explains that we are moving from our lovely Scorton Village to Northampton in the Midlands, the explanation being improved schooling options for Billy and Fay and also nearby is Grandma Burton, Pop's mother. It will also be more beneficial for Daddy when he gets out of the army and restarts his civil engineering profession. It is now late June, Alexander House School will be shut down for the summer holidays and Mummy has come to get me to the train to our new home.

It's exciting to be in a new house, an upstairs apartment really. We are on the second floor of a large house with three bedrooms; one for Billy and me and one for Fay and another for Mummy and Daddy when he gets home. I'm really noticing that Billy and Fay are growing since I last saw them at Christmas.

One very fascinating view from our big bay window from the living room looks over the street front to a big park. A beautiful series of trees is interwoven with a 12-foot fence with barbed wire at the top. Mummy explains that this is Northampton's famous Abingdon Park. It has been partially converted to a temporary prisoner-of-war camp.

We would learn later on that England has accepted thousands of German and Italian prisoners of war. We have no idea when they might be returned home. In the meantime, they are guarded by military police and are very conspicuous for their green overall prison garb. Their clothing has large 18-inch diameter bold red, blue and yellow colours. The Germans are in red, the Italians in blue and yellow ones signify trustee prisoners. These trustees help the guards and help supervise their camp life.

Our first visit from Grandma Burton I do not find very pleasant. She is stern and does not seem to accept little boys gladly. Grandma does not seem to be of the loving family types we read about in stories.

Now we are settling into a big city. It is quite a shock from the convenient Scorton Country life and even the sheltered security of Alexander House School. Mummy says our ration book does not help provide sufficient healthy food. She complains that unlike Scorton where some extra eggs or meat can be obtained from the local farmers to add to our rations, this is not easy to do in the big city of Northampton.

The other day she sent me down the street to a butcher hopefully for some brisket and all he would give me was two pounds of tripe. Mummy cooked it that evening. It's white, tastes like rubber and no wonder I was nearly sick when I found out it is sheep stomach. I vowed never to eat tripe again and I haven't. Amidst the meat scarcity, oxtail has become a staple in our diet. It's good in soup and stew and not too bad really. Bully beef, Spam, powdered eggs and cod liver oil, dripping toast, beans on toast continue to be on our wartime table.

Severe toothache continues and Mummy finally finds a dentist. Off we go to see this doctor. After a very long wait, I'm in his reclining chair, with mouth wide open and a very horrible smell of gas to put me to sleep. I'm subjected to my first operation. When I wake up, I have a horrible headache and a gaping hole in my lower left jaw. The doctor explains that I have too many teeth and they are crowding others so more will have to be removed in the future. I don't look forward to this eventuality.

I've made friends with a couple of lads. They invite me to play in their fort. This kids' retreat for playing is really part of a large garage behind our house. It has a loft upstairs. We can climb a vertical ladder attached to the wall and clamber through a trap door to the room above. There is a large window that opens showing the courtyard below. We play Army, repelling and defeating the Hun and only special people can be invited into our secure fort.

Billy, several years younger, wants to join us and we won't let him up. He's becoming insistent. We push him off the ladder and he runs out into the yard yelling. One of the boys who had assembled some stones for sling shots and ammunition hurls a small rock at Billy. It hits him square in the middle of the forehead. With a terrifying scream, blood and all, he runs yelling for Mummy. We all cheer. The enemy has been sent packing. But we are the ones with haven't won yet. Mummy and the parents are really mad now. Our punishment is being quarantined for two days and the garage locked up and out of bounds and just like school -- 500 lines of "I will not act a hooligan"--- we are severely chastised.

Abingdon Park is much more than a prisoner-of-war camp. It is also one of Northampton's best playgrounds for all the people. Mummy takes us several times a week to enjoy the large lake with paddle boats we can hire for a few pennies. Billy and I enjoyed the freedom of being on the water. Mummy has made a picnic of marmite sandwiches, carrots and apples. The Park's canteen is selling cups of tea, sparkling water and Wall's ice cream. Wall's is the most creamy, delicious flavour I've ever tasted. Mummy finds a few pennies so we can enjoy a very scarce Wall's.

The Atomic Bomb

Through the wireless and the papers, I am very aware there is still a war going on in the Pacific. Our American allies and Commonwealth armies and navies were still battling the stubborn Japanese forces. Prime Minister Churchill's broadcast voices concerns about, *"desperate resistance by the Japanese fighting to the death with Samurai devotion"*.

Winston Churchill: Triumph and Tragedy

The Prime Minister would later write, *"to avert a vast, indefinite butchery, to bring the war to an end by the manifestation of overwhelming power to a miracle of deliverance"* are the reasons behind the stunning news.

On August 6, 1945, the United States Air Force dropped an atomic bomb on Hiroshima, Japan. The resulting mushroom cloud did not conceal the fact that the entire city had been obliterated. Three days later (August 9) with no signal of a Japanese intention to surrender, the second atomic bomb was dropped on the city of Nagasaki. This city was also annihilated. Massive power, unbelievable death and destruction. On August 10, newspapers report, "Japs Quit". They surrendered on August 14, 1945.

We have VJ Day, Victory in Japan. Coupled with VE day two months before, Winston Churchill went on to write: *"The unconditional surrender of our enemies was the signal for the greatest outburst of joy in the history of mankind".*

Our Northampton VJ Day opposite Abingdon Park is one big party celebration. Mummy lets Billy and me out onto the street cautioning not to go too far. Shopkeepers are putting out flags and bunting. On our side street, people are building a giant bonfire of old wooden creates, rubbish and anything they can find. Someone comes out with an effigy of Tojo the infamous Japanese Army General who led all their forces. Some wag wants to burn their Emperor Hirohito but there is no mannequin for him.

Air-raid sirens blare, church bells ring, windows are wide open so we all hear the BBC news and celebratory songs from Vera Lynn, Arthur Askey and more. Big Ben chimes from Whitehall London. They've let out some of the German and Italian prisoners from the Abingdon Park barbed wire fence compound and they also join in the festivities. In accented English, they tell us they didn't trust or like the Japanese anyway.

One friendly Italian prisoner with a big grin presents Billy and me with a very different look at the results of war. He rolls up his left sleeve to reveal about a dozen wrist watches of all shapes and sizes. (Were they stolen, bartered or what?) He says we can buy them cheap and will make great presents. We have no money, laugh and turn him down.

That evening, there is a huge street dance. Bobbies control the crowd, there are all kinds of men in uniform, the pub is open and pints of bitter are consumed on the street. There is sparkling water for us kids and a few Yanks on hand provide the gum for the chums. It's a grand affair and we all go to bed exhausted from the enthusiastic revelry.

Back to Alexander House School

The exhilarating summer days of city and celebratory war's-end activities are over. Mummy takes me on a new train journey to Kent. Alexander House School which had been at its wartime Cheltenham locale, had, over the summer, has relocated to its pre-war permanent school and buildings at Broadstairs. Located between Ramsgate and Margate on the English Channel coast, Broadstairs is a well-known seaside resort also renowned for its several leading public schools, many attended by children of some of England's upper-crust families.

It is good to be back among familiar school faces. Mr. Young continues as my housemaster. The buildings are more like a school, not a great big old house like Cheltenham. The dorms are broken up for boys by age group. There is a radio fusion intercom system throughout all the buildings.

On our first days back, we are treated to long walks around Broadstairs and its magnificent boardwalk and beaches. Remnants of England's Channel defences are still prominent. Large sections of the beach are cut off with barbed wire. There are signs posted – *"Danger Land Mines Keep Off."* Every few hundred yards there are huge concrete pillboxes. Some still have large guns protruding from their narrow window slits with camouflage netting draped around. They also had warning signs and we couldn't wait until the next outing when, with no teachers, we could explore these fortifications.

It's a few days later, September warmth continues and for our Saturday athletics we are going to the Broadstairs beach. It is a special boardwalk section that has been cleared of barbed wire and mines.

There are small cabanas to change into our swimming trunks. There is even a small canteen café for those of us who have tuck money to spend. We like the Wall's ice cream.

Back in school, Doo Da is like a father figure. We chat with him lots. He smokes his mini cigarettes continuously. When he buys his 20 Player's Navy Cut, he immediately cuts them in half. Despite creating two butts to throw away, he explains that this is a habit left over from his life in the Army and First World War trenches. Apparently, to extend the life of a pack of cigarettes, they shared with all the other Tommies by cutting them in two.

Continuing over conversations in his study, we watch Doo Da's woodworking. He makes beautiful carved inkwell stands and matching blotter stamps. He sells them to us students for presents to give our parents. They are very nice and only cost about three weeks of tuck money. I have one precious set even today.

It's Wednesday afternoon for athletics and our gym teacher---yes, we now have a gym---parades us down to the seaside for swimming lessons. After my Tiree experience with Pop a few years ago, I'm not as nervous now. With a bit of instruction from the teachers and some of the boys, I'm learning to float and do the breast stroke. It's smashing fun as I learn how to not swallow the salty sea water or get too much in my eyes.

My dormitory is off the main kitchen and also down the hall from our bathroom. Barry is one of our new boys who kept getting up in the middle of the night to go pee. He wakes us up and we get annoyed. It turns out he is not circumcised and the skin keeps growing over his willy to stop the flow. He's so bad in this department he has to have nurse help make him go. We boys can be critical. One minute we laugh, the next, we jeer his seeming embarrassment.

One night he wakes us up at 2 am. We had secretly been anticipating this and had obtained a bucket of water. When he left for the loo, we jumped out of bed and placed the bucket on top of the door, supported by the frame. Hunkering down under our blankets we couldn't wait for his return, and eureka, it worked. He pushed the door. Bucket and all the water fell perfectly on his head and he let out a load scream and then yelling, "I've been attacked!" We are howling in glee at out super booby trap. But not for long because it seems right away, nurse and the housekeeper come running in, scolding us, comforting Barry. Doo Da is called for: Mr. Young is not amused. He scolds us some more and says it will be Mr. Green's office in the morning for all of us to get to the bottom of this disgusting episode.

After breakfast at 8:30 am, we are all in the headmaster's study. Mr. Green wants to know who the instigator was. We don't say a word: solidarity in silence. Mr. Green singles out the tallest, thank goodness not me. Takes out his six-foot cane and proceeds to give the boys two of the best on each hand. Suppressing a yell but in tears, he's told to stand down. Then we are told to come back before lunch to finish the punishment. What will it be? Six of the best, more lines or, heaven help us, expulsion.

"Come back at lunch time," said Mr. Green in his severe and stern voice. This is frightening. I wonder what punishment am I in for. Now the whole school knows of our prank. The boys are all a-buzz. Surely they are going to get six of the best – which is forceful caning on both palms of your hands – maybe we might get expelled and what a disgrace that would be.

We are now before our judge, headmaster Mr. Green. He admonishes that such coarse and destructive behaviour (Barry could have been severely injured by the blow to the head from the metal bucket) cannot be tolerated. We are to be taught a lesson. Headmaster says our parents will be notified that we came close to expulsion and it will be noted on our term report card. There will be no tuck for several weeks. We are to be gated, or confined to school grounds, so no visiting the village on seaside swims for several weeks and six of the best, three on each hand.

Some of the boys yelp blubber and cry. Now it's my turn. I hold out my left hand, palm up and wham – the pain is excruciating. Number two and number three strokes of the cane and I'm biting my lip, determined not to yell or cry, now my right hand. The three whacks take forever and I really hurt but I am not blubbering, although tears creep down my cheek. Whew it's over, Mr. Green says, "Now you've learned a lesson, go and see nurse for salve on your very red and stinging hands". I determined never to be caned or strapped again, and I haven't.

Alexander House School is proud of the company we keep. Our school is one of four public schools all adjacent to each other on the Broadstairs scholastic mile, as it is referred to. The playing fields of several schools are next to ours and we can yell across to their students.

We are friendly rivals with some of them. It's now autumn and football and rugger are mandatory athletics for all. The young Duke of Kent, several years older than I, is one of our football opponents and we are chuffed to be on the same playing field as this member of the Royal Family.

My lessons continue to be a challenge. I enjoy reading but am told my writing is atrocious and my sums don't add up, so I'm relegated to extra evening study time and more Mr. Brown tutoring, Doo Da helps, too!

Some of the older boys test the school's boundaries and Mr. Green's strict rules. They sneak out at night to go into Broadstairs to see a flick at the cinema. While they enjoyed themselves, they did not notice one of the teachers in the theatre. Needless to say, there was the devil to pay when they are caught.

I'm now in new larger dorm with older boys and I've learned several things. I can still enjoy listening to my crystal set. The antidote for an open-mouthed sleeping snorer is to drop a bit of soap into the boy mouth and then watch the bubbling choking poor sod wake up wondering what happened.

Although the war is over this late in 1945, I have no news of Daddy coming home. Mummy writes that Pop is still at Montgomery's HQ and has mopping up things to do with Jerry. We might not see him until spring of next year. I'm to stay at boarding school over Christmas and until the end of the term, so I continue to settle into public school life.

I'm learning that England's Empire and Commonwealth building has been done on the backs of English schoolboys who are often graduates of public schools. We're taught to have pride.

Our Empire connections also come home as the school turns on the short-wave radio and patches in the play-by-play of the England versus Australia cricket test matches from Melbourne. Due to the time difference, we are awakened in our dormitory at about 5:30 am to listen. We are all England cricket fans and eagerly listen to Richard Dimbleby describe the overs, wickets and captain Dick Hutton's 300 for five---it's a marvelous way to wake up listening in bed. What luxury.

Some of the chaps have gone home for Christmas. A surprising number stay and we are treated to some extra perks for the holiday season. It's into Broadstairs and the cinema; Tom Mix, the cowboy, and cartoon shorts are the entertainment. Movietone news reawakens our relaxed film watching with ghastly pictures from the Nazi concentration camps. These have been found and liberated by American and British soldiers. They reveal horrible gas chamber atrocities; skin and bone, sunken eyes survivors and railway carloads of dead bodies stacked like wood. It's the most revolting scene to a 10-year-old's eyes and senses. So indelible as to never be forgotten. I think Hitler, his generals and their government should be in hell themselves for such acts. These news reports put the damper on the fun of a regular flick.

Mr. Green announces the school has been able to scrounge some turkeys for a Christmas dinner feast. Chef has even been able to do roast potatoes with lots of green vegetables. And our pudding will be special orange cake. We don't know where she got the orange peel; we have not seen an orange in years.

The pudding arrives at the tables, just cooked and out of the oven in large flat tins. The staff cuts each boy large square of the cake. Oops, it's over-cooked, burnt on the bottom and quite firm. The kerfuffle starts when one wag drops his piece on the floor and kicks it down the aisle of chairs. Other boys start to do the same and general a cry ensues: *Let's drop kick the orange cake!* It's so firm and hard, we're calling it toe buster and everyone seems to be in the act when headmaster Green calls a halt very loudly. "You boys are spoiling a perfectly good Christmas dinner and your behaviour is not acceptable, so all of you are to now hand in 1,000 lines by noon on Boxing Day." We are to write: *"Manners make the man."*

This mantra will be drilled into our psyche many, many times before we leave Alexander House School.

Post-war Family Fortune Ups and Downs: Pop's Career and the Decision to Emigrate

While I am at public school (Alexander House School in Broadstairs, Kent and now at Dutch Private School outside Whiston/Liverpool), Mummy increasingly has her hands full raising Billy, Fay and me. We are growing. Whether it is clothing, rationed food, schooling and housing, I learn it's all a challenge with what little money Mummy has available. Pop and Mummy's hopes at "pitching up" as we say, in a new post-war English house were dashed as news that the movers' warehouse near Bedford that held some of our major furnishings for bedrooms, living room and kitchen had been lost. I would later learn there was no insurance on items like this, a rarity in England of the day.

Meantime our father and head of the household, Captain C.C. George Daniels, Royal Engineers, was demobilised and Gazetted with honours in early 1946. His job prospects look really good. In Monty's Army, he had been one of the Royal Engineers (sappers as they are called) being Captain and acting Brigadier in reconstructing some of the largest, most important bridges, railways and other buildings destroyed by the retreating German Army. Chasing Jerry through North Africa, landing in Sicily then on to Naples, Monte Casino, Milan and interim Governor of Bologna, Pop has some impressive credentials.

But it's now peacetime and there are no big projects in England which has tossed out Prime Minister Winston Churchill in the 1945 election. Churchill, a man highly regarded for his leadership in the victory over Hitler is replaced by Labour Party socialist Clement Atlee as Prime Minister. Pop cannot get a job in England.

Later we would come to know the dire situation that would descend upon the British Isles, seat of the Commonwealth and glory as best described by Ingrid Seward in her 1999 book about the Queen Mum, *The Last Great Edwardian Lady:*

" Churchill, the Prime Minister who had led the country to victory and who only a few weeks before had stood triumphant with the Royal Family on the balcony at Buckingham Palace, was ruthlessly voted out of office and Labour was swept to power in a landslide on the promise of far-reaching reforms which amounted to what the King himself called a 'Social Revolution'.

The hard truth is that the Labour government had no intention of listening to any Conservative voice, the King's included. At breakneck speed it set about creating the Welfare State. The coal mines, the railways, gas and electricity, road transport were nationalized. The iron and steel industry would follow.

Taxation soared to punitive levels. Attlee declared: 'Controls were desirable not for their own sake but because they were necessary in order to gain freedom from the economic power of the owners of capital. A more just distribution of wealth was not a policy to soak the rich or to take revenge, but because a society with gross inequalities of wealth and opportunity is fundamentally unhealthy.'

The optimism which had greeted Labour's historic victory ran aground on the banks of austerity, as military victory started to look depressingly like economic defeat. Britain, which within memory had been the richest country on earth, was rushing towards bankruptcy. The pound, the very symbol of national strength, was devalued and gold reserves shrank to crisis level. Rationing was more severe than ever. In 1946, bread was added to the list of rationed goods for the first time. Socialism, it seemed, was being bought at a great cost which even huge American loans could not meet. Conditions were harsher than they had been at the height of the war." (Excerpted from pages 201-203)

It is this intolerable economic and political situation that leads my parents to an obvious conclusion: they must consider leaving England to find a better future.

Family and Lancashire Adjustments to Emigrant Planning

At the end of the spring 1946 school term, I get a letter from Mummy saying we are going to move from Northampton to stay with Auntie Lou and Uncle George Jones at Whiston outside Liverpool. The other welcome news is that Pop will be coming to get me. Yes, what a relief. He has survived the battles and crises of the war and is safe. I cannot wait to see him.

It's an early July day and my Daddy is seeing me for the first time in ages in Mr. Green's study. He is in his very posh Captain's uniform. No doubt he has heard all about my various antics, so-so academic marks and sometime athletic achievements on the playing fields. I'm a pretty good runner if I do say so. Pop gives me a loving hug of welcome. To be wrapped in the arms of one of England's super soldiers (the way I see him anyway) is special.

On the train home, Pop tells me some of his war stories. These recount everything from awful marches and slogs through battlefields to his building temporary bridges and railroads to replace the ones the Germans had blown up in retreat. He also has some funny and interesting stories about the Italians; "Eyeties" he calls them, and their disdain for Jerry. I tell him about the Italian prisoner of war who tried to sell me some watches outside Abingdon Park. He laughs and says, "just like them". Of course, Pop speaks Italian as well as French and knows how to get along with them.

Daddy has met a gentleman who is starting a new school that apparently is modeled after schools similar to our Alexander House School. It will be co–educational, meaning boys and girls. Daddy says it will be not quite as expensive as my school in Broadstairs. He urges me to give this new school a try and says he will take me there at the end of the summer.

We are met at the Liverpool train station by Uncle George in a police car. I learn that Uncle George works undercover for the Liverpool Police. Although he does not have a police car for his job, he is able to borrow one from time to time. Uncle George works all 17 of the Liverpool Docks, Elevated

Railway and countless military posts along this seaside port. Pop and he have an interesting chat about their mutual military involvement in things to do with major wartime ports.

Seeing Mummy, Billy, Fay and Auntie Lou at their house is filled with fun and excitement. Where are we all going to sleep? There are only so many bedrooms. Some extra cots in a large bed room will have to do as Billy, Fay and I share.

News comes that Daddy has his first postwar job, but it is not in England. He has been hired by the Anglo-American Oil Company to work in their Middle East oilfields. His wartime civil engineering experience will be valuable, he says. Before he embarks for Haifa, he is going to take me on a bit of a farewell trip to Scorton and then the new boarding school which is in Yorkshire.

We travel by bus to Garstang and are met by Mrs. Short in her car. "George, oh, how you have grown," she says. "Cecil, (my father's most-used first name), you must be proud of your boy." We drive to Scorton where Pop is going to get our old Austin car that has been in storage and on blocks in the Wyersdale garage all during the war.

It being now Wednesday afternoon, Pop tells me to go across the road from Mrs. Short's House to the Scorton Village Common where all the school children are engaged in their usual athletics.

I arrive on the pitch with a football game going on. I am saying hello to old chums including Norm Farrar. They are all jealous of my stories about boarding school at the Broadstairs seaside. I find myself instinctively reverting to village Lancashire dialect.

Along comes a young fellow a foot shorter than me. Interrupting our conversation he looks up at me and says in a broad Lancashire accent; "Eeh ba gum ! If it ain't Daniels. How's that little bruther o' thine? He wern't half a cute little nipper, wern't 'e?"

I immediately hear the unique Lancashire accent and think, oh my goodness, did I use to speak like this village chap? No wonder my Mother was always saying to stop speaking like one of the village lads. It is an accent that is now part of my repertoire of several dialects.

The Daniels Family arrives in Canada
on the R.M.S. Aquitania
Pier 21, December 20, 1947

"Cecil Daniels on board the Aquitania to welcome his family to Montreal.
Back row (L -R) Cunard line nanny, Bunty Daniels, Cecil Daniels.
Front row (L -R) Bill Daniels, Fay Daniels, George Daniels."

Crossing the Atlantic to Canada on Ship Beautiful

"George, you going to a country with streets paved in gold. A land of mountains, long rivers, large lakes and Red Indians."

What excitement! We have been told by our cabin steward, the purser and the dining-room waiter that the Aquitania is called the Queen of the Cunard Line, also known as Ship Beautiful. Here we are, two English lads and getting into hijinks on this beautiful ship. Billy and I are lucky. Mummy lets us explore, so we have the run of the ship. Going from deck to deck in the lift (elevator) instead of bounding up and down stairs is fun. Playing shuffleboard in the inside swimming pool court---it being winter---finds us competing as friendly brothers.

The highlight of the day is 4 o'clock English tea, served on each deck. Billy and I have become samplers of all the cakes, tarts and sweet goodies they have. Starting on A Deck, we eat lemon squares and crisps with our tea. Fifteen minutes later, we are down on B Deck for their sponge cake and strawberries. At 5 o'clock, we are on C Deck for some chocolate cake and round bonbons with our tea. By five-thirty, we are filled up. But, wanting to catch up on eats that we rarely saw in England, we finished up on D Deck for an ice cream and another "cuppa". When we are back in our cabin, Mummy scolds us. "You boys won't be able to eat supper." Yes we will because we can now pause and rest up for the 7 o'clock dinner sitting. Imagine being this lucky each day of the five-day voyage.

The Aquitania has been refurbished after its work in the war as a troop carrier and it's very spiffy. According to the purser, the Aquitania was floating luxury with fine cabins, porcelain baths for fresh or salt water, colorful rugs from the Orient and large cupboards. Our interior deck areas, including entranceways to the dining room and the purser's office where we would sometimes see the Captain, are nicely decorated. There is a stage for an orchestra and some chandeliers.

Instead of exterior garden rooms designed to resemble English landscapes, there are nice open decks with reclining chairs---padded, of course. As Mummy says, we are certainly not toffs, yet we are enjoying pretending to be almost like them as we sail in this well-appointed ocean liner. We are very fortunate, and although we don't realize it at the time, Mummy's connections have gone a long way.

The sound of a foghorn blasts into my eardrums. We have arrived in Canada and thoughts of all the words I have been given by my English headmaster come into my head. Billy and I scramble out of bed and hurry to get on deck. Weather-wise, it really does not look much different that what we have left at home in England. It is damp and foggy. I expect snow and sleet. The Aquitania's PA system tells us it is 20 degrees Fahrenheit (12 degrees below freezing) yet it does not feel all that cold. I would learn later that we thin-blooded blokes can handle the Canadian cold on arrival, and we will really get acclimatized to our new weather realities in the months ahead.

We peer through the mist to see the outline of a big warehouse and a giant sign that says Pier 21. A tugboat is pushing us to the side of the wharf. The PA says that Pier 21 docking will take some time. We are further instructed to attend the dining room for breakfast, our last meal on board. Daddy arrives from Montreal to meet us on deck. We are dressed in our Harris Tweed finery.

The porters are joined by stevedores from the wharf. There is a lot of hubbub as luggage is being gathered. Daddy says he has everything organized and explains we will have to go through Customs and Immigration. We chatter about what we are going to see. The Aquitania has been our luxurious home for the past five days and now we are heading into a new unknown.

Eventually, we are herded to a point on the departure deck. Our purser is on hand to give us guidance as we all line up alphabetically. We head down the covered gangway, and all of a sudden, we are on land. No more the gentle sway of a giant ship. This is Canada.

We see and hear lots of activity. Porters and stevedores are yelling. Luggage carts seem to be everywhere. Somewhere in the background, we can hear a band playing. This is our welcome to Canada. As Mommy and Daddy shepherd us through the crowd of disembarking passengers, I turn my head to take one last look at the Aquitania. I can just see the tops of the red-and-black funnels. The brilliant blue hull with the odd but of rust showing is a sight I will always remember. What a magnificent ship!

RMS Aquitania is the last of the four-stackers, served as a troop ship in two world wars, and was decommissioned in late summer of 1947. We Daniels were among the first peacetime passengers to travel with her in her new paint job, but its passenger service did not last long, ending in November of 1949.

We now enter a giant warehouse. Mommy and Daddy keep us close together. We notice we are behind a large steel screen which divides the area and has various openings, with counters staffed by very official-looking people. Daddy explains they are the Customs and Immigration officers. Mommy is searching her purse for our passports. All of a sudden, a porter appears with our luggage. It takes a long time to explain what is in our luggage. We have one very large wooden trunk with metal straps that bind the strong leather case. We would have this trunk in our family for many years after, as this type of trunk became a signature piece for many trans-Atlantic immigrants to Canada.

We eventually get through the detailed Customs and Immigration inspection. Bill and I comment that finally, we are through the fence and into Pier 21's new reception area. It is a hive of activity. There are piles of luggage everywhere. Our Daniels luggage looks rather special among mounds of cardboard boxes and luggage that has barely survived handling during the voyage.

People with paperwork and clipboards, some nuns and some from the Red Cross, are running around interviewing families to determine where they are going. Porters seem ever helpful and Mommy and Daddy engage one to help us with our pile of possessions. The whole process is taking a long time. We all are hungry, when out of nowhere appears tea and sandwiches. Among the food offered is our first experience with a truly Canadian tradition---the hot dog. We didn't have these in England. They are very tasty with a sweet yellow mustard that is far more enjoyable (thanks, Canada) than the mouth-burning English Dijon mustard.

Finally, we find our way onto our train platform. Looking back at the building we just left, I can see through a window a railroad telephone operator. He seems to have all kinds of equipment, and his headset and green eyeshade set him apart as a special man.

In front of us is one of the biggest locomotives we have ever seen. It has huge steel wheels and steam is hissing from underneath. We notice a name painted on the side: Ocean Limited. It is a monster compared to what we were used to seeing in England. The *Flying Scotsman and London, Midland and Scottish Railway (LMS)* were 'way smaller as I remembered them from going to Alexander House School from Scorton. What is also different is that there is no platform; we are standing at ground level, which we never experienced in England.

The conductor has a box-like footstool for us to stand on to mount the steps into our coach. "All aboard!" he cries, as the railway takes us on our new road to the Canadian experience.

Pier 21 Immigration Officers interview new landed immigrants.

Luggage and arrivals area at Pier 21.

CNR 4-8-4 Steam Engine used for "Ocean Limited" cross Canada Rail travel. Canadian National Railways 1940's -'50's Engine same as the" Ocean Limited".

CN Railway Station 1940's-50's Tele-Type operator. (George would obtain one of these "Radio/Telephone" Licenses in the mid fifties).

PART II

The Daniels family settles in Montreal with new friends, new schools, new housing and new interests, including athletics and the Montreal Canadiens hockey team.

Part II

High Schools of Montreal, Town of Mount Royal and McMaster University

We have been in Canada for barely two weeks and I am still getting acclimatized, although with my thicker British blood, I don't feel the Canadian cold as much as our new Montréal friends do. And it is 10° below freezing with snow.

We are starting a new year. It's January 1948 and Pop and I are driving in his British-American oil company car from 117725 La Gauchetiere St., our lower duplex home, to the center of Montréal at Sherbrooke St. and University Ave. opposite McGill University to register at the High School of Montréal. Pop is saying that I should pay attention to the transit routes for when I will be doing it on my own. I will be boarding several buses with a transfer stop at the George V terminal.

My dad has pre-arranged a meeting with the principal. His name is Mr. Leonard Unsworth and he is called the Rector. Pop and Mr. Unsworth seem to get along very well. The Rector is a fairly-new Canadian and is from Yorkshire. He and my Dad seem to have various mutual acquaintances back in England.

I am quite nervous and apprehensive when they start to discuss my English school record (not very good at math). My father keeps pushing for me to be in what is called grade 9. Eventually they agree that I will be enrolled in grade 9D. Mr. Campbell, the Vice-Rector, is introduced and takes me to visit my new class on the second floor.

The Winter Term: January-April, 1948

Being at the High School of Montréal is a stark contrast to the small schools I had attended in England. It is over 100 years old, although this massive building, which was built in 1914, seems to accommodate all students very well. It is the major regional high school for Protestant students that come from all over the Island of Montréal. The enrolment is 3,500 with 60 class-rooms, teaching grades 8 to 11. I am learning to juggle my schedule from 9 am to noon, then lunch to 12:30 p.m. with classes ending at 2:30 pm. This early ending of the school day is to accommodate the extra club and sports activities and so that students from far away can get their buses or streetcars home before supper time.

I am encouraged by Pop to join the chess club. Mr. Rivard, one of the Physics teachers, is our coach. We often meet over sandwiches at lunch time. It being winter, I joined the swimming team and tried out for water polo. Water polo is tough. Fred Urquhart, who is head of athletics, is encouraging me to keep practicing treading water in place and bobbing the ball at the same time. The objective is to be able to throw the ball overhand to your teammate and/or on the goal. I will keep practicing.

We have a large history book to study. It chronicles the history of England from 1066 to World War I in 1914-18. I am enjoying it and get good marks. In our biology classes, I learn about dissection of frogs. Mr. Byers' art classes include making papier-mache facial masks. I do one of a Red Indian. Mr. Byers again gives me good marks for this model.

Not too far away from the school on de Maisonneuve is the legendary Kravitz family business, Ben's Delicatessen. Once or twice a week, we rush there to grab one of the counter seats and have Jacques serve us with piled-high, steaming smoked meat sandwiches, French fries and a Coke for $2.50. Delicious. Eaton's is just down the road at the corner of University and St. Catherine Street. I find myself often going there on the way home to check out the latest newsstand magazines and chocolate bars before hurrying to get my bus home.

After the Easter break and as we head into springtime, me and the other students often go to the McGill campus is right across the road. We spread out our sandwich lunches and do some studying. Spring exams are just around the corner. I cannot remember exams being an important part of my life in England. Here, they are. Whether it's academics, clubs or sports, we are being taught that all of this is the foundation for our future. I guess I am becoming a New Canadian.

I do not to do very well on the June exams. Discussions with my parents and Mr. Campbell determine that I will return to grade 9 in September.

I am not discouraged about returning to grade 9 and I'm looking forward to my first Canadian summer. This turns out to be highlighted by my first green-thumb gardening experience with Pop. My dad has discovered that our large backyard garden used to be a chicken pen and explains that chicken poop makes perfect manure for growing tomatoes and cucumbers. From planting to cultivating and weeding to the end of harvest, we pick bushels of cucumbers and tomatoes. My mother, using all her English culinary bottling experience, puts down many jars of both these vegetables. Of course, she makes many, many cucumber sandwiches and by the end of summer, I am fed up with cucumbers.

The Montréal East Boy Scout Troop is not too far away and meets in the local Grade school. We get a visit from District Commissioner Holdsworth who tells us about Camp Tamaracoutta in the Laurentians. It sounds exciting with swimming, hiking, games and living in a tent with other boys wanting an outdoor adventure.

He recommends we save our money earned from shoveling snow in the wintertime, babysitting and in general, doing various chores to earn the dollars to pay for camp. He points out that we will enjoy it more having earned the $17 per week it costs instead of relying on our parents to spend their hard-earned money. By the time I hear of this, I have already saved up nearly $10, so I can easily see being able to earn extra money to go to Camp Tamaracoutta. I am working hard on persuading my mother and Pop that I should go to the camp. They subsequently agree.

Montreal High January 1948 and Pointe-aux-Trembles

I have now been introduced to my 9D classroom teacher, Mr. Lunan. He explains the various subjects and points out that part of the curriculum is an active sports program. This includes gym classes and swimming lessons. The school has one of the few large swimming pools in the Montréal area for student activities. Apparently, I will also be involved with shop and will have my choice of either auto mechanics or woodwork and carpentry. New to me will be homework assignments. I never experienced homework in England. More about my grade 9 class after I say some words about our new home.

Our Pointe-aux-Trembles house has three bedrooms with a large living dining area and cozy kitchen all on one floor. There is an upstairs apartment being rented to another family. Stairs to the upper flat are outside the building. I discover this is typical Montréal architecture.

Pop is determined that I am going to learn French. We know I will be studying French in school but to catch up, I will need some tutoring, so I am now enrolled in a private French Protestant school to be tutored by Father Hurtubise. Lessons are scheduled twice midweek and on Saturday mornings. It is a struggle to not only listen to the teacher but also to understand the French verbs.

It being winter, my English Harris Tweed coat and other clothing are not good enough to withstand the cold and snow, so my Mother and Pop take us shopping for new clothes. We have noticed that some of the boys are wearing what we called jodhpurs, a wide pant with a tapered leg that could fit into high boots. Oh what a shock I have when I show up at Montréal High wearing these pants. I look like an out-of-place farmer, and I'm roundly teased by my fellow students. Obviously, I'm not going to wear these again. An important part of our footwear is rubber galoshes that go over our regular shoes, a nice item of new Canadian wear to battle the snow and slush of winter.

Shopping is a new adventure. There are several types of grocery stores my parents can choose from. We discover almost next door a converted house that is home to Mrs. Bavalack. In what would be the living room and dining room, she has well-stocked shelves of convenience foods. There are cans of soup, packages of cereal, bread and a cooler for butter and milk. The whole place smells of her garlic-laced cooking. She is very friendly and welcomes my mother with a free bottle of Coca-Cola, A glass for both of them and she announces a toast to welcome the Daniels. My mother is taken aback and giggles with this generosity.

At home we also discover our new radio. Its broadcasts are nothing like the BBC we were used to in England. The BBC had only one or two channels, but here in Canada and Montréal, there are at least four stations and several that we can get from the United States. We like this new Canadian sound. The Canadian Broadcasting Corporation broadcasts are similar to some BBC programs, having concerts and interview programs. What we kids like are the other stations which play popular music and family programming such as *Bringing up Father* with

William Bendix. No one celebrated Mothers' Day in England but they do here. And we all have a big laugh when listening to William Bendix announce to his wife that, "it's Mothers' Day so you don't have to do the dishes, dear, we will just pile them in the sink so you can do them tomorrow". Another popular program is the *Bob Hope Show* and his many jokes.

Montreal High School

It's June 1948, and wow, what really-hot weather. This is our first experience with Canadian spring and summer temperatures that seem to go above the limits of the outdoor thermometer. What a contrast to the cold winters. It is uncomfortable and we are not used to it. It's more than seventy degrees and the humidity makes it feel like 100. The Montreal Star headlines that it is one of the warmest summers on record. My mother is trying to re-outfit us with summer clothes to replace our old English winter tweed togs.

Our final term exams are uncomfortable due to the weather. Every classroom has its large six-foot-wide windows pushed up to the ceiling trying to get a breath of fresh air. But there is no breeze---just the rumble of street traffic and the tension of trying to concentrate on math or physics, written French or English. I am not handling it very well and cannot wait to get to our new-found swimming beach at But de Lisle, just east of our house.

Bill and I discover that we can earn pocket money, something we never did in England, by doing various chores for our neighbours. Mowing a lawn can get us from $.50-$.75 and washing dishes for elderly people is worth $.25-$.40. Mrs. Bavelak sometimes needs us to deliver some of her groceries. We get some nice tips doing this. Over the summer months, we both earn more than $25, which we are saving to go to Camp Tamarracuta next summer.

I have still not lost all my English accent. Water comes out as 'wahtter.' Saucer is particularly obvious with the AH sound in the middle of the word. Bill and I get teased a lot by our new Montréal friends.

Every boy looks up to his sports heroes. So now we must forget Stanley Matthews of English soccer fame and Everton footballer

Now he is with the Brooklyn Dodgers, we will also follow his super career in New York.

Being track and field participants, we really cheered when French Canadian Gerard Cote won the 52nd running of the Boston Marathon in two hours and 21 minutes. All of Montréal is quite chuffed by this feat.

In other news, we learn of the Palestine Jews being at war with the Arabs which would lead to the formation of the new state of Israel. The Communists take over Czechoslovakia and in the United States election, Harry Truman defeats Thomas Dewey in the greatest upset in presidential election history.

Pop has told us to keep an eye and an ear on the Union Nationale party and their leader, Maurice Duplessis. Mr. Duplessis is an arch-Conservative, and Pop says his political shenanigans are of concern. One of these is the Union Jack which has been flying over the Québec provincial Parliament buildings since the early 1800s. On July 28, Duplessis wins a landslide re-election and immediately takes down the Union Jack and replaces it with that new flag of Québec, the Fleur-de-Lys. Pop says we can look forward to more dramatic moves from the Union Nationale government.

Make-Believe Ballroom with Mike Stevens on CJAD 800 on the radio dial is Bill's and my preference. We tune in when parents are not around to listen to the CBC, Lister Sinclair and excerpts from the BBC. Some of the music in the top 10 is as a result of the big bands of Tommy Dorsey and others making way for individual stars such as the Andrews sisters, Nat King Cole, Doris Day, Bing Crosby and the Ink Spots to name a few. Hit songs *Slow Boat to China, I'm Looking Over a Four-Leaf Clover* and the *Woody Woodpecker Song* are in the top 10.

I am feeling more comfortable returning to my grade 9 class in the fall. Arithmetic is a challenge and Mr. Griffith often bemoans my performance and says in his Scots accent; "what's the matter, man, don't you know your matter mattics?"

My intramural track and field and cross-country running for the school team are interrupted when Pop has to rush me to the hospital for a burst appendix operation. It's not so bad after all because I am off school for a two-week recuperation. Sports-wise I have to take it easy, but one thing I am allowed to do is easy lengths in our swimming pool, which is shared by the boys' school intermittently with the girls' school on the south side of the building. The adjoining doors and showers are locked and closely monitored by two boys and girls. Our teenage boy hormones are always active when some devious guy decides he's found a peephole so we can look into the girls' showers. It's really not true.

Travel time from the high school to our home in Pointe-aux-Trembles is always an hour and a half. It certainly puts a crimp in after-school activities, but we persevere and make arrangements accordingly.

1949 High School
Montreal--Richelieu

I can feel that this year is certainly going to be my new Canadian adventure. In my Montreal High class I am among a United Nations of classmates. My new-found friends, although teasing me about my English accent, are accepting. They are a cross-section of Poles, Greeks, Ukrainians, Japanese and some Blacks. Vic Podinski, Steve Bobiushka and Karl Hilzinger sit near me in class. Karl is a fan of Frankie Laine's new hit recording of *Mule Train*.

The teachers point out that we are witnessing history. Joey Smallwood of Newfoundland has been able to work with the English Parliament and Newfoundland now officially joins Canada as a province. In other news the Montréal docks are paralyzed by a major seamen's strike.

The friends I make in the Montréal East Boy Scout troop can lead me astray. One Saturday, with time on our hands, we explore a construction site and come across a large vat of bricklayers' lime. We start stirring it with sticks and the next thing you know we are flinging it up against nearby brick walls. This leaves large stain marks. Boy, are we in trouble now. The owner complains to the police who in turn track us down through the Scoutmaster and we are severely reprimanded and have to pay by clearing up the construction site. A lesson learned.

Saving money has paid off. My mother and Pop approve of me going to Camp Tamarracouta near St. Jovite in the Laurentians. Living in a tent with other boys at what was called the Cumberland House Camp is really fun. We have a special kitchen mess that is under a large tent with a refractory table. This is our main eating facility for breakfast and lunch.

Our evening meal is in the camp's main Assembly Hall and always is led by the Factor, Mr. Holdsworth, or his second-in-command. We are required to change from informal camp wear into our full Scout uniforms. We open with a salute to the flags and the singing of God Save the King, as King George VI is our Patron and Chief Scout. We remain on our feet and sing Grace:

Be present at our table, Lord
Be here and ev'rywhere adored.
These mercies bless and grant that we
May feast in Paradise with Thee

Recognition of various Scouts includes awarding of badges and in particular, those to do with swimming and the Royal Lifesaving Society medals. I am in training for the bronze medal. The Tamarracouta dock and swimming facility is huge. The swimming exercises are vigorous and our instructors are hard taskmasters. At the end of my first two weeks, I have earned my bronze medal. One of the Scout leaders tells me I am now being considered for a "Knight of Tamara" enrolment. This is quite an accolade.

My parents decide that our Pointe-aux-Trembles home is really too small. Pop has got to know people from the South Shore and we now move to Richelieu. Our new house is half of a very large, stately-looking mansion. There are huge rooms and an upstairs for bedrooms and on the roof, an impressive turret. It is a Ward home and is called The Chateau. There are large grounds and we face the Richelieu River.

Pop and mother quickly establish new friends. We get to know the Maybees, Jelletts and Tubmans. I want to keep up with Scouting but there are no boys my age. Mr. Bashaw is the Cubmaster and he arranges with Mr. Charlie Phillips that I become a Lone Scout. Because Pop is often away due to his job, having Mr. Phillips as my leader is very helpful.

Commuting to Montreal High is now another challenge. The Montreal and Southern Counties Railroad leaves our Richelieu station at 7:30 am. It is about one hour across the Pont Victoria to Place d'Armes. Then I have an uphill walk to Montreal High. It is a scramble every morning to make the opening bell. If I am late, the teachers are considerate knowing the distance I have come.

We get our first black-and-white small TV. The news says that Mao-Tse Tung has turned China Communist. In Olympic hockey, Canada beats Denmark 47-0 and we discover Hockey Night in Canada. The Montreal Canadiens and the Rocket are favourites.

My first Lone Scout camping trip is with Charlie Phillips and some friends. We are on a hunting trip for deer down by the Quebec-US border. Mr. Phillips and his gun-toting friends have no luck shooting game but we have fun with campfires and exploring the area.

1950: Dude Ranch at Kananaskis

It is the middle of July 1950 and I have completed Scouting at Camp Tamaracouta. Pop has flown east from his job at Seabee, Alberta, where he is building a huge hydro dam on the Bow River. Pop says that I am going to drive West with him to Seabee and Kananaskis on the Bow River where he is the chief engineering superintendent for the Foundation Company of Canada, main contractors building the Bow River dam. Pop points out that the several thousand-mile drive will be an eye-opener to all the things Canadian along the way.

Leaving Montréal, we travel to Sudbury, Ontario and view the large statue of a Canadian nickel.

George at Banff Indian Days
his 1950 Christmas Card

Some of our dude ranch guests are Americans very concerned about Korea and its impact on immediate family members who might have to go to war. Brewster Kananaskis Dude Ranch is a huge spread, as they say here. The main lodge is home to the Brewster family. The large kitchen services the dining room where all meals are served for the working cowboy staff and paying guests. My chore boy duties include collecting the dishes and general cleanup after meals.

We have prominent guests. The Cadbury family of chocolate bar fame is here from England. Their upper-class accents are pronounced. We also have a group of teenage girls from the United States. They have come for the trail rides into the Rockies. One of their chaperones is the Chambers family which has several daughters. Mr. Chambers thinks it would be a good idea if I were return to Boston with them at the end of the summer and become part of the family. When Pop gets wind of this idea, he quickly puts a kibosh on this notion. It doesn't stop me noticing the girls.

The ranch has a large stable area for several dozen horses that are used for riding lessons. From time to time, the pack horses that are the backbone of the trail rides venture into the Rockies every several weeks for a seven-day camping trip. The lead cowboy in charge of the stables is Steve Cody, said to be a grandson of the famous Buffalo Bill Cody.

Steve takes me under his wing to teach me the ropes. The first order of business is to learn how to saddle a horse. First of all, I have to corral the beast. Sometimes it's easy because you just call their names and at other times you have to lasso them. Steve teaches me how to make a lasso so the rope can make a large 4-6 foot diameter circle with a trailing portion of the rope. There is a knack to winding it up around your head and throwing it over the neck of the horse. I am not very good at the beginning, but finally I'm able to accomplish it probably half of the time. Bridal bits, reins, stirrups and saddle blankets all have to be placed on the horse for its comfort and the rider's control of the horse's movements. It takes me several days and much practice to become a junior cowboy. Now I am ready for a trail ride.

One day, I am accompanying a dozen girls on horseback in my baggy Eastern Canadian jeans. A part of the ride includes squeezing through a series of bushes next to a barbwire fence. I am in the middle of the pack when all of a sudden, one of the bush branches whacks the horse in the head and it shies away and pushes us up against the sharp wire. My jeans are caught. The horse takes off on a gallop and my pants are totally ripped down to my underwear. The girls all laugh and giggle. I turn a blushing red and I'm mortified. Steve supplies a jacket which I wrap around my middle for some semblance of modesty on the way back to the ranch. The girls cannot stop talking about this episode and I am embarrassed.

Steve Cody's hobby is to make decorative leather belts and cowboy-themed silver buckles to match. I am honoured that he makes a set for me and then donates a pair of his used cowboy boots and an old Stetson so that I can really look the part. Boy, do I feel posh. Some people say I even look like I am walking bowlegged as if I had been on a horse all my teenage years.

The wide-open spaces of the Seabee flats are an ideal location to learn to drive Pop's grey panel van. It has a four-speed stick shift. On my times off, he takes me several times until I get the hang of it. But I am still not driving on Alberta's roads; that will come later. I will have to wait until I am 16 and back in Montréal to get a learner's license. It is fun getting started.

Canmore's train station is only several miles from the Brewster Ranch on the main CPR line. One day, Steve and I drive to the station to send some parcels. There is hardly anyone around when the train chugs to a stop with a big hissing sound of steam and the squeal of brakes. Steve heads back to the truck and I hang around the platform to see the train depart. A toot of the whistle, a rush of steam and the grind of steel wheels on the tracks sees the engine start to move quite rapidly.

Just then a beautiful Collie runs out of the station barking like mad and runs angrily after the train. It starts to snap at a protruding set of steps. The dog gets too close and with a piercing yelp of pain is almost decapitated by the step. It is writhing in agony and instantly I know what I have to do. Put it out of its misery. Conveniently, there is a large shovel nearby, so I grab it and with all my force bash the dog's head until it is still and dead. I run and yell for Steve and I am shaking. He says I have done the right thing and that the stationmaster will look after the dog's burial. All I could think about was our lovely spaniel Nola in England and our Labrador puppies in Montréal and how I would not want a similar fate for them.

Banff Indian Days is a one-week celebration for all the Alberta tribes. Pop decides we are going to spend a day to view the festivities, which are colourful and exciting. All the natives are dressed in their Indian finery to complement the various war dances. The chuckwagon rides with natives and regular cowboys are quite a sight. To use an English expression, I am quite chuffed, when I overhear a nearby woman spectator casually remark, "Look at that young cowboy, he just fits the part".

Mr. King works with Pop on the Bow River hydro dam project, so it is decided that we will take a few days off to visit the Columbia ice fields, is a vast glacier. It is a beautiful sunny day and we travel up the glacier in a six-person Bombardier tracked vehicle made in Québec and dates from the late 30s. It is a Canadian first in transportation.

The Korean War rages on and the US army is drafting all young men to serve overseas. Pop points out that if I had gone to Boston with the Chambers, I would be eligible for the draft in two and a half years. So it is far better staying in Canada listening to the radio and hearing the Andrews sisters, Ink Spots and the Woodpecker Song and working summer jobs while in school.

My return train ticket to Montréal is on CP rail. At the end of August, the railway workers go on a strike extending through Labour Day for nine days. Hooray, I am forced to stay at the Brewster Ranch for an extra several weeks before returning home and I am delighted.

Fall 1950

Commuting to Montréal High School takes three hours out of a very busy day. My extra-curricular water polo team activity, Chess Club and homework are a challenge. As winter sets in, Richelieu is blanketed in snow. Some of the boys have skis. I take the plunge and give it a try. The wooden skis have what are called a bear-trap harness. You slip into the harness, buckle up with a strap over your regular boots and are ready to go. After several falls and nearly crashing into nearby trees, I get the hang of it. Lots of fun.

Pop buys an English Ford Prefect which is now my opportunity to continue learning to drive. Taking to back roads with no traffic, I navigate, with Pop at my side, several miles with ease. We drive back to the garage next to our house. The door is open and I slowly inch forward to park. I put on the brakes and nothing happens, the car won't stop. Pop yells grab the handbrake, which I do and it pulls out in my hand as the car comes to a gentle crunch on the back wall. We are not too impressed with the Prefect's mechanics. Several months later, Pop gets rid of this car and buys a used 1947 Cadillac sedan previously owned by the president of French-language television station Channel 10 Montréal. Later on, this station would become another learning and influential experience in my future career.

We have friends in a little village called Foster in the Eastern Townships. During a visit in early March we are invited to ski. The soft snow becomes icy in the late afternoon. As I enjoy swooshing the gentle hills, I make a sharp turn in front of a tree and my legs slide out from under me and I crash into the tree. I can feel it---I have broken a leg. After much parental consternation, I am driven to Sherbrooke Hospital and a walking plaster cast is put on my lower left leg where I have a cracked tibia. Now I have a souvenir which attracts signatures and I am told I have now really embraced a Canadian winter.

With the arrival of spring and my leg all better, it is time for track and field. McGill Stadium is our training venue. Canadian track stars Murray Gazuck and Bruce Whaller are some of our coaches. In the world of Olympic athletics, there is talk about breaking the four-minute mile.

Much speculation surrounds England's Oxford University team led by Roger Bannister and Chris Chataway. The Eastern Canadian track and field championships are going to be in Saint-Lambert south of Montréal in early June.

Excitement mounts as Chataway announces he will enter the three-mile race. With much audacity and encouragement from coach Fred Urquhart, I also enter the race. When the big day arrives, I have the jitters lining up at the start with Chataway and other notables. The gun goes off and there is a mad scramble to rush out and try and keep up with Chataway. I hold my own for about a mile and then like a gazelle, he is way ahead. By the end of the race, he has nearly lapped me and many others. Now we understand why he is in a class by himself. Chris would finally go on to be the rabbit or pacesetter who pulled Doctor Roger Bannister through to breaking the four-minute mile in three minutes and 59 seconds at Oxford in early 1954.

Once again we are we soaked and getting a campfire started is virtually impossible. By the third day, we are down to eating our last food; a can of cherries. On arrival back at Tamaracouta, no one seems worried and leaders Wheeler and Ford say we have done well.

The Knights of Tamara is a semi-secret Society of Camp Tamaracouta. Every summer, several boys are selected to become members. The qualifications include continuous work towards Scouting leadership. I am very honoured when camp director Len Holdsworth and Mr. Ford advise me I have been selected to become a Knight of Tamara. A public initiation is scheduled.

It entails being in a boxing ring stripped down to your swimming trunks and then plastered with Vaseline all over your upper body, except one's head, and then being given a bag of cocoa to sprinkle and plaster all over a wrestling partner. The one who becomes Coco Brown all over loses and the cleanest one wins. Amazingly, I am the winner. Several days later at a campfire ceremony on the other side of the lake, I am presented with a leather thong and yellow bead bracelet that signifies I am now a Knight of Tamara. I am tickled by this achievement.

Fall 1951-1952

Commuting from St. Hubert to Montréal High is now easier by bus or in Pop's car. Bill and Fay have to change schools and are now attending in St. Hubert.

Princess Elizabeth and her husband, the Duke of Edinburgh, arrive in Canada. A large assembly of Montréal-area schools becomes part of their itinerary. To plan for the McGill Stadium event, we are all encouraged to dress smartly in navy blazers and grey flannels. Mommy takes me to Morgan's department store to be suited up. Ron Bertrand is in my class and is the head boy of Montréal High. We are all honoured that Ron is selected to present the Princess with a bouquet of flowers. I am sitting only six people away from this ceremony which takes place before various bands and athletics that are performed for the Royal guests. Several days later, the Princess and her husband are in a special parade along the route in Westmount where I am one of hundreds of Boy Scouts and Girl Guides who line the route. I have also joined the St. George's Westmount Scout troop.

This grade 11 year is important as I prepare for the Quebec Provincial leaving exams in the springtime. My math and sciences continue to be a challenge. I am on our Water Polo team and we are all celebrated as we win the City Championship for the third year in a row. I do well in track and field and this is highlighted by me winning the fall cross-country three-mile race around Mount Royal. I even get my picture in the Montréal Gazette.

The news constantly features the ongoing Korean War and Quebec Premier Maurice Duplessis is at odds with the Aluminum Company of Canada workers on strike in Arvida, Québec. However, our youthful enthusiasm centres more on popular singer Nat King Cole. He is featured at the Empire Theatre and one day, we are truant and sneak in to catch one of his performances. The Montréal Alouette football team is a fan favourite and Mayor Camillien Houde is invited to perform the season kickoff. In front of all the TV cameras and radio, and in broken English, he says, "I am delighted to be here to kick your balls off", generating howls of laughter from those in the Stadium and no doubt from folks tuned in at home.

Our stay in St. Bruno is short lived. The house is sold and Pop and Mummy decide to move into a new home in a Ville St.-Laurent subdivision on the Island of Montréal. When the spring term is over and exams are completed, we move into our new semi-detached house on Marlatt Avenue.

I expectantly wait for my high school matriculation results. It is now the summer of 1952 and for the second time, I return to work on the St. Hubert Air Force Base project. I now have a promotion and work in the toolshed handing out everything from a basic hammer, claw bar, shovel, nails and screws for the carpenters and labourers alike. Once again, I am immersed in French and get to know the French names of these tools. I move around the job sites.

We have riggers and most of these are Mohawk Indians who come from Kahnawake. They are not afraid of heights and are fearless as they casually walk two and three stories about the ground on the huge steel I-beams. They encourage me to give it a try. I stand up and walk, looking straight ahead and not down, for about four or five feet before I sink down on my bottom to the safety of the beam---I'm not doing that again.

Not unexpectedly, I have passed only five of the obligatory eight matriculation subjects but am allowed to take supplementary exams at the end of August to complete this requirement. Sir George Williams University on Mountain Street runs a summer school, and this is where I attend, study and rewrite the math and science papers. We have a distraction with the Alouettes' American import players staying at the Sir George dorms. We get to chum with QB Al Dekdebrun, Chuck Hunsinger and Herb Trawick from time to time. Whether I do well or not, all of my marks are marginal, so we decide I will repeat grade 11 at the new Town of Mount Royal High School. The school is only a short 20-minute bus ride from our house and I start there in September.

Readjusting to these new surroundings is fun and challenging. At high school, some of my former colleagues from Montréal High are also there. I take all the classes in each discipline. My new teachers are pleased that I am skilled in History, English and oral French. I join the track and field team and I am often excused from afternoon classes in order to train. Ms. Harrison, our history teacher and Miss Dombroski let me off repeatedly, yet I'm still able to get high marks on their tests. One of my new friends is Eddie Kudlack whose father lends him a new Chevrolet hardtop from time to time. I'm tickled that Eddie includes me as part of the group who takes the girls for rides after school. High-school dances in our gymnasium are now part of my new experience in growing up. The Cartierville Airport is a bicycle ride from our house and one Saturday, Bill and I cycle over to see the airplanes. Standing by the mesh fence, we ogle the planes and their pilots. A man comes over and says, "would you boys like to go flying?" Of course we quickly say yes. The gentleman is a doctor who has a small single-engine Aeronca C5, a high-wing airplane with, he explains, an 85-hp engine. It has no doors but a 6-inch lip that keeps pilot and passengers tucked in after one is strapped in with the safety harness. It has a bench seat with enough room for the pilot Dr. and skinny Bill and me to fit in. After going through this procedure, we taxi out to the runway and with power applied take off. Wow! What exhilaration! The roar of the wind and motor is all around us. We are amazed at the super view from on high. The doctor flies us over the huge landmark Saint Joseph's Oratory Cathedral. It is spectacular. The views from our cockpit perch are amazing. I am hooked on flying.

Our High School is new and construction finished just before enrolment. Bill joins me on our bus rides to school, he being in Grade 8 and me in the final year. Bill's after-school work includes being on the Red Cross and swimming teams.

This fall, I continue my Boy Scout activities with the Westmount troop. My goal is to complete the King's Scout Merit Badge before Christmas. A new NHL season starts and as fans of the Canadiens, we are eager to see them play. Several times Bill and I take the Cartierville streetcar to the Montréal Forum. We discover that for a standing room only ticket in the gods, or very highest level, we can get in for $1.25 each. When the doors open one hour before the opening face-off, we rush upstairs with the rest of the mob to grab a railing position at the highest level in the Forum. We have a bird's-eye view of the rink. The games are exciting and the Rocket often scores as does Boom-Boom Geoffrion. Pop says ware so addicted to Rocket Richard that we probably know when he cuts his toenails and takes a shower. We are not alone being fans of the Habs' greats.

By Christmas, I have earned my King's Scout badge. This is considered a special achievement in Scouting and I will be presented with this honour later at a special ceremony at McGill University.

Montreal is known or its wide-open night life. The nightclubs and entertainment bars turn a blind eye and let older teenagers be patrons. It is not unusual for a group of us to go downtown after a high-school dance and visit such hot spots as the Bellevue Casino or Rockhead's Cabaret. My friends often order quart bottles of Quebec beer while others drink rum and Coke. Being on the track team and with a queasy stomach and ulcers, I do not drink. On one visit to the Casino, I cause quite a sneer from the bartender when I order a glass of milk. My friends laugh but do not disparage me.

It is February 1952 and the world is shocked by the death of King George VI, our beloved monarch who, with Queen Elizabeth, were our moral compass and backbone with Prime Minister Winston Churchill in the resistance to the Blitz in World War II. We experienced the northern Blitz on Liverpool and area.

Princess Elizabeth now becomes Queen. She is joined at her side by the Duke of Edinburgh. This situation makes my King's Scout award special. In late March, I am one of several hundred Scouts to be presented with their various merit badges. It takes place in Moyse Hall at McGill. The well-known CBC Radio commentator John Fisher (known as Mr. Canada) is the MC and presenter. I am one of only six to be honoured with a King's Scout certificate and badge. The presentations are made alphabetically and John Fisher comments on the public address system that I will be the last of the King Scouts. Subsequent recipients will be Queen's Scouts. I am very proud of my

Crown badge. It is one of the pinnacles of Boy Scout merit and I am honoured to wear it. Shortly after this achievement, the Westmount Scoutmaster enrolls me in Rover Scout leadership training. All is going well, and then Pop announces he has accepted a position with a major construction company in Hamilton, Ontario and tells Mother to get ready to move. We know that the summer months will include packing boxes and suitcases for our end-of-August trip. I will still be able to work for about six weeks on the St. Hubert air base construction site. News comes that I have passed, barely, my Quebec Grade 11 Matriculation. Hurray!

We have been in Canada five years and have moved five times in Montréal and the surrounding towns. Pop and Mummy are always striving to improve our lot in our new country. This new relocation to Hamilton, Ontario brings a lot of expectations. I had been planning to go to McGill in the fall, but my parents say I can now set my sights on McMaster University. This will be our sixth move in Canada as we travel to what is called Steeltown on Lake Ontario. My Canadian journey continues.

Fall 1953: McMaster University

Kenwood Westmount Movers jockey our St. Bruno household goods into a giant van and move everything to our new home on the Hamilton Mountain. We are on 10th Street in a square bungalow and squeezed into three bedrooms. It is early September 1953.

My Quebec high school graduation marks are not very impressive. Pop uses his Baptist background and is able to negotiate my enrolment at McMaster, founded by the Baptist Convention. The Principal is George Gilmore. He takes me under his wing as a student and I start on September 4.

After filling out numerous registration forms, I quickly learn the informality of university life. There are no regimented classes, rather optional subjects one can take. I opt for a mix of social studies and science. Second-year students are called sophomores, and tradition has it that they conduct a hazing week on the first-year students. I find myself lined up with approximately 100 other frosh, as we are called, in front of the Ivor Wynne gymnasium drill hall. All the sophs are wearing maroon McMaster jackets. One chap has a very long pair of scissors. He patrols the lineup of the newbies and brandishing the scissors under the nose of many who have long hair, such as myself, threatening that if "you do not get a half-inch brush cut before 3 o'clock in the afternoon, I will be forced to do the barbering myself". The sophomore rule is that all frosh be readily identified by a very short brush cut.

When I get home, Mummy is horrified about my brush cut. I told her this is only the beginning of hazing week. My dad thinks my new look is amusing. He mentions that many of the workers at his Olmstead and Parker construction company have brush cuts. He says he experienced hazing when he went to school and remembers it's part of building one's character and learning to get along with others.

Sporting a new McMaster frosh schoolboy hat, a group of us is taken to downtown Hamilton for another initiation. The sophs have a bag of peeled and pungent onions. We are forced to our knees and must push an onion with our noses approximately 24 feet along the sidewalk. Passersby gawk and laugh at our predicament as we are egged on by our sophomore masters.

We make time to go to our new lectures. Sitting in a large amphitheater on the first day towards the end of the period, I am asked by a chap next to me what I am doing after school. I reply I do not know, being new to McMaster and just arrived from Montréal. Introducing himself as Owen Boris, he says that he is looking for several fellows to help him after school by putting up television antennas to earn some money. He goes on to explain he has a small truck and equipment for the installation work. He also says he has just got his pilot's license at the Hamilton airport and we can go flying with him after an antenna installation. This sounds intriguing so I say, "Count me in". Owen asks several of our seatmates the same question. Fred Warren replies that he already has a pilot's license from Air Cadets but he will go up on the roof to earn some money. Bob McCullagh says, "I am not going up on any damn roof, but I will go flying with you." The three of us sign on to Owen's TV antenna business and would go on to make some bucks that helped us also pay for flying lessons. This became the start of five to six decades of friendship for the four of us.

Being the subject of outlandish hazing escapades has its memorable moments, one of which was being challenged to invade the girls' dormitory and retrieve a set of brassieres and panties. Fred Warren was driven miles away, blindfolded, dumped out of the car on Highway 5 near Clapperson's

Cut in the dark and told to find his way home. Thank goodness for friendly drivers, he made it back.

Owen Boris enrolled at McMaster after two years working on the Westinghouse television assembly line. Their plant is nearby on Longwood Road. He recognized Hamilton household television sets' limitations. On the small black-and-white TVs currently installed, there were only several channels available. The CBC from Toronto and reception from Channel 4 Buffalo were often spotty.

Owen's research proved that a 40-foot TV antenna mounted on the roof of a two-story Hamilton house properly directed to the South could receive a Buffalo signal from 50 to 60 miles away. Thus, a new antenna would clearly receive Channel 4 but also Channel 2 and with a smaller separate antenna for Channel 17. This is a huge TV news and entertainment viewing spectrum for the homeowner as there were not many companies providing this service.

Several times a week, 3 to 4 hours at a time, we install these antennas in Hamilton's West End. We buy four-inch galvanized pipe for the masts, guy wires, turnbuckles, Benko boosters and 300-ohm TV wire to lead from the all wave antenna on top of the masts to the television sets. Total cost of materials is about $60 to $70. We charge $120 per installation and split the profits three ways, so my weekly take-home pay averages $40-$60. This is pretty good and it all goes into the bank to help pay for flying lessons. Yes, I have signed up for pilot training. Furthermore, I am learning about this new broadcast TV signal technology. It is my first broadcast-related apprenticeship and will be significant in years to come.

The Grand Finale for McMaster Frosh Week hazing is a greased pole rotten tomato fight. It works like this; a four-inch metal pole is securely anchored into the Campus athletic grounds. It is lathered with axle grease and a frosh hat is placed on top, 25 feet in the air. Four feet wide, all around the pole, is spread with 6-8 inches of axle grease. Armed with sacks full of rotten tomatoes, our tormentors, the hazing sophs, stand a dozen feet away.

Male frosh, (the girls are excused this ordeal), are all naked except for our swim trunks. Three dozen of us surround the pole ankle deep in disgusting old axle grease. The objective is to form a pyramid and capture the hat from the top of the pole in under 15 minutes. Our heaviest and strongest males form an arms-locked "base step." On top of them is another tier, and then another. Most of us are smeared with grease and footing is hard to maintain. All the while, we are being pelted non-stop by rotten tomatoes thrown with super force and accuracy by the sophs. Being light weight, I become a pillar of one of the top tiers. It worked. We were able to retrieve the hat in 12 minutes. We win and a loud roar of hurray went up from the hundreds of spectators. A photo of the high jinks would make the rounds. Hazing, Fall 1953 style, is over with a popular bang.

Our mountain home is in a mundane, blah neighborhood, so our parents are looking for a house in a more tony area. They find it on Hillcrest Avenue in west-end Hamilton near the Chedoke Golf Club. Later in the fall of 1953, we move to 172 Hillcrest Avenue, a two-story three-bedroom home with a beautiful backyard garden. Towering above us is the Hamilton Mountain and behind the garden is an abandoned railway/pathway that leads to the golf course. Bill quickly finds the golf course and becomes a caddy. I am now closer to where Owen Boris lives, which is several blocks south on Dundurn Ave. where the Boris garage, truck and TV antenna installation shop is located.

In addition to becoming friends with Owen, Fred Warren and Bob McCullagh, I am getting to know others from our neighbourhood, most of whom are also at Mac. After-classroom activity often centers around some popular hangouts and Cal's Delicatessen is one of them.

For out-of-town student residents, Cal's five-dollar meal coupon purchased in advance buys $5.60 worth of meals. This is a good deal, especially when you can buy a whole chili con carne meal for just $.60. Going downtown for shopping or a movie, Robinson's Soda Fountain sells popular Cherry Cokes for only $.20.

Our 1947 Cadillac requires service from time to time. Pat Hare has become a nearby friend on Hillcrest. He works for Johnny Long's Sunoco station across the road from Cal's deli as an apprentice mechanic. When I drive our '47 Caddy, I take the car to Pat for oil changes and tire rotations. We become friends, and Pat dubs me, "Cadillac George".

My classroom work is a challenge. The Buttery is our cafeteria and student lounge, a between-classes and after-hours hangout. Paul Burns and his jazz musician pals, Don Wingfield being one of them, often put on a late-after-noon performance. Card games include Canasta, Euchre and Bridge. I start to play Euchre but quickly graduate to Bridge. I might be having difficulty in math but I quickly learn Bridge mathematics and its importance in the bidding process. I've become quite adept. We often play for a tenth of a cent per point. This amateur gambling turns out to be, when you are bidding and playing successfully, quite lucrative. I become addicted to Bridge and often earn my weekly two to four dollars in pocket money. I really should be studying.

McMaster '54

The fall and early winter of 1953 at Mac are a whirlwind of academic and extra-curricular activities. My classes are scheduled Monday to Friday 8:30 am to 3 pm. I enjoy English and history which are my strong subjects and try to knuckle down on science and math. The Ivor Wynne gymnasium is a hive of a varsity and intramural sports activity. The campus football and soccer fields are, in part, home to the McMaster Marauders football team. It has a strong group of seasoned players such as Sam Daragh, Lorne Wrigglesworth, Jimmy Dodd and up-and-coming quarterback Russ Jackson. The Marauders are invited to join, on a trial basis, the prestigious four-team league of Queen's, Western, U of T and McGill. We are all fans and become trekkers to support the Marauders at away games.

On one such trip to Varsity Stadium, the University of Toronto's home turf, I pal around with Bob McCullagh, his friends Tony Phillips and Rick Irwin, who include me in Bob's car. Our Marauders hold their own but lose to Toronto. After the game, it's time for a beer. Although I am under 21, the legal age for drinking, McCullagh organizes our way into the King Cole Room of the Park Plaza Hotel. I am fast becoming a jazz fan. The headline entertainment in the King Cole lounge is the famous Cal Jackson. On vibes is Peter Appleyard, who will become another great. Tony Phillips is in geology, a course that is interconnected with the Queen's University engineers. We get to know some of the visiting Queen's students.

Many cars do not have radios but Bob has one and we all sing along with Rosemary Clooney to *This Ole House* or the Crew Cuts' *Sh-Boom*. Doris Day and Perry Como also have popular hits.

Harrier is another word for cross-country running. I qualify for the McMaster Track team. Running alongside David Moule and others including Fred Horton, we are respectable athletes as we compete against our nearby rival the University of Western Ontario in London. Capt. Cornelius is the Hamilton area's top track coach and we become one of his athletes in training at Ivor Wynne Stadium which becomes a focal point. Next door is the home of Isabel Kaprielian, a campus favourite and one of the McMaster cheerleaders. She becomes a friend and I get to know her mother and brothers Norman and Paul.

In October, Pop accepts a new job with the Foundation Company of Canada. His assignment is to be one of the senior engineers on the new Bell telephone cross Canada Microwave link. He has recently traded in the '47 Caddy and bought a nice green used 1950 Cadillac. We decide that I am going to drive Pop to Union Station in Toronto where he will be taking the train north. As I tune in to the car radio, the announcer issues a warning about Hurricane Hazel which is about to hit Southern Ontario. It is October 15 and as I join the Queen Elizabeth Way, the rain is teeming down. By the time I get to Oakville, it is 2-3 inches deep on the highway. I am praying, as I splash through, that the car's electrics stay dry and I get back to Hamilton safely. On the outskirts of town, the radio announces that they have just closed the Queen Elizabeth Way. Whew! I've made it back in the nick of time. There is significant damage; trees are toppled, roofs are torn off and flooding bungs up basements and culverts. It is quite a disaster.

My Christmas exam results are not very good. I commit to more evening study at the McMaster Library. Still, there are too many distractions. I have become friends with Walt Fraser who drives a trendy 1947 Ford Woody station wagon. Walt and John Sullivan are neighbours near our Hillcrest home. We are keen fans of the NHL teams. The Canadiens' Burt Olmstead sets an NHL record for eight points in the game. The Habs score a record three goals in 56 seconds in a playoff game against Detroit. We are disappointed when Detroit wins the Stanley Cup. I am starting to switch allegiance to the Toronto Maple Leafs. A lot of this sports chatter takes place in Paddy Green's Pub across the street from Westdale High School where Bill is a student.

In the news, Asia is making headlines. The Korean War is winding down but the French are battling the Communists in Vietnam. President Eisenhower is warning the world about the dangers of the hydrogen bomb. Senator Joe McCarthy is censured by his colleagues and Congressmen John F. Kennedy makes an appearance on Meet The Press. It has taken a long time, but rationing ends in Britain. Sam Snead wins the Masters golf tournament and Roger Bannister breaks the four-minute mile in 3:59.4 at Oxford. Exciting. We are all bemused as a Devil's face is found in the Queen's hair on the dollar bill. It is a topical story.

Rooftop antennas become difficult to install in the winter months, so campus activity prevails. My studies are interrupted by Buttery bridge, intramural basketball and indoor track-and-field training. Needless to say, when spring exams are over, I have not done well. I will be forced to repeat my freshman year.

A career opportunity seems to be in aviation. The airlines are looking for more pilots. Airline cockpits with larger aircraft now need a third pilot as a navigator. I continue learning to fly at the Royal Hamilton Flying Club.

This takes money and Owen's antenna business is intermittent. The Hamilton Golf and Country Club at Ancaster offers me a job as a clubhouse steward. This is almost a seven-day-a-week job with room and board included. I am hired by Mr. Lord, the Chief Steward. Ancaster is known as one of Canada's premier golf courses. Dick Borthwick is the pro. Bill gets a job as a caddy and I get to play a few rounds from time to time. Eric Nesterenko of the Chicago Blackhawks and Don Peebles of the Toronto Maple Leafs are some of our golfing mentors.

Picking worms at Ancaster is a midnight-to-2 pm part-time job. A local fish bait shop has a contract with the club to allow worm harvesting. For those skilled enough, one can make good money. I am game to try. Joined by several of my working buddies, one night we are dressed for worm picking by the bait shop man. All it takes is two 20-oz. pails attached to either side of your waist belt and a miner's lamp on your head. The worms come out onto the dew-covered greens. My head lamp shows 6-8 inch slithering worms. The trick is to grab them quickly before they squirm and retreat into their holes. Boy, do they move fast. I catch a few over a half hour, but adept pickers can fill up two pails in under an hour and are earning $1.25 per pail. I am a dud and not cut out for this midnight crawl. I will stick to my clubhouse job.

Ancaster's stewards have multiple tasks. We are shoeshine boys in the men's locker room, providing fresh towels for post-golf showers, and cleaning members' clubs and spikes is all part of our service. The Canteen Café adjacent to the locker room cooks delicious hamburgers and fries to order for the ravenous members. We are also waiters who serve soft drinks, ice and mixes for the liquor many members bring to a 19th-hole scorecard wrapup. We get good tips from the wealthy members. Dick Borthwick is a generous head professional. He gives us an occasional lesson and allows us to play free after hours. We often can get in three or four holes before dusk and our evening meal. Bill sometimes plays with us and we might also be joined by Don Peebles and Eric Nesterenko.

Back at McMaster in September, I buckle down to my studies. Dr. Gilmore, school president and my assigned faculty guide, is encouraging. I take some extra tutoring in sciences. They allow me back on the track-and-field team. Once again, Owen recruits me to help install TV antennas. I am a pretty good worker on the roof as we wrestle those 40-foot pipes. This is tricky as we have pre-mounted the all-wave sensitive, multi dipole TV antenna to the mast. The slate roof on the steep-pitched Art Scarlett house is a challenge.

Mr. Scarlett, an executive with International Harvester, is very impressed with our work and recommends us to others. We get to know his family and in particular, his daughter Joan. Mr. Scarlett thinks it is marvelous that we are learning to fly, suggesting that should we ever be flying a float plane in Muskoka, we should come to visit him at his Lake Joseph cottage. We like this idea and Owen and I plan to get our float endorsement next summer.

The McMaster Marauders continue to field a good team with quarterback Russ Jackson at the helm. Although the Marauders will not be accepted into the league with Western, Queen's, U of T and McGill, they play some challenging rivals. Isabel Kaprielian and her cheerleaders stimulate our raucous Marauder football support at Ivor Wynne Stadium.

The Hamilton Tiger-Cats football team is a community-owned icon. They train at the Hamilton AAA grounds not too far from our house. Coach Jim Trimble puts such stars as Bernie Custis, Angelo Mosca, Bernie Faloney and other notables through their paces as we watch them practice. Owen's cousins are the proprietors of the Strand Tavern and also Directors and supporters of the Ti-Cats. Bill, Pop and I are keen Tiger-Cats fans and from time to time get some priority tickets to see them play by lining up at the AAA ticket booth. Their major CFL rivals are the Toronto Argonauts closely followed by the Montréal Alouettes.

Hamilton is abuzz about Tiger-Cats '53 football. They rule the CFL Eastern Conference and have won the playoffs and the right to go to the Grey Cup. Pop, Bill and I are as excited about this as the rest of the community. "How can we get a ticket to the Grey Cup?" is on everyone's lips. We are not season ticket holders and there is a limited number available for a few early hours at the AAA ticket office. Bill and I line up the night before the box office opens. We take turns in three-hour shifts amongst a long line of fans. Success! We obtain three seats for the November 28 game at Varsity Stadium.

Game day is perfect football weather. The Winnipeg Blue Bombers have a well-known gunslinger at quarterback in Indian Jack Jacobs. The Tiger-Cats in their gold-and-black uniforms have lots of talent. We are seated in the end zone at field level close to the action. It becomes a hard-fought game and with several minutes to go the score is Tiger Cats 12, Blue Bombers 6. Winnipeg gets the ball and Indian Jack Jacobs starts throwing accurate bullet passes to his top players and they march down the field. They are within yards of a field goal. The Tiger-Cats' defensive line of such stalwarts as Eddie Bevan, Vince Mazza, Angela Mosca and brute force cunning hold off the Bombers until the final gun sounds. Whew---our Tiger-Cats win the Grey Cup by a thrilling 12-6 score. We go home elated.

As the fall progresses, the weather is not conducive to pilot training. Working to keep us in airmanship mode, chief flying instructor Reg Spence teaches us all aspects of flight as we wade through the basic Bible of instruction *From the Ground Up*. I am also learning Morse Code and voice communication skills to get my Radio Telephone Operator's license. This is another basic requirement for a commercial pilot's license. Between flight ground school and McMaster academic school, I have a lot on my plate.

The McMaster Drill Hall is a WW11 converted aerodrome hangar, with a first-class hardwood gymnasium floor. Its name is the Ivor Wynne Drill Hall and is often a hub of activity. Offices for coaches and change rooms for male and female athletes surround the interior walls. It's my Track Team

HQ. Rollaway bleachers can accommodate five to seven hundred spectators for a basketball game. Our McMaster Varsity basketball team is good and popular, and a number of Marauders football stars such as Jackie Jerome, Sam Daragh, Bert Kellock and Russ Jackson are centered by tall Mr. Basketball, Burt Raphael.

Our co-ed campus life includes dances either with a disc jockey or our own bandsmen. Hit songs from Rosemary Clooney and her chart toppers *Mambo Italiano* and *This Ole House* drive the music. The *Ballad of Davey Crocket* and *I'm a Country Boy* from John Denver are in the mix. Percy Faith's Orchestra is very danceable with the hit *Baubles, Bangles and Beads*.

In mid-December, the Drill Hall is converted into a giant classroom for Christmas exams. Oh, what a challenge for me. I'm working hard and keeping my fingers crossed for positive results to be reported in January.

McMaster 1955; Flying 1956

January's winter weather starts as drearily as my Christmas marks. Once again I defy the odds for a first-year repeater as I have results just as negative as last year. However, I am not deterred. I soldier on with more tutorials at the McMaster Library.

Campus life is varied. Buttery bridge consumes a lot of my time, but I am winning several dollars per week which is good pocket money. Buffalo is only an hour and a half drive. One of our entertainment thrills is to go and see the burlesque theatre. There is nothing like it in Hamilton. We young studs get titillated by the striptease performers. What a disappointment; the girls don't really strip down to nothing and always retain G-strings and flimsy bras. We come back to school bragging about these escapades.

In class, the profs teach us to keep abreast of important news e.g.: Canada agrees to resettlement of Palestinian refugees. In the United States, Rosa Parks, a black woman, makes headlines as she refuses to move from a whites-only seat on a segregated bus in Montgomery, Alabama. The Vietnam War is underway. Prime Minister Pearson joins President Eisenhower to open the St. Lawrence Seaway. This huge Canal and various locks allow ocean-going vessels to travel from Montréal to the United States and Canada's Great Lakes ports.

With Pop away, I have the luxury of driving the family Cadillac to and from University. Bob McCullagh decides we should put the car to good use and visit the nurses in training at Toronto's Sick Children's Hospital. Bob is a tease who persuades David Eckmejian, who because of his dark skin Bob calls Farouk, to be our Cadillac chauffeur when we pick up the nurses. Bob has a chauffeur's hat which Farouk wears. Bob treats David as if he is just a hired hand and we act like snooty playboys. Sometimes it goes over and when it doesn't, everyone has a good laugh.

We take the girls out to the clubs in Toronto. From the jukebox Bill Haley and the Comets, Chuck Berry and Fats Domino are belting out their memorable songs. It's all fun with the damper being we have to get the girls back to residence before midnight. Nurses Lynn Fairburn, Shirley Pretty and Joan Jellett would become regular dates.

McMaster student council elections are a competitive affair. Our Buttery bridge group wants to elect Gord Carruth as Student Council President. *Vote for Gord Carruth* flyers are produced. Someone comes up with the idea that pilots George and Owen should bomb the Mac quadrangle mid-morning when classes are changing and there will be a large crowd. We are game for the plot. We arrange for Owen to fly an Aeronca Champ with me as the passenger/bombadier on this mission and 600 Vote for Gord, we all embrace pop culture. On Broadway, Damon Runyan has a smash hit musical called *Guys and Dolls* featuring Nathan Detroit and his floating crap game. Also on radio, Louis Armstrong's *Mack the Knife* and Guy Mitchell's *Singing the Blues* are popular. Johnny Ray comes to the Grange Tavern and underage or not, we get in to hear his big hit, *Just Walking in the Rain.*

Train Driver at Stelco Metallurgical Lab

I continue working with Owen and I am often at his apartment above the family-owned Strand Tavern where we plan our TV installation work. We have become close buddies.

The expansion of new television stations and accompanying technology are all part of my Father's new job, which is building microwave relay station towers from northern Ontario to western Canada.

Most people can afford a $100 black and white TV set. Local TV news now competes with radio. James Dean is a Hollywood star who tragically gets killed in a car accident. *Gunsmoke* and the *$64,000 Question* are several of the highest-rated television programs. The news tells us about Disneyland opening in California and that Coke will now be sold in cans.

I barely squeak through on the final exams, but the faculty advises me my marks are not high enough to be promoted. My parents are not too amused by this situation but agree that I should pursue my aviation dreams. Although I am making satisfactory part-time money, I will need a steady income to pay for flying lessons. A good break occurs when Mr. Leonard, our neighbour and General Manager of the Canada Crushed Stone company in Dundas, offers me a job.

The Canada Crushed Stone Dundas Quarry and railway line to their large crushing complex on the Niagara Escarpment will be putting on a second shift of workers for the summer months. I am hired as one of their Electric Train Drivers. These small engines tow 4-6 open boxcars. The cars are loaded with 10-12 tons of rock. The train then descends a three-mile series of tracks to the crusher. The heavy stone load is tipped into the machinery where the rock is pulverized into various sizes. The ground-up stone then finds its way into various highway and construction projects.

My wage is $.90 per hour on the 7 am-7 pm 12-hour shift (the average construction wage is $1/hr). On the night swing shift, I am earning $1.25 per hour. These 60-hour work weeks are lucrative and allow me to pay for my flying lessons. I also learn a lot about railway engines. Being electric, ours have large copper wire dynamos and have to be driven carefully. One guy got fired for trying to force excessive speed out of the engine and blew the motor, which cost the company thousands of dollars to repair. Overhead electric wires on either side of the track provide power to Pantagraph Wands which connect the train engine to our power source. Axle Journal boxes need to be frequently oiled or the wheel bearings will burn out. It is hard work that requires attention to many facets of the railway business. This experience should look good on my resume.

In September, no longer driving a railway engine, I am now driving an airplane and learning to fly an Aeronca Champ at the Hamilton Flying Club. Reg and Grace Spence run the club. Reg is famous having been one of the top Mosquito bomber pilot instructors in WWII. I will often fly with Reg. My day-to-day instructor is WW11 pilot Ken Parr. After many hours practicing circuits around various Hamilton airport runways with Ken in the back seat as my instructor, I am nearly ready to solo.

In my Aeronca C-FMP on a clear November 6, 1955 day, I land on Runway 06. Ken tells me to come to a full stop and pull over to the side of the runway. He opens the door, gets out and tells me to take off. Wow! Gently applying power, raising the tail and obtaining airspeed, I carefully pull back on the joystick and the aircraft immediately pops into the air. No wonder I am airborne so fast because of having less weight as Ken no longer is my passenger.

I am exhilarated. My head is on a swivel as I survey everything. I am all alone and it's a magnificent feeling. I am flying solo! I diligently proceed with standard Aircraft Circuit procedure, enter the base leg and then final approach and execute a perfect three-point landing. I come to a full stop by the waiting Ken Parr. He climbs aboard and I taxi back to the Club with his congratulations ringing in my ears.

My summer railway job is at an end and I am looking for other work. My Dad is home from up north. Through his professional engineering circles, he has got to know Dr. Szebakin who is the head of metallurgy at the Steel Company of Canada and arranges for an interview, after which I am hired as an apprentice technician in the metallurgical laboratory. I sense that my father feels that this lab job might offer me more career stability in case the flying options don't work out.

My new job is shift work. Days are 7 am to 3 pm and I earn $1.10/hr, while evenings are 3 pm to 11 pm at the same wage. The night shift from 11 pm to 7 am is $1.20/hour. I have to join the United Steelworkers of America Union. The union deduction is several dollars per week and the company provides various benefits including medical. They even have a small hospital clinic with a full-time nurse on staff.

Ron Patterson, the union steward, is one of my bosses and a well-known amateur golfer at Chedoke Golf Club. Bill often caddies for him. Ron knows of my flying ambitions and from time to time, lets me off work early so I can get to the Mount Hope Airport in time for a scheduled training flight. The shift work hours are ideal for flight training. I can often fly in the morning before going to work at three in the afternoon. After a night shift, it's home to bed from eight until 2 or 3 pm and then off to the airport for a late-afternoon flight. Several of the Met Lab guys think I am crazy setting my sights on being a commercial pilot. They say I am now set for life with this secure, well-paying Stelco job. However, that is not in my plan.

In order to build up flight time towards the 150 hours required for a certified Commercial Pilot's License, Owen and I travel to Orillia on weekends. We now both have Transport Canada Private Pilot licenses. Harry Stirk's Orillia Air Service on the Bay at the foot of Main Street offers float plane flying endorsements and on August 2, 1956 flying an Aeronca Champ CF-JAX with instructor Hans Meneke, I am certified as a Sea Plane Pilot on my license. Owen also gets his float plane designation.

We now proceed to rent the Aeronca Champ or Piper PA 11 on floats for the weekend and the Air Service gives us permission to fly north to Muskoka. One of us drives Owen's snazzy 1955 Chevrolet hardtop to Milford Manor Resort while the other flies the airplane to the same place. There we dock and offer airplane rides at three dollars for 15 minutes. The aircraft rental is $12 per hour. You can read more about *Wings Over Muskoka*, the story of two guys' summer resort hopping, later in this book.

During the Fall I continue to log more flight time. Reg Spence now instructs me in our two-place, side-by-side Cessna 140 taildragger. The instrument panel is fully radio and NavAids equipped. I now go under the hood for IFR

Inspector Moe Louch and am awarded my Commercial Pilot License No. HQC 7071, subsequently upgraded to CA 22467 (current in 2017). My parents are very proud of this accomplishment. I have finally passed a University grade series of tests and exams. They present me with a Rolex Oyster Chronograph Pilot's stopwatch which I cherish to this day.

Grade XI-D

GEORGE DANIELS

"It is wiser to keep quiet and let people think you're a fool than to open your mouth and prove it."

Origin—Bedford, England, June 23, 1935.
Favourite Pastime—"Holy cow!"
Ambition—Civil Engineer.
Probable Destination—Sanitary Engineer.

THE BOYS' SWIMMING TEAM

First row, left to right: P. Rutherford, A. Grant, P. Lowndes, W. Windsor, R. Dykes, Mr. A. R. Scammell (Coach). *Second row, left to right:* G. Robinson, J. Atcheson, K. Thiesmeyer, I. Ahern, D. Farquharson. *Third row, left to right:* G. Philips, D. Irwin (Manager), G. Daniels, P. Neroutsos.

THE BOYS' PHYSICAL ACTIVITIES COUNCIL

Mount Royal High School Yearbook

Boy Scout camp Tamaracouta, in the Larentians.
George - in Pork Pie hat..Patrol Leader of Cumberland House Tent.

George enrolled in 1949

THE HONOURABLE SOCIETY OF THE

KNIGHTS OF TAMARA

ESTABLISHED IN 1933

Scouts Tamara

George Daniels: far left.

Varsity Harrier Team

FIRST ROW: Daniels, Schenk, Beard, Sibbald, Moule. SECOND ROW: Stone (Trainer), Hurst (Mgr.). ABSENT: Perozak, Wilkinson, Whalen, Roussell, Brown, Mason, Miller.

1953-'54 George earns his Varsity letter.

Varsity Track Team

FIRST ROW: Sibbald, Yates, Stone (Mgr.). SECOND ROW: Fawcett (Coach), Daniels, Moule, Horton, Simpson.

1953 Christmas Dance, in the Mac. Gym
George 4th from the right with date Sue Boomer

McMaster University
September 1953

Freshman Week

1—Freshettes enjoy a square meal. 2—The parade assembles before the Western-Mac game. 3—Cinderella Ball: Joan McIlroy, Peter Jankowski, Sally Northey, Don Jones. 4—Gord Carruth and Chuck Evans grease the pole. 5—Cinderalla Ball again. 6—Community Service. 7—Chain gang led by Dianne Thomson. 8—One of the floats in the football parade.

Frosh vs Sophs - hazing à la innocent highjinks
Greased pole tomato fight to retrieve the hat on top.

Photos:
Spring '54 Marmor Yearbook

Christmas the Canadian Way

Father Christmas or as they call him here in Canada, Santa Claus, has been generous to Bill and I and we get new skates for Christmas. There are many ponds and home-made rinks on which to learn and practice. Our new friend Insley Maybee is showing us how to skate and avoid many tumbles as we awkwardly start gliding along the slippery ice. One of our skating adventures includes following a meandering frozen stream for several miles south towards Merivale. The ice is thick enough and the snow is windswept so as not to cover our convenient outdoor rink. I am starting to get the hang of skating on crackling sheets of ice on streams that wind through farmers' fields. It is exhilarating.

Back home in front of the Château, Pop helps us build our own rink, approximately 70 by 20 feet. Several of the Cub pack join us for fun and games as we all pretend to be Montréal Canadiens, known as the Habs. We have all become fans of Rocket Richard, Doug Harvey, Butch Bouchard and other famous players.

I sometimes wonder what my old Scorton chum Norm Farrar in England would think of me now in all my winter clothing; fur-trimmed parka hood on my coat, hockey sticks and pucks with padded shin guards above our skates. Smashing, he would probably think.

As springtime approaches, I am looking forward to summer. Frankly, I am not a very good student except in certain subjects. I like biology, history and shop where we learn everything from basic carpentry and making items for home use to understanding how an automobile engine works.

Bill and I have discovered how to make pocket money. We wash dishes at Mr. Bashaw's house for 10 cents a time. He is the Cubmaster and his wife is not well. Bill takes on a newspaper boy delivery route and I start to mow lawns for half a dozen people in the Village. I earn $.75 for each lawn and in the case of Mrs. Austin, where it is very large. It is hard work with the hand mower (no gas mowers available in the village). I get $1.25 for cutting her grass. We start saving this money for Camp Tamaracouta, the Boy Scout Camp and we are encouraged by the Cubmaster and my lone Scout mentor, Charlie Phillips, to save our money as a two-week stay costs $17 per week. It does not take too long or too many lawns plus babysitting at $.25 per hour for me to earn the money.

PART III

Moving to Ontario, George enters McMaster University, discovers a love for flying, takes a variety of jobs to pay for it, and earns his pilot's wings.

Part III

Stelco Metallurgical Lab and the Hamilton Flying Club.

I graduate from the Royal Hamilton Flying Club with my Transport Canada-certified Commercial Pilot's License November 29, 1956. This is recorded in my Log Book Number 1, with 197 total hours and endorsed by CFI Reg H. Spence. With a return to McMaster now out of the question and after much soul searching with my parents, Pop in particular, I decide to pursue a career in professional aviation.

My first opportunity to put my commercial pilot's license to work is with Jack Murphy Aircraft Sales at Mount Hope Airport. Jack has been following my commercial pilot learning and progress and invites me to go with him to the Taylorcraft factory in St. Paul, Minnesota.

Murphy Aircraft Sales has just obtained the Canadian rights to sell a revolutionary new single-engine four-place Taylorcraft. Its major benefit is a fiberglass skin over its tubular frame, ensuring low maintenance, outdoor weather resistance, light weight and long life. Jack employs me to fly with him in one of these new aircraft to St. Paul, Minnesota to visit the factory and make arrangements for further deliveries.

We will be flying in the new Taylorcraft M20, its registration is CF–I KV. It's my first hands-on experience with a four-place aircraft. Our December 17 flight planning for the long trip includes careful plotting, VFR (Visual Flight Rules), with our Southwest Ontario/Toronto chart and those in the United States for MI, IN, IL, WI, and Minnesota. Outbound, we fly to Windsor, then to Detroit Wayne Major, clearing Customs. We then fly to Chicago

Miegs Field, on the waterfront (sadly this field was decommissioned in 1990) and then to Minneapolis Crystal airport, Taylorcraft's home HQ. We arrive on December and spend two days working at the factory and discussing Aircraft Sales and Marketing. This is my first sales-related experience.

The Taylorcraft M20 is not fully IFR equipped. We do have an ADF, which we certainly put to good use on our return flight. As we depart Minneapolis December 24, winter is coming and we start to encounter snow squalls, yet are above VFR limits. All is going well until we get near the Green Bay, Wisconsin Airport. Radio communication with the Airport Tower is very good. Our ADF radio really helps with the airport frequency so our navigation is accurate. The snow is now seriously curtailing our visibility.

In talking with the Tower, they indicate they can "perhaps" hear us but do not have us in sight. It becomes imperative that we land. Although without seeing the Airport, I set the runway heading and decide to land in a field. We do so successfully, but just as we get out, a large twin-engine airplane screams overhead on its final approach. A near miss---scary. We are lucky to avoid a collision. We have landed about half a mile short of the runway and without visual separation from other aircraft. What a learning experience. Over the next two days, we fly the M20 out of the field and get fuelled up for our next leg to Port Huron. Weather continues iffy and we have to stay overnight for Christmas. The locals treat us well in the spirit of the season.

On December 27, with the weather forecast promising, we fly East via London where it is marginal VFR and do some scud running (flying below the clouds) before arriving at Mount Hope. I have flown a total of 12 hours, 25 minutes in the Taylorcraft in 10 days and to various airports the USA. It's all in my Log Book Number One and an experience I will never forget.

Stelco Metallurgical Lab and the Hamilton Flying Club.

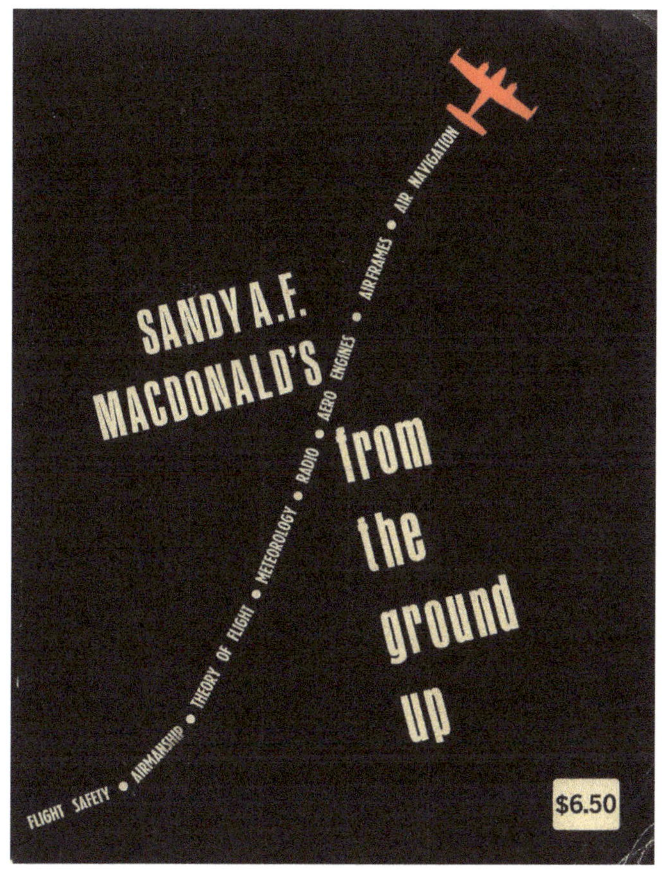

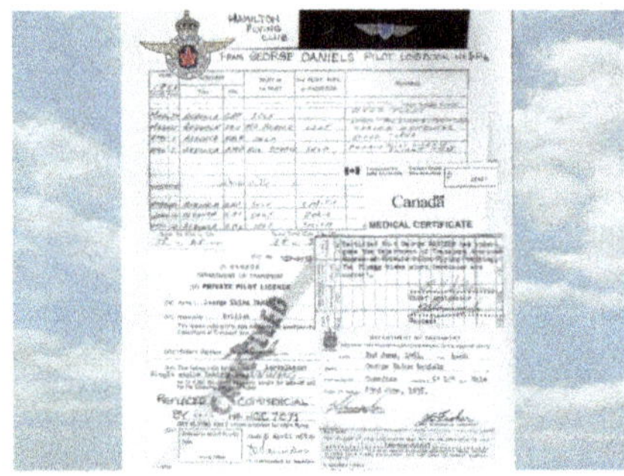

Hamilton Flying Club slides

Elliot Lake Mine Works: January-April 1957.

The Hamilton Flying Club is very helpful and allows me to run a tab for the cost of flight time in the last quarter of 1956. It was nearly $700, and I promise to pay off this no-interest loan in early 1957. This is how I did it.

Once again, my Pop helps by employing me and fellow new Commercial Pilot Glenn Waldick at the Denison Nordic uranium mine at Elliot Lake. Pop was the Chief Superintendent on this vast construction project and uranium was the new Gold Rush. Although only eight miles north of the Trans-Canada Highway, Elliot Lake was largely undeveloped northern bush. Potholed dirt roads and teetering telephone poles and no local shopping were the norm. As senior management, my father had a three-bedroom mobile home where Glen and I stayed. Our 6 am breakfast cereal was different as Glen lathered ketchup on his cornflakes.

It was luxury compared to the massive steel Butler buildings that housed the hundreds of workers. The millwrights, mechanics and riggers bunked three tiers high in conditions that were largely smelly jockstraps and overalls. We often joined them in the Crawley McCracken Community canteen mess hall to feast on overcooked greasy bacon and eggs at breakfast. Gallons of weak coffee, slabs of bread & jam with jugs of milk filled our stomachs under not the most sanitary conditions. Menus at lunch and dinner were often soggy cooked cabbage from the bathtub kettles with gristly meat and mash. There was little or no fresh fruit (scurvy anyone?). Hungry after 10-hour shifts, we would eat anything. No wonder many contracted hepatitis.

The Denison Nordic Mine was one of 12 in the Elliot Lake area. It operated from 1956 to 1968 and produced 13 million tons of ore. It kept its Dry Pack plant open for other nearby mills until 1990. Its chemical leaching and grinding process produced Yellow Cake Uranium powder that was sold by Rio Algom into the Uranium market as U3O8. The Nordic Mine was totally closed in 1992, covered over and landscaped to Elliot Lake's beautiful community environmental standards.

I made good money at $2.50 per hour working in the garage and toolshed. The winter was bitterly cold at -20° most nights. One of my jobs was to restart the half-dozen bulldozers early each morning. Using a three-ounce ether bomb capsule and flinging it into the open carburetor at the same time as activating the start button would result in a mini- explosion as the 'dozer engine grudgingly turned on. It was dangerous, but fun work. Assigning tools to the various skilled labourers, counting returns and keeping inventory was my routine. The days were long and seven-day weeks were the norm. Every two weeks, we would get a day off and visit Spanish or Espanola Hotels 30 or 40 miles away for a few beers in their men's lounges. When Elliot Lake's first hotel opened in early March, there was a riot caused by unruly drunken workers. I decided it was my time to leave, get back to the Hamilton Flying Club, pay off my debt and get on with flying.

TCA Evaluation

Reg Spence welcomes me back after my winter in Elliot Lake with a Cessna 140 CF-JFG refresher check flight. I buy more flight time. I now have over 212 hours total time with my Commercial and Radio Licenses. Reg nominates me to Trans-Canada Airlines' pilot evaluation interviews in Montreal at its Dorval Airport Headquarters. Not every commercial pilot gets an invitation and I feel somewhat special.

Airlines and general aviation are in need of pilots as we enter the late 1950s. In Canada's North, the Pine Tree, Mid-Canada and Dew Lines are all being serviced by charter regional air services. The airline industry is rapidly expanding service all over North America and to overseas. Business executives are starting to use air transportation to gain markets.

Trans-Canada Airlines is the county's flag carrier. It originally was a subsidiary of the CN Railway when it launched in 1937. The Lockheed 10 Electra, the Douglas DC-3, North Stars and new Viscount turboprops are the backbone of the fleet. New, larger, four-engine long-range aircraft like the TCA Lockheed Super Constellation (also famous with Howard Hughes and his Trans World Airlines) require a 3-4 pilot cockpit crew and are now being integrated into their fleets. Jet airliners are coming and in 1965, TCA officially changes its name to

It is in this environment that I set off for TCA's Montreal one-week pilot evaluation and testing. Glen Waldick, my fellow Hamilton Flying Club graduate, joins me. Two hundred and fifty new commercial pilots have been accepted and invited. They will select the top 200 at week's end. The navigation tests, engine reviews, instrument Link training requirements and many airmanship exams are part of the course.

Furthermore, we undergo an extensive medical including eyesight, hearing, cardio and muscular strength and balance examinations. I really enjoy it and work hard to pass. However, it is not enough. I am out of the running having scored 203, just missing by three spots and will not be accepted. Glen makes it and I am quite disappointed, but what a learning experience. It will stand me in good stead for my next career flight.

PART IV

Now a qualified commercial pilot, the author embarks on a series of jobs and adventures leading to his uniquely-specialized career as a Canadian bush pilot.

Part IV

Adventures of a Bush Pilot

I arrive in Fort William-Port Arthur by train in mid-May. Pop has paved the way and I obtain an interview with Orville Wieben, owner of Superior Airways. The company is well known as a major charter air service in northwestern Ontario. The headquarters base in Fort William includes a seaplane facility on the Kamanistiway River and operations at Sioux Lookout and Armstrong. The company had several dozen aircraft including Norseman Vs, a Bellanca Skyrocket, a Douglas DC-3 and a number of Cessna 180s. They are also an official Cessna Aircraft sales and service facility for northwestern Ontario and eastern Manitoba.

Orville Wieben is an excellent pilot and savvy aircraft owner-operator with a fleet of high-performance bush planes. These aircraft had to be relatively low maintenance, easy to fly and carry a diverse cargo of passengers or freight. Two aircraft are the workhorses of the Superior Airways fleet. The first is the Nooduyn Norseman, almost a flying truck. With a 450hp Pratt and Whitney radial engine, it can cruise at 120 mph on floats with a 2,700-pound payload. The other is the fairly-new Cessna 180 on floats. It has a 230hp Continental engine, consumes 11 gallons of gas per hour with an 800-pound payload and competes nicely with the de Haviland Beaver which is a bit slower than a Cessna 180 and consumes twice as much gas.

Mr. Wieben reviews my logbook, asks questions about my southern Ontario flying experience and in particular, my float endorsement for pontoons I earned at Orillia Air Services. He apparently has a high regard for Orillia's Harry Stirk and his pilot training.

He also says my 200 hours commercial pilot license represent a modest experience but hires me and sends me off to the Sioux Lookout base.

There I would be under the guidance of chief pilot and manager Ranny McDonald. On May 25, 1957, McDonald checks me out on Cessna 180 CF-HZY on floats. We fly to several nearby lakes where I perform a float plane landing, a pilot's most difficult maneuver on water. They are glassy water landings and docking in an adverse crosswind---difficult, as the aircraft wants to weather cock into the wind. Being on the controls requires aileron, water rudder and power manipulation. Ranny says I did well. Before he assigns me to my own aircraft, I am scheduled for familiarization and navigation of our extensive North Western Ontario Charter Air service territory as a co-pilot.

For the next six weeks I fly co-pilot for Captain Gord Norell in the Norseman V. I also co-pilot a Bellanca Skyrocket, similar to a Norseman, with Captain Alex Maxwell. Flying with these senior pilots, I learn a lot. Our jobs are very diverse and include flying prospectors to find mineral ore. We augment the Ontario Provincial Air services and fly people requiring Sioux Lookout Hospital medical help. The company has four or five hunting and fishing camps throughout our territory. Flying fishing and hunting parties with an Indian guide for a week's fun in the bush is big business. Other aspects of our work are written about my January 2016 talk to the Collingwood Historical Society.There have been various books written about bush pilots. We are great storytellers about our many escapades, but a lot of what has been published does not get to the crux of what makes a bush pilot. So here is my take. When I visited Orval in his Thunder Bay office in the mid-70s, we reminisced about my experiences with his company in the 50s. I was proud when he said, "George, you are one of the last real bush pilots." So, this is my definition:

A bush pilot should be categorized as an adventurous, resourceful Grade A pilot-come mechanic-technician. He or she should have the instincts of an explorer to fly and navigate over Canada's vast geography of forests and lakes above the 49th and 50th parallels north of Lake Superior and James Bay. By comparison, most of southern Ontario straddles the 44th parallel.

"Be Prepared" as the Scouts say, often seven days per week. Pushing the limits responsibly to get the best power and fuel efficiency to reach the destination. Bush

sense includes how to fend for yourself when downed by weather in a remote area. A fishing rod, 410 shotgun, Arctic sleeping bag and camping on the shore under the wing while waiting for weather to clear areas part of the job. So is fuelling the aircraft by oneself from a cached 45-gallon drum of gas with a wobble pump and chamois in a funnel.

Bush pilots need to have the courage to face hardships and danger. Bush pilots flew aircraft at the time with basic flight instruments; an airspeed indicator, turn and bank and sometimes an artificial horizon, if it worked. Navigation equipment was a magnetic compass and directional gyro. Reading and interpreting the VFR Nav charts over wide swaths of barren terrain is vital. In some aircraft, we were lucky to have a UHF radio to communicate with our base. These signals were often erratic and dependent on us trailing 200-foot antenna.

An essential ingredient of being a good bush pilot is having strong self-discipline and in its modern sense flying and working with situational awareness. Today, pilots have the luxury of advanced high-tech satellite, GPS, transponder, T-Cast and glass cockpit instrument panels to aid their flying.

In late July 1957, I was assigned my own airplane, Cessna 180 CF-JEV. Flying engineers and equipment to the headwaters of the Great Divide along the 51st parallel was one of my jobs. The streams and rivers flowing from this terrain's high point descend north into Hudson Bay. A series of dams was devised to divert the water southward to Lac Soul and Lake Joseph's hydro projects. By mid-August, I had done this trip many times. One day I took an engineer who had not flown with me before and he asked if he could follow our journey by reading my map that was on top of the instrument panel. After a while he remarked, "you are going straight to our destination."

I said I hope so and why do you ask. He said, "I was recently flying with one of your other pilots and he got lost. We had to land on a lake and ask an Indian in his canoe where we were." I recalled the pilot he referred to. He would go out on a two-hour trip and come back four hours later. He was getting lost. Apparently, the Indian took the chart, turned it over several folds and stabbed his finger at the correct location which was about 50 miles away from the intended route. Quite laughable if it wasn't so serious.

Our contract with the Federal Government Department of Entomology biologist meant that once every several weeks, one of us would fly the bug Doctor, as we called him, to collect samples from various lakes in the territory.

Ours was an avid fisherman. We would take off early in the morning and go to three or four lakes, pull up on a sandy beach and the doctor would collect various insect samples from the trees and bushes and place them in tagged bags. He always scheduled our flights so that about 1 pm we would arrive at one of his favourite fishing holes. We would then de-plane and fish for pickerel for several hours. It was like being on vacation. We cooked some of our catch and had a shore-line lunch. I even became adept at landing fish from the teeming schools of prevalent pickerel. What a lot of fun amidst a very busy bush pilot's week.

The Ojibway and Cree, indigenous aboriginals of Northwestern Ontario, are a special group of natives who are everything from fellow workers to customers of our company. The Albany River Oji-Cree have a good fishing business. Our contract requires we pick up freshly-caught sturgeon every several weeks. The Indians catch the fish, keep them alive and tethered by a rope through the gills to a stanchion on the riverbank. When they hear the aircraft arriving, they kill the fish and prepare them for transport. This means cleaning out the innards and saving the roe/eggs from the females.

I have the interior prepped for this cargo. All seats have been removed except mine and the interior lined with a waterproof canvas tarp. I have taken a 16-ounce glass jar with me to be filled up with eggs. It cost me only $.50 for a full jar. On returning to Sioux Lookout with my sturgeon cargo for the Fish Monger Warehouse, the company did not mind me selling my jar of sturgeon eggs which I do and earn the princely sum of $5. I later find out that when this is made into caviar for the big city restaurants, my 16 ounces of eggs are worth about $100.

Forced landings can occur at awkward times. Flying the Norseman with Gord Norrell, we are near Big Cat Lake when one of the cylinder heads blows off. Instantly, the windscreen is doused with oil and it is hard to see. We are flying at approximately 2,000 feet and losing manifold power pressure so we determine that Big Cat Lake will be our emergency stop. I am on our UHF radio with a Mayday call but get no response. Landing safely, we pull up to a nice sandy beach in front of the only habitation we could see. We are warmly welcomed by a family of Indians who live in a hut. They help us tie up, clean off our oily overalls and invite us for supper and to stay overnight while we wait for a new cylinder and our mechanic. No doubt, our absence would be noted and a search made.

In the meantime, I really get to know these Indians. Their modest shack was immaculate. They hunt and fish and explain their spirituality and sacred respect for their land. The recent Federal Government Indian Act has not affected them yet, but they are aware of the potential of being relocated to another reservation and they are unhappy about that. They go on to explain that their ancestors taught them that they had the right to live on their land, which had been theirs for hundreds of years, but they were not entitled to squat or live on another's Aboriginal land which belonged to their brothers for centuries and is sacrosanct. I find all of this very educational and subsequently become very sensitive to indigenous peoples' relationships with the land. I learn more about this from my son Andrew who reads a lot about our native people, and Dr. Robbie Keith from the University of Waterloo. I have become very concerned about our Canadian Government's management of our native Canadians ever since this experience. We spend two days there before a replacement cylinder and the mechanic arrive.

Flying Band-Aids

Superior Airways provides Medevac services that augment the Ontario Provincial Air Service and the Sioux Lookout Hospital is the central facility operated by the Medical Services Branch of Health & Welfare Canada. This zone service area covers 385 000 square kilometres. We transport people requiring hospital or nursing station care from roughly one-third of the total area of Ontario. Nursing stations are at Sandy Lake, Big Trout Lake, Osnaburgh, Pikangikum. Webequie, Fort Hope and Round Lake. They provide treatment and public health programs for 28 scattered communities, mostly accessible only by air.

A not-so-typical emergency flight is a call to get passenger Mary Blue Bell from Fort Severn, northeast of James Bay. I was the next pilot on the list for Medevac work. My Cessna 180 was in the shop for its 100-hour inspection, but Orville Wieben's personal Luscombe was available. This is a small two-place, side-by-side 85hp aircraft that cruises at 85 to 90 mph on floats.

My fellow pilots tease me that I will be picking up an Indian princess. I almost believe them but get a rude awakening when a very sick and old Mary Blue Bell, belching a hacking cough, not speaking English, is somehow sandwiched into the tight passenger seat. Luckily, I have a box of cough drops, concerned I might catch her ills, give them to Mary as we boringly fly a nearly two-hour flight to the Trout Lake nursing station. Whew, mission accomplished and I remain healthy.

Cockpit Levity

I learn how to play this joke on our passengers from one of our seasoned pilots. It works like this; after loading a group of hunters and fishermen, I climb over the baggage and supplies to my pilot's seat. Looking around curiously, I notice the small blue covered booklet called *How to Fly on Floats*. Grabbing the book I open it to the first page and read, "it says make sure the water rudders are down." I then start looking for the water rudder lift. I then read, "make sure the controls are free and clear." I pull the control column fore and aft for the elevator and turn left and right for the ailerons. I continue to read instructions. In the Norseman you can pop the Control Wheel stop button and flop it over into the Co-Pilot/passenger seat as a dual control. I would do this and say," Hold this for a minute." By now, my passenger is looking very concerned. As I read more instructions from the manual, sort of indicating I might not know what I am doing, the passenger is just about to abandon the flight. Putting the book down, I explain my joke and everyone has a laugh. I get back to the flight plan and deliver my customers to the outfitters' camp.

Assembling and staging passenger baggage often includes several cases of beer and hard liquor brought for a week in the bush by the tourists. Sometimes they hired one of our most experienced Indian guides. This chap enjoyed his drink. When asked what day we plan to fly in and pick up the party, Joe would eyeball all the booze, estimate how long it would take him to help them consume it, to finally catch their limit and then announce the day we should pick them up.

US Border crossings

American hunters and fisherman liked to charter our aircraft for a week vacation at our various campsites North of Sioux Lookout. We offer a service of picking them up at International Falls on the US side of the border opposite Fort Frances. Several times, when I showed up, I was asked by US customs where I was born and I would answer Bedford, England. I would then be held up for an hour or so while they tried to determine if I was an alien or not. They were working from the Senator Joe McCarthy playbook. His infamous Committee on un-American Activities promoted that if you were not born in the USA, you might be a Communist. They were trying to tar me with this brush. I was being paid by miles flown, not by down time or in the air.

This type of delay was costly and frustrating and became my motivation to become a Canadian citizen. I really did not have to take this step because all my documents showed I was British and perfectly acceptable in Canada. To cross the border and travel would be good for my future. The following year, I go before a Citizenship Judge in Toronto and proudly obtain my Canadian Citizenship Certificate.

Prior to the Canadian Government passing a Canadian Citizenship Act in 1967, (Part of Expo 67) I was a British National;

(III) No. YZP-6758
(I) CANADA
DEPARTMENT OF TRANSPORT
(II) **PRIVATE PILOT LICENCE**
(IV) Name : George Eaton Daniels
(VI) Nationality : British
This licence valid only to date mentioned on accompanying Department of Transport form 2496
(VII) Holder's signature

Replaced by Commercial Pilot Lic. No. HQC 7071, Nov.'56.

I apply for Canadian Citizenship. The decision "turning point " being treated to McCarthyism at the Fort Frances -USA border.Read my Bush Pilot Adventures. Part IV.

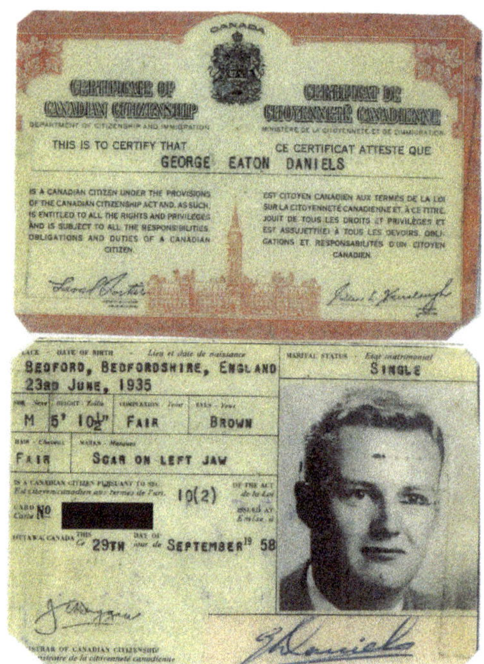
CANADA
CERTIFICATE OF CANADIAN CITIZENSHIP
CERTIFICAT DE CITOYENNETÉ CANADIENNE
THIS IS TO CERTIFY THAT
CE CERTIFICAT ATTESTE QUE
GEORGE EATON DANIELS
IS A CANADIAN CITIZEN UNDER THE PROVISIONS OF THE CANADIAN CITIZENSHIP ACT AND, AS SUCH, IS ENTITLED TO ALL THE RIGHTS AND PRIVILEGES AND IS SUBJECT TO ALL THE RESPONSIBILITIES, OBLIGATIONS AND DUTIES OF A CANADIAN CITIZEN
EST CITOYEN CANADIEN AUX TERMES DE LA LOI SUR LA CITOYENNETÉ CANADIENNE ET, À CE TITRE, JOUIT DE TOUS LES DROITS ET PRIVILÈGES ET EST ASSUJETTI(E) À TOUS LES DEVOIRS, OBLIGATIONS ET RESPONSABILITÉS D'UN CITOYEN CANADIEN
BEDFORD, BEDFORDSHIRE, ENGLAND
23RD JUNE, 1935
SINGLE
M 5' 10½" FAIR BROWN
FAIR SCAR ON LEFT JAW
10(2)
CARD NO
29TH SEPTEMBER 1958

Eleven years after becoming a Landed Canadian Immigrant at Pier 21.. George is a New Canadian Citizen. I am one of the first 97,000 since Expo 67.

Canoes, Cargo and Courage

Our company has a contract with the Hydrographic (water) Survey Department of the Federal Government. One week, I am scheduled to fly out of our Fort William base to ferry a two-man team with canoe and equipment into Malone Lake, about a 45-minute flight north.

My concerns about aircraft weight and balance increase as I look over the survey team's cargo. They have half a dozen large lead weights and depth lines, similar to those of a fisherman. One or two weighed 10 pounds or more. In addition, we have to load sleeping bags, provisions for a three- or four-day camp plus a two-person tent. The canoe comes next.

Strapping the canoe on the side of the aircraft pontoon is an art. First, it has to be placed with its open deck facing inward to the underside of the aircraft and should be located well back of the propeller. Strong hemp rope should be cinched around the front of the canoe and anchored to the float plane struts. This procedure is repeated towards the rear of the canoe.

I am always careful to calculate the effects of this added weight and aerodynamics change to the aircraft. One must double the weight of the canoe, approximately 300-400 pounds and add this to the gross weight calculations for the flight. The exterior on-board canoe will now increase the air speed necessary for takeoff and in turn, reduce our cruising speed by 5-10 mph. This canoe add-on is all in a day's work for a bush pilot.

At nearly gross weight we take off for Malone Lake. I unload my passengers and cargo and return to the Lakehead. Several days later, I return to pick them up. Prepping for the flight I estimate our weight to be several hundred pounds less than on arrival, after they had eaten all their grocery supplies. I load the two men aboard with all their gear including the heavy lead weights, minus the canoe. With the short narrow lake, I am left with not much takeoff room and it is safer to leave the canoe and retrieve it later. Then things get interesting.

I taxi to the downwind end of the lake and enter the mouth of a wide stream, prepared to turn into the wind. All of a sudden, the front left float crashed into an invisible jutting rock just below the surface of the water. Shutting off the engine, I climb out of the cockpit and onto the rear of the float. Bouncing up and down I free the pontoon from the rock, but now of course I have water rushing into a major float compartment.

I attempt to take off and although I am able to get on the step, water being forced into the float compartment inhibits my speed for takeoff. Solution is to turn back to the campsite and unload one of my passengers and some of the gear. My Cessna 180 has a manual flap. This is a godsend for a quick departure when airspeed is achieved while skimming over the lake surface. That's what I do on my second takeoff attempt. I get on the step with the flaps. I am just able to attain airspeed and retract the flaps to gain more speed. As the trees are almost right in front of me, I quickly pop the flaps, the aircraft jumps from the water and with the stall warning screaming, I just ease the aircraft over the treetops. Whew---what a courageous moment, accentuated by the swoosh, swoosh as we skim over the treetops for the next several miles, gathering more airspeed before I can gently lift the bird to altitude. My passenger thought it great fun and really didn't feel the apprehension I was experiencing.

When we land in Fort William, the aircraft taxiing with a pronounced tilt of the wing because of the flooded float, I am not expecting the boss to meet us at the dock. After unloading the passenger and gear and out of his earshot, Orval Weiben really lit into me.

"Daniels, what is the big idea of driving my airplane like a tractor? There are no excuses. You get back to the lake and return with your other passenger and canoe, then you are going to stay here all evening and all night until you and our mechanic have repaired the damage." So that is what I do. I really get to appreciate the zinc chrome putty and pop rivets and guns, working in tight corners to get the repair done. We finally finish at 1 am and I have another bush pilot adventure under my belt.

The Work Horses of Bush Flying

George flies these Cessnas

Top; **Cessna 180, 230 H P, 11 gals/ hr. 800 lb. payload**

Bottom; **Beaver - CF - PCG, 450 H P, 20 gals/ hr. 1100 lb. payload**

Superior Airways Norseman V-CF-HEV
(Look a Likes)

Flying Prospectors & Mining groups on Exploration work. Shown two photos of mineral site in the mid fifties, N W Ont.

1957 - June. On the Superior Airways Sioux Lookout dock in front of Cessna 180 CF - HEQ. L to R, Pilot George Daniels in his McMaster U. Jacket, Imperial Oil Mngr., Arnold Davidson Chief Mechanic, Pilot Alex Maxwell, Randy (Ranny) MacDonald Chief Pilot & Base Manager.

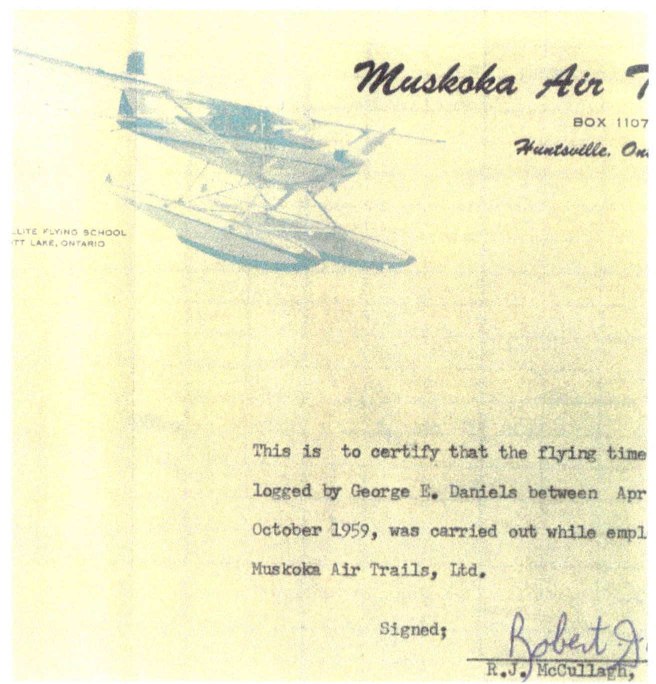

Muskoka Air T

BOX 1107

Huntsville, On.

...LLITE FLYING SCHOOL
...TT LAKE, ONTARIO

This is to certify that the flying time logged by George E. Daniels between Apr October 1959, was carried out while empl Muskoka Air Trails, Ltd.

Signed; Robert J.

R.J. McCullagh,

Moving on

The 1957 Canadian Federal Election results in C. D. Howe, the Liberal member for Fort William-Port Arthur being defeated, as was his Government and being replaced by John Diefenbaker's Conservatives. Superior Airways has 11 contracts for servicing the Mid-Canada Line, largely due to Orville Wieben's connections with C. D. Howe. With our member now out of power, the company's contracts are cancelled and many of our pilots are laid off. I am offered a modest contract to stay in Sioux Lookout, but work prospects do not look promising and I resign. Orville and Nanny McDonald give me good references and I go back to Toronto in late October 1957.

Sanderson Ackfield Aviation: Cessna Aircraft dealers

I walk into General Manager Trevor Ackfield's Malton office in mid-November and say, "I am applying as a pilot to ferry your Cessnas from the Wichita factory to Toronto."

After reviewing my Log Book, Trevor asks me to describe all the different Superior Airways charter work I had flown. I explain the diversity of my bush flying experience. He seems pleased and says, "Fine, I think you will make a good aircraft salesman and we will train you." I am tickled and cannot wait to get started. My next career flight is underway and will prove to be very formative in my chosen profession.

Trevor Ackfield, who it turned out was a RCAF pilot in WW 11, literally takes me under his wing. My Log Book for January 10, 1958 records Trevor giving me a check flight in the company's brand-new Cessna 182 CF-JUG. This four-place aircraft is the top of the line in the new Cessna high-wing, tricycle gear fleet of modern aircraft. The 182 ranks ahead of the Cessna 180, Cessna 172 and the Cessna 150 trainer. After my half-hour dual, I fly with co-pilot Trevor to Hamilton and Welland before returning to Malton Airport.

The Cessna Aircraft Company of Wichita, Kansas has a comprehensive Sales Manual. In part, it teaches the basics of salesmanship. It recommends getting to know the potential customer and fitting the ownership of a Cessna airplane to their needs.

Cessna breaks down the potential for aircraft sales into several categories. They point out that many current pilots learned to fly on fabric-covered taildragger aircraft. My learning to fly on an Aeronca Champ was a good example. The new Cessna tricycle airplanes are easy to taxi and so straightforward to fly that they almost seem like an extension of one's car. This is a big selling feature. Beginners find them a lot easier to learn than on a taildragger.

One of the main sources of potential customers is pilots hanging around flying clubs. I am already a member of the Hamilton Flying Club and quickly join the Toronto Flying Club, which has a nice clubhouse and restaurant on the south side of Malton airport. This Club is also quite sociable with several hundred members who enjoy the fly-in barbecues and weekend dances. I attend many of them and get to know some super prospective customers.

Sanderson Ackfield Aircraft also sells used airplanes that can become trade-ins on new Cessnas. Without a check ride or much difficulty, I get to fly Cessna 172s, 170s, Piper Tri-Pacers and Cessna 180s. The uniquely amphibious Republic Seabee is on our used lot and Trevor gives me a check ride. The Seabee is heavy with its retractable landing gear, 165hp Franklin engine and thick cord wing. A pilot really has to fly hands-on at the controls with attention to airspeeds in all aspects of flight. I get my first real test of a Seabee when Lloyd Nourse of Wyxx Corporation and member of the Toronto Flying Club asks me to give him a demo flight.

On a hot spring day, I ask our gas jockey to fill up the Seabee tanks, climb into the left seat with Lloyd in the right and radio Toronto Ground Control. We are directed to 11,000-foot runway 05, then contact the Tower and are cleared for takeoff. Under full throttle for maximum power, the aircraft slowly, oh so slowly, starts to gain speed. It seems to rumble along forever until we near takeoff speed. I use at least half the runway, nearly a mile, before I am able to rotate and lift the Seabee into a climbing attitude. Lloyd seems to enjoy it. Being used to the high-speed prompt response from Cessna 180s, I think this is not a very good airplane.

Nevertheless, after a very large circuit of the airport, we land and much to my surprise, Lloyd buys the plane because he wants to fly and land on water at his cottage on Lake of Bays at Baysville. On his first attempt at Baysville, he had had a crash landing and the plane was going to take several months to repair. It was my luck as he came back to buy another Seabee, which we have to find through another dealer. On review about Seabees I learn to fill the tanks only to half and for water flying, to remove the retractable landing gear.

We work closely with the Cessna Marketing Department. One of their sales strategies is to target business professionals needing to travel two- to three hundred miles from home office. We follow this plan and I am successful in selling Cessnas to car dealers, mining companies and cottagers throughout the Muskoka Lakes and beyond.

Lawyer David Humphrey is a pilot and member of the Toronto Flying Club. One day he says he had a client interested in buying a Cessna 180 on floats to fly to his Kawartha Lakes cottage. David arranges several meetings with his clients Vincent Feeley and Joe McDermott. They are novice pilots and give me a large deposit on the Cessna 180. It is arranged that we will finalize the sale at our Island Airport office. David mentions that Joe is bringing out a lot of cash for the final payment. I have reserved the airport terminal boardroom for the handover of the aircraft keys, at which time I will receive payment.

The clients often appear to be somewhat shady. I see them coming off the ferry carrying a large paper bag. When we get into the boardroom, Joe McDermott says, "Here is your $20,000 for final payment." He proceeds to turn the bag upside down and dump the money in $20 bills onto the table. He then says, "Count it". It takes me an hour and a half, I give them the keys and they decide to not fly it that evening. I am extremely apprehensive about holding onto all this cash after hours on a Friday evening. I phone Trevor Ackfield and persuade him to come to the Island Airport and take custody of this cash. Which he does.

A month later, it appears at the CNE Toronto International Airshow along the waterfront. All pilots are given NOTAMS (Notices to Airmen) advising flight restrictions around the show. On the second day, Feely and McDermott fly into the airshow zone with their C180 on floats and are told by the Tower, in no uncertain terms, they cannot land in the harbour due to the airshow. They are told to land in Oshawa, but ignoring instructions, they land in heavy swells outside the breakwater. Being inexperienced on landing floats in rough water, they capsize the aircraft. The plane stays afloat upside down and they are rescued by the Harbour Patrol.

This incident will come up several years later in an Ontario crime commission hearing about money laundering, as they had dumped bags of money from Fort Erie race track into the lake. The airplane had suffered a buckled wing and some water damage.

Several days later, the intrepid pair walks into my office and offer to trade in the damaged aircraft on another brand-new Cessna 180. Trevor and I huddle to discuss a fair but modest trade-in value and sell them another brand-new Cessna 180. A year or so later, I became nervous that I might be called to testify as a witness at the crime hearings, but relieved that I never was.

One of my key sales is a Cessna 150 trainer to Bobby and Tommy Wong, owners of Central Airways Flight School at the Island Airport.

Central is well known for its training on the two-place, side-by-side Fleet Canuck and Trevor says getting them to move up to Cessna is a coup.

Flying out of Toronto International in 1958 gives me some milestone moments. The Avro Arrow test flights are underway and on April 20, I am in the circuit with test pilot Jan Zurakowski. As he slows down, I keep up speed in my 182---what a sight, what an experience. Later on, Howard Hughes flies into Toronto in his TWA Lockheed Super Constellation and during my circuit, I had to fly well clear on Air Traffic control instructions. It was a thrill to be in the circuit with this aviation icon.

1958 Memories of being in the Toronto Malton YYZ Circuit with Aviation Pioneer Howard Hughes & his TWA Super Connie.

Avro Arrow 1958

I fly the new Cessna 182 CF-JUG demonstrator with quite a few customers all over Southern Ontario and build up a fair number of hours on this high-performance aircraft. I am becoming a successful aircraft salesman, my bush flying experience enhances my reputation and customers seem to like dealing with someone with this background.

My alma mater, the Hamilton Flying Club, buys a new Cessna 172 from me. My university friend Bob McCullagh purchases Cessna 180 CF-ICE with a set of floats for the summertime to fly to his Lake of Bays cottage. Don Weir of the Canadian Scale Company is also one of my customers. Don, Bob and I hear that Tommy Douglas wants to sell his Muskoka Air Trails on Lake Vernon, Huntsville. This company operates charter air service, maintenance base and flight school.

By the fall of 1958, I have sold over a dozen new and used aircraft and receive a Cessna Achievement Award. Cessna also sends a thank-you gift; a red plastic, electric $12 kitchen clock. Whoopee! I still have it.

Bob McCullagh is well connected with the T. Eaton Department Store family. They have their own float plane and base on Georgian Bay.

Bob's uncle Don MacIntosh is a Director of Eaton's. Bob sounds out these connections on the potential of owning Muskoka Air Trails and gets a positive response. The result; using mostly Bob's money and a token shareholding from myself, we buy Muskoka Air Trails. Bob keeps his stockbroker day job in Toronto and I take over as resident General Manager. My article in Muskoka Life Magazine headed *Wings over Muskoka* provides a unique insight into this entrepreneurial adventure.

Muskoka Life Magazine May 1991

Wings over Muskoka

On floats, every lake is a potential runway

BY GEORGE E. DANIELS

Heather Douglas

GEORGE DANIELS SLIPS THE 'SURLY BONDS OF EARTH' IN CF-JCT.

It was the year the King had really arrived with his "Don't you step on my blue suede shoes"—the year the Montreal Canadiens won the Stanley Cup for the third year in a row and I flew into Milford Manor Lodge in a Piper PA 11 on floats. The place was jumping. Gorgeous mahogany boats glistened in the sun and the college guys were checking out the waitresses with the King's music blaring in the background.

Not to be outdone by sleek-looking boats, my friend and I invited the guests and staff to go for a joy ride in our shabby-looking PA 11. Sitting in the front pilot seat with a flabbergasted passenger "ooing" and "ahhing" at the magic panorama and blue waters of Muskoka below, was exhilarating.

That summer of '56, I was trying to build up solo pilot time to earn my commercial pilot's licence. I worked part-time putting up television antennas to earn the money to rent airplanes from Orillia Air Services, where I was instructed and checked out by some pretty professional pilots — Hans Meneke, Rick Belamy, Cliff Lewis, John Richardson.

Names of a by-gone era were then an integral part of the economy and aviation life in Muskoka—the Red Wing Flying Service, Georgian Bay Air Services, Muskoka Air Trails in Huntsville and the fledgling DC3 Toronto Island to Muskoka air service. The noble yellow Beaver airplanes flew the Department of Lands and Forest fire, hydro and pipeline patrols.

The aviation fraternity had strong roots in Muskoka even then, with pilots like Paul Tapley, Ted Hungerford, and Muskoka's own Orville Wright swapping tales when they'd meet. Phil Garratt Sr., president of DeHavilland, would fly from Toronto to his Baysville cottage, a tradition his son Phil Jr. continues today.

In the mid '50s Orville Wright rented a Piper PA 11 on floats to take Bob Seagram for a ride. After gassing up on Lake Vernon they flew west across Skeleton Lake heading for Lake Rosseau.

"Halfway between Skeleton and Rosseau we noticed the fuel gauges were showing nearly empty," he says. "I concluded that the fuel cap had not been placed on the gas tanks correctly and the wind was sucking the fuel out by the gallon. It was too late to turn back into Skeleton Lake.

"I put the aircraft into a gradual glide for the nearest bay, and as we got close the aircraft was just above the treetops. On a straight-in final approach we could hear and feel the swoosh of the trees hitting the bottom of the pontoons and then, after some frantic moments, we were down on Skeleton Bay, Lake Rosseau. A boat towed us to shore.

"We called the aviation service where we had rented the plane. They told us to top up with car gas and make sure the fuel tank caps were properly secured. We flew back to the rental service without incident and would you believe Bob gave the owner such a hard time about our flight and the plane, we got away with having to only pay half price for the rental."

After university I launched into my aviation career with Superior Airways and was a bush pilot in Sioux Lookout for a year and a half. My university friend Bob McCullagh and I bought Muskoka Air Trails in the fall of 1958. No doubt many readers will fondly remember the air service's former owner, Tommy Douglas.

Tommy could fly a Stinson station wagon loaded to the gunwales and get in and out of any lake in Muskoka or north. The Stinson station wagon plane gets its name from its interior cabin, which was lined with wood similar to the Ford station wagons of the late '40s and early '50s.

How to fly: Tommy was a character. He'd pack a plane full of excited New York fishermen, along with their baggage, their fishing gear and the finest of LCBO products, then pick up a booklet from on top of the instrument panel — "How to Fly on Edo Floats." He'd thumb to the first page and read aloud. "Make sure water rudders are down for taxiing, check all aircraft surfaces, controls and the water and lake take-off area for obstruction. Do extensive cockpit check." Then he'd deliberately check out everything while the increasingly startled eyes of the passengers reflected their near panic. Of course, Tommy, who was inwardly killing himself laughing, eventually got the passengers calmed down and airborne. Tommy had his Aircraft Maintenance Certificate and stayed with us in the first several months to affect a smooth transition.

These were great times for us at Muskoka Air Trails. We obtained a Cessna distributorship and introduced the 180 to Muskoka. We sold aircraft, ran a flying school and operated a charter air service between Toronto and Muskoka.

George Daniels

BOB MCCULLAGH, HIS SON DAVID AND FRIEND MARIA PREPARE FOR A FISHING TRIP.

Some of our passengers had such notable names as Bassett, Hatch and Atwell. John Bassett was publisher of the then well-known *Toronto Telegram*. I would fly down from Muskoka to pick him up from the Toronto Island Airport to fly him north to his Muskoka cottage. The in-cockpit chatter consisted of John reading passages from his competitor's newspaper, the *Toronto Star*. He would make many remarks about the *Star* and how it compared with the *Telegram*, often laughing at the *Star's* editorial write-ups compared to his own current stories. Discussion of business and the trends of the day were part of the dialogue during these flights.

Our flying school was so successful with two or three Aeroncas and Piper J3s that in 1959 we expanded to the uranium boom town of Elliott Lake, Ont. and set up a satellite flying school. Everything was going along very well until one day the chief pilot we hired to manage Elliott Lake absconded with two weeks' receipts, which put an end to our new satellite venture. I don't think the RCMP ever caught up with him but it certainly forced us to regroup in Muskoka.

During this period of time, the local community was very supportive of our efforts. Mr. Rice, the owner of the *Huntsville Forester*, gave us a lot of publicity.

We developed Muskoka's first aviation traffic reports, after persuading the new Huntsville radio station, which was then called CKAR, the reports would be a valuable service to cottagers heading to or from Muskoka on Friday and Sunday evenings. Flying our new Cessna 180 CF-LGB, Gar Thomas (who is still with radio station CFBK-FM) and I flew from Huntsville down to Gravenhurst, north on Highway 169 to Bala then back to Lake Vernon in approximately 20 minutes.

Gar would report continuous traffic information into an old reel to reel tape recorder. Upon landing, he would dash back to the station, which was then on the corner of Highway 11 and the Lake Vernon Road. He injected the previously recorded traffic information into the following hour's programming. Of course, what was amusing is that these reports, although accurate, were obviously somewhere between 20 minutes to an hour and a half behind the real traffic conditions at time of broadcast. However, it was a service and we were able to generate some revenue through sponsorship and the listeners got a bird's eye view of the traffic from the wings over Muskoka.

The Queen's tour: In the summer of '59 the Queen, with Prince Philip, made her first visit as sovereign to Canada. The royal yacht *Brittania* came to Muskoka and Parry Sound. The Queen and Prince Philip used the *Brittania* as their floating hotel and she did side trips around Muskoka by train and limousine. I was hired by some Toronto journalists to fly them from spot to spot. Speedy aircraft coverage was necessary because the

Halfway between Skeleton and Rosseau we noticed the fuel gauges were showing nearly empty

Queen's itinerary was fast and with brief and various stops throughout Muskoka. At one point I flew the reporters into Gravenhurst's Gull Lake Park while the royal couple watched a concert on "the Barge" and then took the reporters immediately over to Parry Sound to see the royal party board the *Britannia*.

I got married in 1961 and was immediately transferred to Montreal. I saw less of Muskoka then, and I cherished those glimpses of Algonquin Park seen through the window of a DC8, flying the Montreal-Ottawa route with my fellow commuters.

In 1972 Harold Ballard solidified his hold on the Toronto Maple Leafs—Jean Beliveau retired from the Montreal Canadiens and a diligent group of Muskoka's leading citizens and business people accelerated the process of raising funds toward getting the *RMS Segwun* restored and afloat in time for its pending centennial. We moved back to Ontario to get closer to our Muskoka cottage. We also started to become more familiar with the Gravenhurst Airport. The airport handles a wide range of general aviation traffic and in the mid-'70s was one of my main twin engine training venues, as I got my twin endorsement on Cessna 310 CF-DAY.

Flying a light twin at 200 knots over Muskoka, northwest to Parry Sound and down into the Toronto control aviation corridors is an exhilarating challenge every flight.

Like many pilot cottagers in Muskoka I've enjoyed the value of flying over congested highways and beating the automotive traffic back to the city by several hours. Of course, being on floats makes every lake a potential runway.

However, aviation does have its attendant difficulties. Many times each summer a morning mist shrouds a nearby island, just a half mile away. It's days like this when I'd planned to take off at 7:30 a.m. to be back at the office at 9 a.m. that the old expression, "Time to spare. Go by air" came into effect as I waited for the morning sun to burn off the mist.

My perennial love affair with the Cessna 180 was rekindled in 1982 when Bob McCullagh invited me to share the cockpit in his CF-JCT. Ever since, he and I have shared flight duties from early May to late October, flying all over Muskoka and much of Ontario.

Emergency landing: All aircraft require, by federal law, an annual and thorough maintenance servicing by specially licensed aircraft mechanics. This includes a complete check of all flight and engine instruments, propellers, and the replacement of worn parts. It's called the annual C of A — Certificate of Air-worthiness. CF-JCT's turn came up again last June. We planned the flight carefully from Lake of Bays to Orillia Aviation, one of the best specialists in Cessna 180 bush plane maintenance.

Bob McCullagh was to drive his car down to Orillia with my wife Ruth and friends while my son Andrew was to come with me to deliver the aircraft.

I checked the North Bay and Muskoka Aviation weather centres, which reported a significant weather trough around Lake Erie—the forecast called for strong winds around Toronto, scattered skies over Lake Simcoe and strong headwinds all the way. But since most of the distance was under good weather and we had bright sunny skies in Muskoka I took off for the half-hour flight to Orillia.

Ten minutes into the flight Andrew and I could see dark, ominous clouds by Baysville. I radioed Muskoka flight services who reported strong winds developing in very light rain showers.

I flew towards the airport and the potential safety of Lake Muskoka. Just then Andrew noticed a significant streak of lightning about 20 miles due southeast. We were proceeding west. The cockpit became a little tense with me working the radio to Muskoka—keeping up a reduced but safe speed and descending below developing lower clouds. Andrew was anxious.

As I came up on Muskoka Airport we also saw a Beaver plane with the tell-tale red and black colors of Air North Bay flying almost alongside me—he was also working Muskoka radio.

Heather Douglas

In the early 2000s, this service became Timmins-Muskoka Radio on the same frequency.

Ed Scammell is the flight service specialist at Muskoka Airport.

By now the weather was getting fairly lousy with diminished visibility and lightning (not the pilot's best friend) appearing to get closer, although the worst turbulence was to the east of us.

I made a quick emergency landing on Sparrow Lake, while the Beaver landed in Lake Muskoka. Just before a horrendous squall line went through, we'd moored at Port Stanton Aviation. Andrew sighed with relief. We later heard that Toronto had been severely buffeted by a storm. It passed through southern Muskoka in about 40 minutes and we were able to achieve our Orillia Aviation objective shortly afterwards.

The good days: There are many beautiful flying days, too. Today when I fly over Lake Rosseau I remember the Royal Muskoka, one of the classic resorts of the area, which burned in the 1950s. My mind does a quick flashback to the Royal's heyday as I look at the sparse vacant land below. In the meantime I'm

Muskoka Airport: fact sheet

Muskoka Airport has a 6,000-foot paved runway, a 2,700-foot east-west grass runway, a Ministry of Transportation weather station and aircraft advisory radio service.

The 24-hour departure and arrival frequency is 122.3 VHF. For en route traffic it's 126.7 VHF.

The airport is 925 feet above sea level. Its annual traffic is a little over 30,000 movements a year, of which 13,000 are visiting aircraft. The balance is circuits and bumps and other student training activity from Sandy Ferrari's flight school. At any one time there are several dozen student pilots on course. They have two Piper Cherokees, a Cessna 172 and a twin engine Piper Seneca available to them.

Lake Central Air Service does valued maintenance and repair for a wide range of aircraft.

The airport frequently hosts Lear Jets, Cessna Citations and other executive jets such as the Challenger. C 130s from the Canadian Forces Base at Trenton use the airport, too. The largest plane to recently touch down at Muskoka Airport was a DC9.

For information, call 687-2194. ✣

Muskoka Life May 1991 23

suspended in glistening sunlight between the blue water, and clear, blue sky as we fly a typical Muskoka summer day.

Bob McCullagh and I are flying CF-JCT over the Royal Muskoka site on our way to visit Alex and Joanne Menzies—and we decide to give them an aircraft "fly-by" salute. This also includes a magnificent view of the twin towers of the Morinus church. And as you pull the aircraft up, you soar over Doug Bassett's immaculate cottage complex and are immediately confronted with the spectacular Clevelands House Resort, accentuated by postage-stamp-sized, red tennis courts. As I make a Rate 1-1/2 turn over Clevelands House we are flying out of the west to come back east and be on final approach to land at the Menzies'. I'm only 500 feet above Henry Wilson's neat little island with its classic early 1900s cottage.

I'm suspended in glistening sunlight between the blue water and clear sky

After our visit we fly south over Lake Muskoka. A sudden excitement mounts as we see the grand old lady of the lake—the *RMS Segwun*. We fly lower to get a better look at that gorgeous white and green hull and dip our wings in salute to another pilot—Captain Jim Caldwell—the *Segwun's* skipper.

We then fly east via the Muskoka River and see another of Muskoka's great attractions as the top of a bright ferris wheel shines in the sun. Yes, it's Santa's Village and there is Rudolph's Roller Coaster Sleigh Ride—another of Muskoka's flying phenomena.

But it is not always a pretty sight that greets Muskoka's pilots these days. There are still some landfill sites that look like raw wounds on the landscape. Large new developments seeming stark and prickly amidst the the natural settings. And there's no denying the water has turned brown in places where it used to be pristine blue. Many flight plans have been written and Muskoka trips taken since those early days in '56. Today another king, No. 99—Wayne Gretzky, dominates the hockey headlines and Elvis's songs and memorabilia continue.

Flying over Muskoka will always have a very special feeling for me and many of my pilot fraternity. It is best expressed by the first five lines of John Gillespie Magee Jr.'s famous poem *High Flight:*

Oh, I have slipped the surly bonds of earth,
And danced the skies on laughter-silvered wings;
Sunward I've climbed and joined the tumbling mirth
Of sun-split clouds—and done a hundred things
You have not dreamed of—wheeled and soared and swung
High in the sunlit silence . . . ❖

Heather Douglas

George Daniels is a licensed commercial pilot, immediate past president of the Lake of Bays Association and executive vice-president of Marketing Plus Inc., in Toronto.

PART V

Facing health issues which prevent his continuation as a commercial airline pilot, George changes gears, enters the world of advertising and sales and meets THE girl.

Part V

A Change in the Cockpit: Navigating a new Career: Fall 1959–March 1960

On my return from Europe in early fall of 1959 aboard the Italian liner SS Irpinia from Genoa to Montreal, it was obvious to me that a new career path was in order.

What to do? Now grounded from flying and with an invalid commercial pilot license medical category A4 due to my third gastrectomy in several years, my chances of being "pilot in command" seem years away. Discussing my options with my Dad and Mum, it was obvious that I might be accepted into the Aviation Disciplines Department of Transport Canada which was looking for air traffic controllers and other ground support staff. Meteorology School was also an option. The airlines continued to expand both Trans-Canada Airlines, Max Ward's Wardair and even TransAir Charters had openings.

However, my mind could not contemplate returning to the routine of shift work I experienced with success at the Stelco Met Labs. This, after all, had proven ideal at the time, working 3 pm to 11 pm at Mount Hope, flying in the morning or 11 pm to 7 am overnight shift, home to bed and then to the Hamilton Airport in late afternoon to build up more flying time on the Aeronca Champ and Cessna 140. The 7 am to 3 pm stints were more normal, but happened only every three weeks, so one's body was constantly in readjustment mode to accommodate the shift rotations. I could not see myself doing this for the rest of my life in a control tower or as an airline ground handler or Met Office technician.

Pop suggested I reenergize my career with some professional advice, so I searched out several management consultants who specialized in professional business placements.

I responded to several companies who were advertising in the business pages of the Toronto newspapers. As I found out, the benefits of responding to the ads meant I did not have pay for their search work. The prospective clients' employees did.

J.B. Fraser, with impressive oak-paneled offices at Bloor and Bay, was one company that took me under their wing, while several others listed me as a candidate.

I was assigned to a Mr. Moore after meeting *the* J.B. Fraser. An aptitude test and various other academic and personality evaluations took place over several weeks. Mr. Moore and Co. was ready to market me at the end of October 1959.

Now here comes the interesting part. J.B. Fraser had prominent major corporations as clients, with a few modest-size companies and placed people in all sorts of disciplines from engineering and accounting to transportation. They had me earmarked for the media and advertising world. At the time, I often wondered what my background---24 years of age, plus their test---had shown to steer me in several directions. Thus started a round of interviews J.B. Fraser arranged that turned out to be pivotal in my new career.

Young and Rubicam Ltd., then as it now, was one of North America's leading advertising agencies. They were located in the Royal Bank building on lower University Ave. at Queen with a stellar list of name clients who were looking at *me* as our account executive trainee. An account executive in an ad agency is the main conduit between the agency and the clients, selling, communicating and getting feedback for the agency's recommendations for ad campaigns. One part of the trainee program was to spend time in the media department crunching numbers! Initially my reaction--ugh!

The General Motors Marketing Department in Oshawa was located in the 1920–1930s department-store style with plate glass walls separating each office so you could see from one end of a 100-yard office floor to the other. Little did I know at the time that I would see much more of these General Motors open-concept offices in about 10 years.

I remember my interview with the assistant marketing manager very well. It began with, "what car are you driving?" (Answer – my '56 Volkswagen) "Well of course, we'll have to get you into a GM product when you start here. Question: what are your creative and copywriting skills? Can you write slogans, such as the '62 Chevrolet is ______? Several years later, I would become a quite proficient advertising/sales writer and more. The second part of the interview saw me with the ad manager, a Mr. Taylor, and much to my surprise he knew me, and remembered our family from Chambly-Richelieu in the late 40s and 50s. He also remembered my involvement in Scouts and my early days of entrepreneurship, mowing lawns, babysitting and general handyman activities in the community.

Surprisingly, he dissuaded me from pursuing the GM marketing department opportunity. His reasoning was that I would just be a little cog in a great big monolith and in his opinion, I would be uncomfortable in this work environment. I'm glad he sold me on not becoming a GM employee, but that proved to be a hindrance to me being a GM man in other ways in the future.

Gould Murray Outdoor Ltd Outdoor Advertising: Large Billboards National Sales Representative

This company was a unique career opportunity. With headquarters in Brantford Ontario, they were a division of Gould Outdoor Advertising. Gould originally started in the 1920s in southwest Ontario. I learned that Hal Gould Senior was a friend of Henry Ford of Model T fame. Apparently, Henry Ford worked with Mr. Gould to build large poster billboards to advertise his Ford cars. The company had grown in six large southwestern Ontario towns from Windsor, Sarnia, London to Brantford.

In the late 50s, John Gould hired Tom Quigley, ex-RCAF, a national space-on-billboards sales representative firm in Toronto. The company teamed up with Tim and his son Vern Murray of Montreal to have an office in Canada's other major advertising market.

This is the iconic Coppertone 24-sheet outdoor advertising poster.

The company provided coast-to-coast sales and service to the six or seven major billboard plant owners as they are called. This meant over 20,000 boards in all major Canadian cities. The prominent clients who buy this space are the banks, car, soft-drink, cigarette and chocolate bar companies and they all needed to be sold on why they should put their media advertising dollars in outdoor advertising in tandem with radio, TV and print. Gould wants me to be a sales representative calling on clients and their advertising agencies with some of the latest research studies show that the outdoor medium reaches thousands of people at a very efficient cost.

I find this opportunity to be up my alley. I'll be a reasonably medium-to-large employee in a modest-size company with a chance to get ahead, so I decide to work for and be taught and mentored by Tom Quigley at Gould Murray, 69 Eglinton Ave. East Toronto office starting February 1960.

How do I love thee? Let me count the ways."—
Elizabeth Barrett Browning

In January 1960, while Canada was entering a decade of economic growth (although not on a post-World War II scale), Prime Minister John Diefenbaker (Dief the Chief) shattered our aviation world by bowing to pressure from the United States and cancelling production of the Avro Arrow, our finest and most-respected jet fighter.

In the previous six months, I had gone through the J. B. Fraser executive search mill after deciding to leave the world of aviation and Muskoka Air Trails and go in a different direction. Fraser set up interviews with General Motors marketing, Young and Rubicam Advertising and Gould Murray Outdoor Advertising, and I determined that Gould represented the best starting point for a new career. I was scheduled to begin work there February 10, 1960.

But I felt the need for a break from the round of interviews, the stress and nervous energy of a career change and the pressure of paying our bills without a pay cheque. While I had saved enough to buy a used 1954 Volkswagen ($600 from a dealer at College and Bay), I needed to relax, and decided that a ski weekend in Muskoka would be the get-away-from-it-all solution.

So, I called up Jack Hatkoski, a new friend from the Lake of Bays area whom I had met through Bob McCuallagh. Jack was a skier, fellow pilot and teacher who enjoyed the outdoors, so I suggested we check into Limberlost Lodge for a Friday-to-Sunday bit of R and R. He readily agreed.

I had good reason to choose Limberlost, one of Ontario's first all-season resorts built by the Hill family in the 20s and 30s, having flown my Cessna 180 (CF-ICE) into Lake Solitaire while flying for Muskoka Air Trails. I knew Mrs. Hill and was always welcomed by her son-in-law Maury East (another pilot) along with the family and staff. It seemed a natural place to go. We registered Friday morning and were given rooms in one of the Fine Olde Cabins, complete with cozy fireplace and other amenities.

Josle Uter was the resident professional overseeing a 400-foot T-bar lift, so I laced my new ski boots, purchased during a September trip to Germany, and signed up for a lesson on the Stem Christie, a manoeuver used by skiers to make difficult turns. That evening, we enjoyed a Limberlost home-cooked meal, followed by a hay ride, and on returning about 8 pm, we noticed some weekend guests arriving.

We awoke Saturday to bright sunlight---CAVU or Ceiling and Visibility Unlimited in aviation terms---with a balmy 25F on the thermometer and a delicious bacon-and-egg breakfast. We were in the midst of a magical winter's day and, as planned, far away from the angst of world politics (the Arrow cancellation and a Catholic Presidential candidate in John F. Kennedy). We were enjoying skiing at Limberlost and recharging the batteries.

By mid-morning and with no lessons scheduled, Jack and I were on our own and began checking out a group of very attractive young women exiting the T-bar lift. Three young women in particular: two in blue ski pants, and a girl in a fur hat, blue jacket and red stretch ski pants (the new Austrian pants known as Bogners) who seemed exceptionally attractive. As Jack expressed his appreciation of these lovely ladies and suggested we might try to get to know them, I said, "Jack, you take the two in blue and I'll try the one in the red pants. She turned out to be Ruth Ditson.

Ruth's recollection:

"It was Valentine's Day weekend in 1960 when teaching colleague Mary King invited me to accompany her and another friend to Limberlost to ski. I had never been there, so I agreed. We arrived Friday and skied all day Saturday, and,

après-ski, we collapsed into soft leather chairs. I closed my eyes, but then heard a voice talking about the virtues of the soft insoles in the new ski boots he bought in Germany. As I had spent the summer hitch-hiking through Europe with my friend Anne, I was not impressed.

But later that evening in the lodge, and dance was being held, and I was sitting across from the entrance when in came the young man who had been entertaining the guests with stories about his new insoles. He headed directly for me and we danced together for the rest of the night. He then asked me to go to a party at the manager's house, but as that didn't happen, he then walked me back to the cabin I was sharing with my friends.

Before we left the next day, he asked me for a date to go to a movie in Toronto, where we then planned to meet the following Saturday at the barn in Collingwood. And the rest, as they say, is history."

"True love is not looking into each other's eyes---it's gazing together in the same direction." ---Thomas Jefferson and historian David McCullagh.

Courting

July 1960, Ruth Ditson, George Daniels at Balm Beach.

At Limberlost Lodge
the newlyweds.
L to R:
Ruth and George
Henk Ploeger and Isabel Kaprielian
Vivian Kummer and Walt Fraser
March 1961

Daniels—Ditson Rites Held at Collingwood

COLLINGWOOD — Ruth Elaine Ditson, daughter of Mr. and Mrs. John A. Ditson, Collingwood, became the bride of George Eaton Daniels, son of Mr. and Mrs. Cecil C. G. Daniels, Toronto, in All Saints' Anglican church here. Rev. Phillip Downer officiated.

Given in marriage by her father, the bride chose a short dress of white satin peau de soie, styled on classic lines. The skirt was bouffant and her shoulder-length veil of tulle illusion was held by a matching circlet featuring a French rose.

The bride's sister, Ann Louise Ditson, was maid of honor in a short frock of larkspur-pink satin peau de soie, with matching headdress. Her flowers were pink and white carnations.

The groom's brother, William Daniels, was best man. Walter Fraser ushered. The reception was held at The Georgian inn. The couple will live in Toronto.

Da[illegible]

Rev. Phillip Downer officiated at the ceremony in All Saints' Anglican Church, Collingwood, uniting in marriage Miss Ruth Elaine Ditson, daughter of Mr. and Mrs John Almer Ditson of Collingwood, to Mr. George Eaton Daniels, son of Mr. and Mrs. Cecil Charles George Daniels of Toronto.

Given in marriage by her father, the bride wore a short gown of satin peau de soie in ice white, the empire bodice fashioned on traditional lines with lilypoint sleeves and a circlet neckline. The skirt was bouffant, and her shoulder-length veil was gathered to a circlet of peau de soie offset with a French rose. She carried a bouquet of gardenias.

Miss Ann Louise Ditson was her sister's maid of honor, and her short peau de soie gown was in larkspur pink. The empire bodice was fashioned with a midriff fold offset with bow-knot detail, and featured bracelet-length sleeves and a scoop neckline. She carried a bouquet of pale pink and white carnations.

Mr. William Daniels was best man for his brother, and Mr. Walter Fraser was usher.

Cutting their wedding cake are Mr. and Mrs. George E. Daniels, who were married in All Saints' Church, Collingwood. The bride was Miss Ruth Elaine Ditson, daughter of Mr. and Mrs. J. A. Ditson.

PART VI

His new career and family find him back in Quebec, where they build their first cottage, and then back to Ontario where the author begins work on a new cottage, enters the burgeoning sport of skiing and becomes a father.

Part VI

George and Ruth pioneer Shack Charmant, their first cottage

In the spring of 1961 and five months after our February marriage, we were transferred to Montreal. My boss Tom Quigley persuaded us to move to Montreal. There, I would get more experience working with Tim Murray and his son Vern as they spearheaded the Outdoor Advertising Sales and Service of four of the largest-spending national advertisers in Canada. Their products were on billboards from coast to coast. My job was to work with the clients' advertising managers and their agencies and in addition, to coordinate all the Poster/Billboard paint with the plant operators' companies with the actual billboards with space to rent in municipalities and surrounding highways.

Arriving in Montreal, we find a very nice apartment on Sherbrooke Street just behind the Montréal Forum. Mr. Murray and Vern are most welcoming. Shortly after settling in, we are invited to their St. Adolph Laurentian cottage for a Saturday barbecue with the family. The lake was small with a very nice beach in front of the Murray's cottage. The setting looked like that featured in the *Apprenticeship of Duddy Kravitz* movie.

After a delightful lunch and getting to know the various Murray family members, Mr. Murray asks me to take a walk on the beach. He asks, "What do you think of this setting?" I reply, "I think it is super". Then Mr. Murray says something that will be my motivator for a long time.

"George, remember God does not make any more land. I suggest you get some."

Several weeks later, I am in the office reading a Montreal Gazette classified ad saying; Quebec Government offers north Laurentian Crown land on a ten-year lease at $10 per year subject to minimum $3,000 building improvements during the life of the lease. Remembering Mr. Murray's words, I take the newspaper into his office. He reads it and says, "Well, what are you waiting for? Go for it." An application is available at the Government's downtown office. I do not have time to tell Ruth and hustle to get an application.

In the evening, Ruth and I review the application. For a small deposit, we can obtain a half-acre lot on Lac Simon in the village of La Conception, several miles north of St. Jovite and an hour and half drive from Montreal. We apply and get accepted.

Excitedly we drive to Lac Simon. There is a small population with a marina at the south end on the only road into the lake. Our new property is on the opposite shore with no road where we meet marina proprietor Raoul Giroux. He is affable but wary and speaks no English. I speak some French. We negotiate a trip in his boat to see our lot. The shoreline is sparsely tree-covered with 20-30 feet of flat land back from the water. White Birch trees are prominent with towering pines atop a steep cliff. Access is by boat as the new road is not planned for several years. Now we know why it is so cheap.

Setting about pioneering our new land, the shopping list includes a small aluminum boat with a 9hp Scott outboard. We decide to build a platform for a tent and front fly. It will be our campsite while we build. Several of our new-found friends from the Advertising and Sales Association of Montreal, where we have become members, will help us from time to time. Most of all, the indispensable Raoul Giroux is our carpenter.

Being our own design engineers, we decide to build a first phase multi-purpose room. Our specifications require building a rock-filled crib foundation along the waterfront. It will be four feet above the water line and 24 feet wide. Using our own rocks and logs from the property takes us most remaining weekends in 1961. The following year, we build the tent platform and outfit our camp kitchen with a used gas stove converted to propane and an icebox refrigerator. On a minimum budget, we scrounge for our needs. Up the hill and out of the way, we build an outhouse with plywood salvaged from Rothmans billboards.

George and Ruth pioneer Shack Charmant, their first cottage

George and Ruth pioneer Shack Charmant, their first cottage

George & Ruth's Laurentian Shack Charmant.
Lac Simon near Ste Jovite and Mont Tremblant Resort.

Building a Dream: The Cottage at Lake of Bays

In the spring of 1965, we had been transferred to Toronto by Paul L'Anglais and continued to own the property at Lac Simon in Québec.

I received a call from old friend Rick Irwin, our insurance agent. He said he wanted to rent his cabin on his Lake of Bays property near Port Cunnington and I remembered visiting his land several years before. He said he wanted $500 rent for the month of August.

That was quite expensive at the time. Rick suggested we share it with someone, so we approached Ruth's cousin Carolyn and her husband John Macdonald about the idea. They agreed. We drove the three hours from Toronto and immediately noted the contrast of basically a flat lot compared to the steep terrain at Lac Simon. Furthermore, we could drive to the door without having to boat as we had in the Laurentians.

The one-room cabin was well equipped with a stove, fridge and sink. The bathroom was in the adjacent sleeping cabin with a toilet and sink. A quick swim in the lake would have to serve as bath and shower.

We settled in on August 1 and our second cottage dream began. What an adventure it has turned out to be. That October, we bought it and also bought the 17-foot Shepherd launch and complete set of outdoor cedar furniture. Getting to know the residents and summer cottage neighbours launched long-standing friendships.

Setting out in the launch, we felt it was time to introduce ourselves to the neighbours and on a lovely late August afternoon, we noted a young couple on the Montgomery dock. Andy and Joy Montgomery were having cocktails and invited us to join them. We had a merry time and before we knew it, the whole evening had gone by and we left, at what is now a memorable "five of eleven" point in time.

Andy explained how his grandfather had pioneered and developed the Montgomery point. The family had a policy of keeping the various lots for their siblings. Apparently, we are one of only three outside families within the mile and a half of shoreline the Montgomerys own. Andy pointed out that our lots are prime southwest facing with gorgeous pine trees. The Slatter and Kirby/Ransom families have a similar exposure. All dwellings are well spaced for considerable privacy. The original 1920s shoreline survey road is the connecting driveway around the point.

As the summer winds down, we become acquainted with the Hamlet of Port Cunnington. It is significant for its St. James Anglican Church, Port Cunnington Lodge and Gord and Alice Allinson who would become our cottage custodians in our absence.

Bigwin Inn on the nearby island of the same name is famous. Built in the 1920s by C. O. Shaw, mogul of the Huntsville Tannery, it had become a destination for the rich and famous. Its magnificent rotunda, separate ballroom, stand-alone dining room and lakeside bar and observation deck were also a magnet for Lake of Bays cottagers. We discovered the Friday night ritual; cottagers boated over to the Round Room bar for the start of their weekend socializing. Many people arranged their recreational socializing, boating excursions, picnics and more formal family dinners at these get-acquainted cocktails.

The fall of 1966 ushered in exciting times for us. Career changes were in the works and I was recruited and moved from Paul L'Anglais's Toronto sales office to Standard Broadcast Sales (CFRB). Ruth signed on with the Toronto Board of Education as a supply teacher. With a number of moves in our first five years of marriage, we set a goal to put down family roots at our new Muskoka cottage.

Towards the end of 1966, our property acquisitions continued. We moved out of our Forest Hill Village apartment. Anticipating the need for more space with a new baby, we bought a three-bedroom house at the end of Glenrose Avenue in the convenient Mt. Pleasant and St. Clair area of North Toronto.

Andrew was born Dec 16, 1966. We saw our adopted baby when he was seven days old and took him home on Boxing Day. Wow! What a gift. Bottles, diapers and responsible loving care were now part of our busy careers. We are parents.

Like most Canadians, we ushered in Canada's 100th birthday in 1967 with patriotism. Bobby Gimby's catchy musical anthem *CAN-A-DA* was widely broadcast and on everyone's lips. Baby Andrew became our contribution to the Centenary celebrations.

Ruth became a stay at home Mom, and while I learned the intricacies of representing half a dozen major market radio stations from coast-to-coast, Ruth's homemaker energies were rewarded by nurturing baby Andrew.

We had joined Devil's Glen Ski Club in 1965 and on many winter weekends we checked in at Grandma Ditson's downtown Collingwood house. Doris' babysitting while we skied was appreciated.

Planning for spring and summer at our Lake of Bays' cottage included equipping our 1967 Ford Mustang convertible with a portable crib, playpen and all items young babies require. It was a tight fit. A growing trend among young families with hectic careers was the mother's helper. Cathy Morrison, the 13-year-old younger sister of a good friend, joined us at the cottage when school was out at the end of June. For a modest weekly wage, good food and water-skiing recreation, Cathy became the ultimate babysitting mother's helper.

Port Cunnington
Lake of Bays
July 6, 1990

Dear George,

Just a note as you step down from the presidency of the Lake of Bays Association to express my admiration of the accomplishments you have achieved during your term as president.

Your dedication, leadership and innovation have been instrumental in developing a vibrant, responsive organization at a critical period in the history of Lake of Bays. You have been truly professional and the right leader for the times in tackling the important issues and bringing along new, young energetic board members who will determine the future of our lake.

I am pleased that you will be remaining on the Board and have done such a good job in grooming Betty for the Presidency. I am sure she will carry on your excellent initiatives, especially in dealing with the potential impact of upcoming development proposals for Bigwin.

It has been a pleasure to serve on the board of directors under your guidance and inspiration. I am both sorry and disappointed that I was unable to be more active while on the board. Unfortunately, having moved into two new positions within the last two and one-half years required my putting in very long hours combined with a heavy travel schedule from coast to coast. Perhaps in the future, when my business commitments have substantially reduced, I will again be given an opportunity to participate more fully.

Anne and I look forward to seeing you and Ruth at the Lake as the years go by.

All the best to you and your family.

Regards,

Dave Johnstone

Devil's Glen is Golden

The 50th Anniversary Celebrations of the Devil's Glen Country Club
The *jewel* in the valley, 1965 - 2015

Glen Huron, Ontario L0M 1L0

From the Devil's Glen Country Club 50th Anniversary Coffee Table Book and George E. Daniels (Ruth) an original club member and Director of The Lodge and Building Committee 1967-1969.

The 1968/69 Lodge Expansion: Innovative Architecture

Devil's Glen Lodge. Note the original architect Eb Zeidler sloped shingled roof line continues today.

Towards the end of the first full season as a private ski club, the need for more lodge space and amenities was obvious, from food services, seating in the dining area, clothing and boot lockers to looking after toddlers, the areas of concern were real. We were a growing, active and enthusiastic group of keen skiers needing a host of items to be able to enjoy our fairly-new club. So, servicing the members and their requests, the Board of directors acted. The Lodge Expansion Committee was formed.

George Daniels was one of four new directors who joined the original founding directors and brought professional skill sets to the Devil's Glen Management Group that would be invaluable to our Lodge Expansion Committee.

In addition to George Daniels, director in charge of Lodge Expansion were Doug Skelton P. Eng., Bill Dawson P. Eng. and Brad Henry, Finance. Our Committee was part of a group of other sub-committees responsible for sourcing and installation of a new chair lift, other T-Bars and trails improvements. We were assigned a whopping $46,000 budget. Although a significant amount, it would still require many volunteer man hours and pro bono work to build to everyone's expectations. Directors, members and friends of the club came on board to make everything work.

Our first task was to get architectural drawings, which would also require creating specifications to comply with the Ontario Building Code. We were also faced with complying with the parameters of the Niagara Escarpment

Commission, due to Devil's Glen being in their jurisdiction and laws designed to protect the natural valley, landscape and the Mad River flowing through our property. George Hamman of the highly-regarded firm of Bregman, Hamman Architects was one of our new members and also a friend of the Daniels family from our Lake of Bays summer cottage community. He stepped forward to put his experience into the project.

It is important to consider how the original Lodge look came about. As reported earlier (The Racers Edge) one of the key figures in the Devil's Glen Lodge was Toni Spiess, a Giant Slalom Olympic medalist hired by Mike Gee and the Devil's Glen owners to run the ski shop and be the ski pro. The Lodge was to also serve as his home apartment. He was involved with guiding the architects on how a ski chalet should look, so Toni suggested a chalet look and roof line such as you would see in the Austrian Alps. One could look out the windows and down the mountain. However, our Lodge with its overhanging awning effect did not allow this—we are in a valley with mostly an uphill view of the Inferno or Limbo. So our priority was improve the view.

George Hamman and his team of architects did a superb job. The fairly new post-and-beam structure was prominent and our windows were almost floor to ceiling Thermopane glass to the cathedral ceiling. We achieved a distinctive look with solid attractive beams. Don Mills Construction was chosen to be our contractor. Don Mills himself spent many hours with our building team to construct the new 1,000 square-foot addition.

We had one hiccup. The original bridge across the Mad River was determined to be not strong enough to absorb the tons of weight that had to be transported (including giant steel chair-lift pylons) to our site. So we had to shore up and almost rebuild the bridge. This entailed large strong steel I-beams and more timber. This bridge works very well to this day.

Expansion also involved food service. The members were asking for a speedier cafeteria line. Pat McCann was a recent graduate of Ryerson Hotel Management. I met him as he was advising Paul Weber for his soon-to-be-popular hamburger restaurant on Hwy 11 just north of Orillia. Paul helped put in the "Get the customer's order up front and then instruct the kitchen to produce" system and new cafeteria manager Mrs. Rigney implemented it to most members' satisfaction. Member Jerry Hesser was with Consumers' Gas and he enabled us to equip the kitchen with more up-to-date commercial appliances.

There have been two other major expansions since. Member Ken Vogel and his construction company worked with manager Alex Wilson and his staff in 1991 on an 8,000-square-foot addition. The budget was $600,000. In 2004, the Club approved another addition on the north side of the lodge.

Whatever the decade, Devil's Glen Lodge has always represented some of the best in winter or summer country-club ambience to the benefit of its members and guests.

The Devil's Advocate

Newsletter launch September 25, 1968
The official publication of the Devil's Glen Country Club, Glen Huron, Ontario

In the spring of 1968, one year after Canada's Centennial, the Board of Directors met at the Fischer Hotel in Guelph, chosen because it was halfway between the homes of various directors in London and Toronto. On the agenda was my recommendation to improve our communications with members by starting a Newsletter.

This initiative came out of my experience as a second-wave director, not having been on the founding Board of Directors two years earlier. I was part of a new group of keen skiing families, including Brad Henry, Finance; Doug Skelton, Trails; Dr. Bill Samis, Ski School Ops and John Mingay, Membership. Our President and leader was Mike Gee and the membership was asking questions such as, I need more information about Devil's Glen Club benefits and the Waterfall scares me and what are you doing to develop more intermediate skiing, will we have a Ski Shop for ski service & rentals, will the Ski School accommodate various age groups, how many guests can I bring and I've heard we can build on the property, please explain cost and rules etc. were some of the many queries heard. We needed a platform to explain to our 200 family members what we were managing.

Our membership got their news mainly from Toronto and London media. This was long before today's 500-channel universe, Internet, e-mail and social media. The 1968 print and broadcast scene was three major newspapers (Globe, Star and Telegram), half a dozen radio stations with my employer CFRB 1010 leading the ratings, several Canadian TV stations and a similar number out of Buffalo. Our London members tuned in to CFPL Radio and the London Free Press but none of these covered the Collingwood private ski club world. Reports on skiing, snow and road travel conditions were hit and miss. There was a need to inform not only about activities but who to contact. A newsletter would be our communications voice.

My recommendation included a name that would have continuity with the novel *Dante's Inferno,* source of our club's nomenclature, which is why the names of our main ski runs are Inferno, River Styx, Waterfall Limbo and the Mad River, eventually adding Stairway. In conceptualizing a Masthead name and researching options, we added the name Advocate to our brand name--Devil's. The Oxford Universal Dictionary reinforced the recommendation; "*Advocate is one who pleads or intercedes for another to recommend publicly; 1767, to a publication, a view; advocacy.*" Using the attractive green-and-red club logo and incorporating the Tri-Devil's Forks in reverse illustrative design, we created *The Devil's Advocate*, with the positioning statement;

The official publication of the Devil's Glen Country Club, Glen Huron, Ontario.

By Issue 3, we incorporated the Devil's fork and bold type you read to this day. Below the logo was printed the Publisher/Editor contact info, which was my address and number. (No e-mail or website in those days.)

It was an exciting time to appeal to winter sports enthusiastic members. They also had broader interests fueled by the 1968 news of Canadian golfer Sandra Post winning the LPGA Championship at 18 and the Toronto Maple Leafs winning the 1967 Stanley Cup. Tennis allows professionals to compete for the first time, our Medicare System is introduced and Pierre Trudeau wins the Liberal leadership. Really motivating our keen Devil's Glen Alpine skiers was the first World Cup Series. All three disciplines---Slalom. Giant Slalom, and Downhill---were won by Jean-Claude Killy and the women's by Canadian Nancy Greene. Little did we realize how these milestones would go on to propel our club and racing venues to name and include the Nancy Greene League and furthermore to see our Alpine athletes succeed at the Provincial and National FIS Levels. David

Roth and Nancy Gee make it to the Canadian National Ski Team. Wonderful stories to write about in the Devil's Advocate.

Here are a couple of highlights from our first September 1968 first issue;

"FROM THE PRESIDENT'S DESK: All clubs thrive and develop on the active participation of the members and, I for one was very pleased with the excellent turnout for our work party in September. See you soon. Mike Gee, President."

And, "Three seasons ago when we started, Devil's Glen Country Club was a $275,000 development. Since then, it has grown to a $400,000 entity. Dave Midgley, formerly from Camp Fortune, Ottawa, the largest ski club in the world, is appointed Manager of Devil's Glen." Also, five new chalets are under construction. This brings the total to 18, advised co-chair directors Bill Leckie and Bill Dawson."

Being the volunteer guy, supported by my wife Ruth, putting together our Newsletter was a labour of love. The work had many facets; chasing up directors for their stories, interviewing members for their input and planning ahead. Also, reporting what would be timely and worthwhile for the family member and their need to maximize their investment in the club. Arranging and paginating the page layouts, highlighting items, creating, writing and typing, working with printers and direct mailing within a budget of several hundred dollars per issue was satisfying.

As Founding Publisher and Editor, 1968, I salute my successive Publishers/ Editors for keeping the Devil's Advocate tradition alive to this day. Long may it develop and prosper in the new media world.

THE RACERS' EDGE by George E. Daniels

Novice to Elite; Self-imposed excellence every time!
Have fun, ski safely, succeed.

When Devil's Glen founders lured Austrian Tony Spiess, Giant Slalom medalist and one of Europe's top Olympians to help start ski racing on hills next to the Mad River Gorge/Valley in 1963, it is hardly surprising that they set in motion Schuss, Wedelin, G.S. and Slalom, now so familiar to any ski buff setting foot on Limbo or the Stairway.

During the first full season ('65–'66), instructors and coaches nurtured novice-to-advanced programs for members and their children. Skiing instruction became well established early on and racing soon followed. Bamboo slalom poles became the norm for setting courses down the sides of Paradise, River Styx and Limbo on Saturday and Sunday mornings. The child-friendly Nancy Greene Little League evolved. Teens' race training for inter-club and those 55 and older in the Masters category began, with all of them racing at our Devil's Glen home and away at Osler, Craigleith, Georgian Peaks and Blue Mountains to name most race venues. Striving for elite racing performance and influenced by the famous Crazy Canucks Steve Podborski, Ken Read, Dave Murray, Jim Hunter and Dave Irwin was a dedicated group of our teens. Devil's Glen has produced some fine Alpine athletes of FIS calibre, leading to NORAM and Olympic renown for David Roth and Nancy Gee.

In the early 1970s, we were a typical family getting our children on skis at two and half to three years, and Pluto Hill with its rope tow was the exercise. It was a several-fold achievement, including bundling up our toddlers in winter clothes, fitting a specially-made pair of 4-inch wide skis cut down to two feet in length with kids' bindings to give little legs platform stability. Insulated little rubber boots fitted with a rubber tire calf support worked for the Pluto Rope tow journey. Our adult frames bent over the little child between our legs, we managed to grip the rope tow and holding on for dear life for about a minute or so, made it to the top several hundred feet away. Wow! With encouraging words to our novice, we are set to ski down Mount Pluto with our darling between our legs. With a controlled snow plow, we turn and traverse through Disney Cartoon, Snoopy, Mickey Mouse, Goofy, Dumbo slalom gates. A racing first for three-year olds; the Pluto Disney Slalom.

Andrew Daniels - Daffie, Jump
Snowmass Colorado March 1980

Eight years into our Devil's Glen membership and now with three young sons, our involvement and commitment to the racing program accelerated. The oldest, Andrew was a good Devil on skis at an early age. He and older buddy David Skelton relished skiing in the powder at the edge of any run-in particularly next to the Hall T-Bar lift and Inferno. The top eastern outcropping of the Inferno precipice was their favourite jump-off spot for spectacular 'Daffies and Wheelies', to the awe of everyone and the concerns of the staff and ski patrol.

We thought Andrew would be a natural in the ski race program, but it did not turn out that way. His first cold Christmas break morning in 1974 (he was eight) had him lined up number 30 out of about 60 youngsters ready to ski race down their first season course. We hovering parents consoled the bundled up freezing kids in the ten-below and howling wind saying, "your turn will come, it won't be long now, be patient." After a while with tears streaming down his face Andrew said NO-NO-NO so he did not participate.

Timothy, son number two, was perfecting his all- round skills in the Paul Munro Ski School. He looked very good even at age 6. Timothy "Tiff" also went on to racing. Christopher, son number three, joined his buddies John Coffeng, Scott Little and Neil Monroe as the Ski School now actively promoted their charges to hone their skills in the racing program. Chris did very well racing in the Nancy Greene, McKenzie Juvenile Leagues, Club Championships and FIS Circuits. These achievements resulted in ribbons, trophies and positive comments from peers and parents. In the meantime, older brother Tiff had earlier joined the Devil's Glen Hershey League Team.

This League and its competitive teams were for teenage boys and girls. Tiff relished the competition and did very well. Teams from all over Southern Ontario competed. Points were awarded for order of finish to decide the winning team each week during the eight-week season. The Devil's Glen team was frequently successful. In March1991, the League Finals were held at Mansfield Ski Club. In addition to Team awards, individual trophies were also presented. Timothy won the Men's Championship Medal and a spiffy Hershey Gold Jacket. Fergie Olver of CFTO–TV filmed the event and interviewed the athletes. Great ski coverage and good public relations for Devil's Glen.

Have Fun, Ski Safely, Succeed, Excel: Themes of both the Paul Munroe Ski School and the Mike Weiss Devil's Glen Racing Program

It takes an army of volunteering parents, race assistants, safety officials, technical delegates from the Ontario and National Alpine Ski governing bodies, Devil's Glen staff and a knowledgeable race committee to run a professional high-performance race. With an entry list of 125 boys and girls, safety will be paramount. The staff will be moving willy bags and hay bales into position around two lift pylons course marker barriers and more. A start gate with electronic timing and its finish gate system must be put in place. The leading time Score Board is located in the finish area. A large Results Board with the names of all 125 entrants will be located and it has space for the finish times for each of two runs. Several volunteers enter the results as they are broadcast over the PA. The Devil's Glen Race Committee became a smooth functioning team. Chair Rusty Gee could count on some of the following, but not limited to, Red McConnville, Kay Gee, George and Ruth Daniels, Gary Thompson, Tom and Pat Bain, the Samis family, Dr. Peter and Libby Fowler and the Lickrishs.

Devil's Glen Toddler Learning to Ski: The U4 Daniels' Boys early 1970s

Most shops sold narrow 2" wide by 3-3½" foot skis for three- and four-year-olds. They were proving to be hard to steer and did not provide sufficient lateral stability. Solution: Shorter two-foot long skis, wider cut-down 3-3/4" wide adult skis and calf-supporting boots.

All three Daniels' boys learned to ski on this modified equipment engineered by Bruce Brereton, who pioneered the rear-entry ski boot at the same time.

Devil's Glen became a magnet and host venue for some important races in the Southern Ontario Zone. They included Nancy Greene, McKenzie and Hershey leagues, FIS competition for long-term international Alpine events such as North American Cup, World Cup and the Olympics. The expansion of the Stairway became a choice location for advanced Slalom. The Stairway and the Club were awarded Federation International du Ski accreditation (Homologation) for Slalom races and became the only hill in the Collingwood area approved for FIS races so elite racers could earn World Slalom Rank Points.

Cox Electronic Timing comes to Devil's Glen

The world of ski racing is largely ruled by the Europeans. Up to the mid-seventies, timing of a race was by stopwatches at the Start and Finish lines. Officials had to co-ordinate their watches using portable radios and set them to the Starter's audio command to the racer. It was not an exact results system and was based on the ability of the Timers to press the stopwatches at the start while out of sight of each other and at the exact time. There could be an error of a fraction of a second because of human delay in pressing the watch as the racer crossed the finish line.

The Swiss are famous for watches and timing devices and in the mid-70s pioneered Leading Time Electronic Precision Systems (compared to reducing time for hockey and football) for swimming and ski racing. North American companies were quick to follow with this technology. My company OTACO Electronics where I was General Sales Manager was in the scoreboard business and had obtained orders for electronic scoreboards for the 1976 Montreal Olympics and Edmonton Coliseum. We used this expertise to negotiate with Cox Electronics of Salt Lake City for a race timer for Devil's Glen. The company approved my pro bono sales time so that the club had to pay only for the unit and its hardware. We were in good company as Cox had just sold a similar system to the US National Ski Team. Our Devil's Glen cost was just under $2,000.

We were now really on the Racers' Edge as the only ski club in the Collingwood with electronic timing. Getting it installed challenged our volunteer committee as we had to install an electronic cable alongside our preferred race hills. Limbo was our choice. A group of us using shovels and pickaxes dug a trench to bury a reel of special wire from bottom to top on the east side of Limbo. It was anchored to start and finish boxes so the start gate wand and finish electronic eyes could be easily attached at any time. We were now in business with state-of-the-art timing, a vast improvement for all our races.

Not everyone was happy about the races and attendant training. From time to time, some members complained that too much hill space was being used for this discipline and taking away groomed areas for the other members. To help put ski racing into perspective, I wrote a front-page article in the Devil's Advocate to explain that all sports have their marquee events the average amateur can look up to. For golfers, it is the Masters. For car buffs it is the Indy 500, for fitness and running folk, it is the Boston Marathon and for Alpine skiers, it's the World Cup and the Olympics. At the Devil's Glen Alps, it's our own training to achieve podiums for many of athletes from house leagues, club championships to SOD, all helping members achieve their own standards of excellence in our super club. They are to be admired.

CTV WIDE WORLD OF SPORTS - Devil's Glen, New Year's Day 1987

Wide World of Sports - 1980's Saturday Primetime

The hype for the Calgary 1988 Winter Olympics was the talk of the race fraternity in 1986 and certainly within the Devil's Glen community. On the early FIS schedule for '97 was the Devil's Glen New Year's Day Slalom. It was billed as a major invitation event for athletes from Quebec, Northeast US, Northwestern Ontario and our own Southern Ontario Division. We could expect some of the world's top-ranked racers in this part of North America. Here was a super publicity opportunity. I had good connections from my Standard Broadcast/CFRB days and in particular with Johnny Esaw, Director of Sports for CTV. This was before the days of sports cable proliferation. i.e. TSN and Saturday's CTV Wide World of Sports was the Number One show of its kind in the country. I phoned Johnny and told him about our January 1 FIS race and the elite athletes who would compete.

"Johnny, I do not know who but you can be sure at least six to eight of our competitors this day will be in the Calgary '88 Winter Olympics and we think it will be worth your while to televise this race," to which Johnny replied, "OK, George, get me a sponsor for our out-of-pocket production costs ($20,000 or about $40-$50,000 today) and I will be there with my Wide World of Sports crew." So, Devil's Glen member Tom Bain convinced his client NEC Electronic Communications to be our Platinum Sponsor on Wide World of Sports. Wow, we were about to hit the big time.

A New Year's Day race following the various parties the night before ensured that many of the average club members would not be out in the early morning. Quite a pity really as we hosted a traditional Japanese Protocol for Opening Ceremonies at the parking lot entrance before the bridge across the Mad River. Mr. Yamamoto, President of NEC, came from Japan and with Tom Bain and careful introductions to Race Chair Rusty Gee and some directors, presents were exchanged with warm greetings and best wishes for a successful event.

The Wide World of Sports setup included three cameras on the Stairway. In addition, CTV's announcer/presenter George Duffield had his own cameraman for individual interviews with organizers and some of the top 10 male and female athletes. We were able to get some of our future achievers in the race as Fore Runners; John Coffeng, Chris Daniels, Cam Fowler, Sarah Hood and Paula Wilson. We were able to fax results to local and national media within 30 minutes of the medal presentations.

The Wide World of Sports edited program was completed within several days and broadcast on the CTV National Network the following Saturday. It was picked up by ABC in the US. Over the next month, CTV re-ran the half-hour show twice. Furthermore, they used excerpts to promote the Calgary Olympics. This was invaluable publicity for Devil's Glen racing fans. And Nancy Gee went on to compete in Calgary.

Where are they now? As Devil's Glen turns 50 and with their formative years largely spent at the Glen, here's a snapshot; sadly, Andrew Daniels died in 2004. Interviewed for this editorial, Tiff said, "The Devil's Glen experience is a big reason why I have travelled extensively and in particular to the French Alps and Meribel where I set up a ski holiday company." He further elaborated about inviting brother Chris to come and join him (which he did) in what is called Les Trois Vallee and to see the 1992 Val d'Isere Olympics. Tiff worked his Meribel business for eight years. "Without the Devil's Glen grounding, my life could have followed a totally different path." Tiff and his wife Leah live in North Vancouver with their two young children and Tiff maintains an Out of Town membership in Devils Glen. Chris Daniels stayed in Meribel for 15 years. He obtained his French National Diploma Premier Degree and started his own international ski racing team called Alpine Performance. Chris returned to Collingwood several years ago to subsequently become the Men's FIS coach at the National Ski Academy and frequently takes his athletes to train and race at Devil's Glen.

Devil's Glen is a significant venue with fond memories and milestones for the Daniels' family.

- Toni Spiess Giant Slalom Bronze Medalist, 1952 Oslo Winter Olympics
- Dr. Peter Fowler CDN. National Ski Team Surgeon - Operated on Chris Daniels' knee in the early 90s
- Photo of Tiff Daniels with Brian Stemmle, National Ski Team, Albertville, France 1992

Brian Stemmle Canadian NTL. Ski Team & Tiff Daniels
1992 Winter Olympics, Albertville, France.

George and Ruth pioneer Shack Charmant, their first cottage

Photo of Chris with Meribel trophies

George & Robin Cumine
Co-Chair the Launch of the
Lake of Bays Heritage
Foundation 1985

Seen at the 1985 Annual Meeting, Lake of Bays Association: Members of the Steering Committee, Lake of Bays Heritage Trust Fund, left to right:

Association President and member ex offico: Jack Hanna
Committee Chairman: George Daniels
Committee Members: Robin Cumine, Ed Brazina, and Simon Miles.

George Daniels

Betty Day Award Winner

George Daniels (right) is presented with the 2009 Betty Day Award by Lake of Bays Association Director Fraser Govan at the Annual Meeting held in July in Dwight.

2009 Betty Day Award

Fraser Govan's introduction.

Good morning everyone...

In 1992, the Lake of Bays Association initiated a recognition award in memory of Betty Day who was president from 1990 until May 1992 when she died suddenly from cancer. Betty was a dedicated, committed volunteer who characterized a range and combination of qualities that few achieve.

This award is given out annually to a director or LOBA member who has made an extraordinary effort as a volunteer and whose activities have furthered the goals of the Association. It gives me great pleasure to present this year's Betty Day award.

This year's recipient has been on the lake for about 5 decades.

In the mid 1970's he became a director of the Association for the Port Cunnington area.

I remember meeting him about that time since my father was also a Director. My first impression of this person was that he was a lot younger than the other LOBA directors that I knew, and that he was very dynamic.

In the following years, our paths crossed many times at various lake functions, whether it be the Lake of Bays regatta, the Annual Church regatta, or a LOBA function. He always had a cause or event that he was involved with and promoting, and encouraged everybody to get involved.

It was in early 1987 that I received a telephone call from this person, asking if I would attend a winter weekend meeting, along with a couple of dozen others, to discuss various issues pertaining to Lake of Bays, and what we could do to improve upon them. At the time I was single, had a ski chalet in Collingwood, and wasn't very keen on missing a weekend of skiing by spending it in a meeting with a lot of people, many of whom I didn't know. But, I bought this person's sales pitch, and attended the 2-day meeting weekend meeting.

Looking back to that weekend, it was the Genesis of a new, more youthful, dynamic Lake of Bays Association. Personally, he was responsible for motivating me and many other younger people to get involved with LOBA, and invest time and energy to institute changes that would ultimately benefit not only our members, but also the entire Lake of Bays region.

Since that time, this year's recipient has been responsible for motivating so many others to think outside the box, and make positive changes happen, in all the projects he has been involved with around the Lake.

Here are some of the accomplishments of this person's leadership and marketing savvy:

- The Yearbook 1976 soon after joining the LOBA Board of Directors he becomes chairperson of the yearbook committee, and turns it into a publication that people will actually want to have and read; it is a major benefit of the Association and ought to convey that message; he expands the advertising base to generate revenue for the Association so that we can expand our programs; shortly thereafter he secures a Wintario grant for $1000 to publish the 50th Anniversary edition;
- The Heritage Foundation - He and others determine the need to be able to accept charitable donations and bequests from members and issue tax receipts. This thinking leads to the creation of the Lake of Bays Heritage Foundation in 1985 – He becomes 2nd VP of the Foundation.
- 1988 - He takes on the role of President of Lake of Bays Association with a mandate to get the Association more pro-active and less re-active.
- shortly thereafter a Marketing committee is struck within LOBA and the idea of a publishing a newsletter is born; about a month later the 1st issue of Current Connection is published. Since I worked for a computer company and had access to all the equipment, I was nominated to type it – one page, black & white, no pictures. A few months later the 2nd issue is published – it is 2 pages with an advertisement. He found an advertiser who paid most of the costs.
- Another outcome of this committee is the development of the "Mission Statement" that appears on our letterhead, yearbook, newsletters, and website;
- During his tenure as president and past president he introduced many new "gung ho" volunteers to the Board, and instilled a new culture that continues to this day.

Since officially retiring from the LOBA board a few years ago, he has continued to give selflessly of his time & skills:

- The Anglican Church Regatta is another beneficiary of his marketing skills. While Nancy Tapley now emcees, for several years, he was the shaker of this Annual fundraiser for the churches. On the days leading up to the regatta, we hear him on MOOSE FM doing his pitch. When the St. John's and St. James Anglican parishes serving Port Cunnington and Fox Point were in need of financial help, he worked on developing the fund raising program & brochure.

- A few years ago, we started to hear about a group of volunteers who were spearheading a fundraising effort for the Fire Department to acquire a proper fireboat for this Lake. Again, by lending his marketing skills and support, he helped the group to focus on promoting the cause, and collectively the group was able to raise the funds and our volunteer firefighters now have that Boat.

- While there are countless other examples of his tireless volunteerism this is my final example -

- After the tragic passing of his son in 2004, two of his son's friends (Bob Ransom and Bruce Montgomery) initiated & created a fish stewardship program in memory of his deceased son, who was passionate about fishing. Under this man's guidance and coordination this project has grown immensely since it was first conceived, and has involved many residents & stewards, Ministry of Natural Resources, the LOB township, consultants, contractors, landowners, & LOBA. And it is still growing. Just last week it was major featured article in the July edition of the Muskoka Magazine.

By now I'm sure you all know who this year's recipient is. In my mind this has been long overdue.

This guy is just like the Energizer Bunny – he just does not stop!

Please join me in congratulating and thanking George Daniels for all his great volunteer work over many decades.

George come on up.

George displays his 1990 President LOBA Carving & New Loon Award From 2009

Daniels family at the cottage 1998.

George and Ruth Daniels and Family - 1988
Front: George, Ruth   Rear: George Andrew, Timothy (Tiff) John, Christopher (Chris) Alexander

The original cabin, 1965 with bunky in the background.

Roger Pimm and George enjoy the winter of 1965-'66.

Ruth, John & Carolyn Macdonald 1965

George with Caretaker Gord Allinson, winter 1966-'67.

The Daniels' 17 Ft. Shepherd Launch 1966

1978 Daniels dock scene; Ruth, George, Tiff, Andrew, Christopher and Teddy Pimm.

George and Ruth relaxing 1966.

Andrew at Lake Rosseau June 1991.

1991, Andrew and Bob McCullagh at Camp Caugnawanagh, Que., Pickerel catch, Cessna 180 CF- JCT on floats.

2007 Andrew's memorial Inukshuk, built by Chris and Tiff

1998 Sons; Andrew, Christopher the Birthday boy, and Tiff.

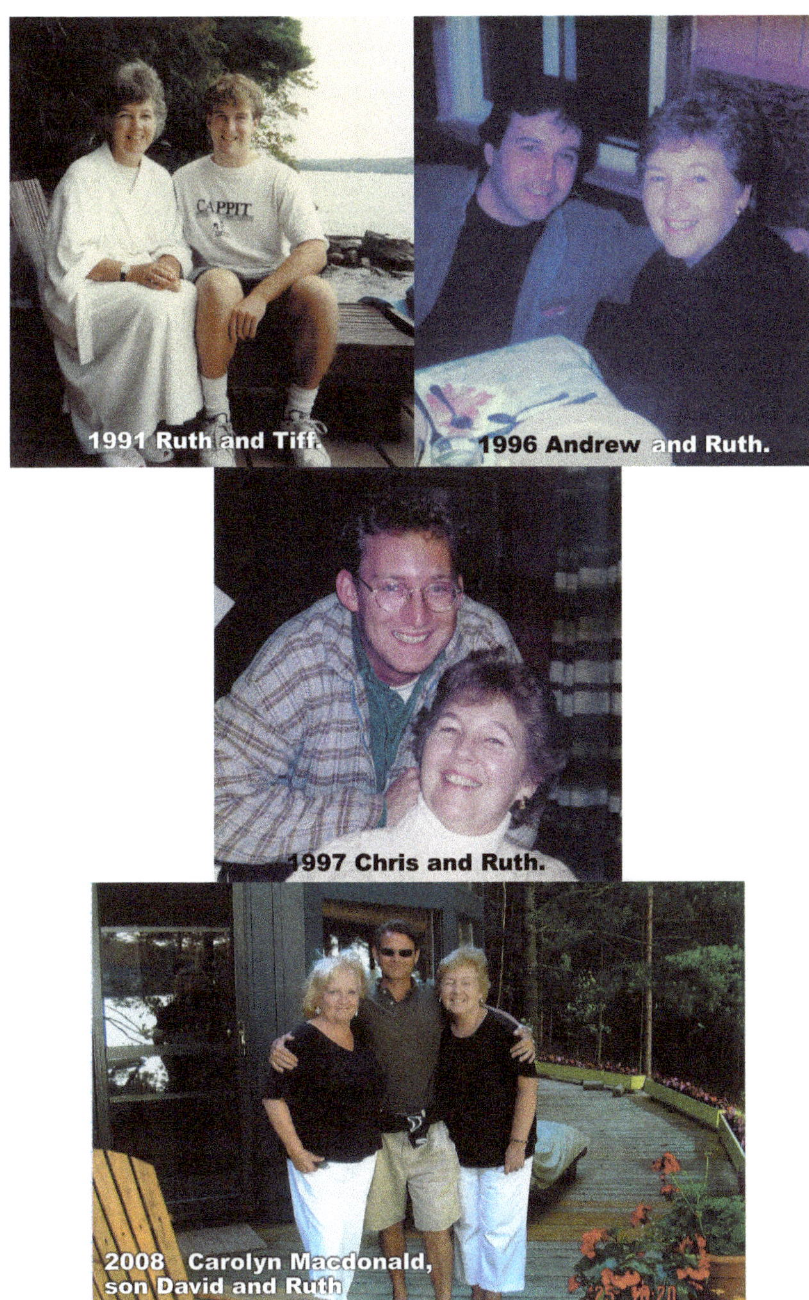

1991 Ruth and Tiff.

1996 Andrew and Ruth.

1997 Chris and Ruth.

2008 Carolyn Macdonald, son David and Ruth

2013 Daniels' Deck with Roddy and Scott , Jam session.

2008 The Bear in front of our window.
"Anything to eat in that kitchen?"

2015 Tiff, Bennett and Chris , cottage horseshoe pitch.

PART VII

Leaving the world of outdoor advertising, George joins Standard Broadcast in Toronto, eventually becoming national Advertising and Sales Manager for the leading radio broadcasting company in Canada and moving back to Montreal once again at a critical time in Canadian politics.

Part VII

Shifting my Sales Focus: Paul L'Anglais to Standard Broadcast

From 1965 through 1966, I worked out of the Toronto office of Paul L'Anglais in the print division representing Montreal Matin, the largest French-language tabloid in the world.

I also helped launch L'actualite magazine, forerunner of the French version of Maclean's Magazine. Among Toronto advertising agency media departments, I earned a reputation as an effective sales representative which did not go unnoticed in the media and in particular, Standard Broadcast Sales.

Waldo Holden, President and Director of CFRB, gave me an attractive offer to join the company and now, I was representing the number one-rated AM stations in Canada's major markets. We had a decided edge in CFRB 1010, the number one station in Toronto and much of southern Ontario. Our sister stations, CJAD 800 AM Montréal, CJOB Winnipeg and CKNW Vancouver, became a must buy for most national advertisers.

ANNOUNCEMENT

STANDARD BROADCAST SALES COMPANY LIMITED

R. R. "Dick" Moody **George E. Daniels**

Waldo J. Holden, President, Standard Broadcast Sales Company Limited, announces the following appointments:

R. R. "Dick" Moody, Vice President, Planning and Development. Mr. Moody will be located at the company's Head Office, Toronto.

George E. Daniels, Vice President and Manager, Montreal Office.

Marketing September 15/69

THE MONTREAL STAR, TUESDAY, SEPTEMBER 22, 1970

Business Today 23

CJAD Limited Announcement

WILLIAM F. HAMBLY

GEORGE E. DANIELS

H. T. McCurdy, president, CJAD Limited, which owns and operates Radio Stations CJAD & CJFM, Montreal, announces the appointments of William F. Hambly, vice-president and director of programming; and George E. Daniels, vice-president and director of sales, CJAD Limited.

Mr. Hambly has been program director of CJAD and Mr. Daniels, vice-president and Montreal manager for Standard Broadcast Sales Company Limited.

Frequency Modulation Radio came on the dial in 1966 and FM signals offered listeners clarity of sound that in some ways is superior to broadcasts on the AM dial. CKFM launched as CFRB's sister station as did CJFM in joining CJAD in Montreal. CJOB-FM in Winnipeg and CKNW-FM Vancouver were now part of our sales representative portfolio.

Producing the dollars for these new stations was tough. Although their limited commercial time seemed attractive, their highbrow programming attracted a limited audience, and it would be several years before these stations offered radio personalities, news and information similar to AM stations. When they did, ratings went up and they became more competitive.

Sales manager Arnold Stinson was a taskmaster who pushed us to place media dollars on these FM stations. When the Bureau of Broadcast Measurement ratings were publicized, some of these FM stations had no numbers and blank lines in some of their morning and afternoon time periods. In the spite of our excuses for not getting some FM money out of the advertising agency media departments, Arnold would remind us of the Foster Hewitt/ CKFH story. Keith Davey was his sales manager. CKFH did not belong to the BBM rating service and becoming frustrated that he had no audience numbers to back up his sales efforts, Davey (later Senator Davey) finally persuaded Foster Hewitt to join BBM.

When the first report came out listing CKFH, there were many blanks and very little audiences to report and he was chagrined when Hewitt reminded him that, ratings or not, he and his reps still had to sell the station and generate dollars. So, it was the same story for our FM sales job. It took a lot of creative salesmanship to get the advertising agencies and their clients onto the FM dial.

These were heady times for Ruth and me, now back in Toronto. We moved into a two-bedroom apartment steps from the heart of trendy upscale Forest Hill Village. There was every convenience from grocery and banking to our Anglican Grace Church on the Hill and I could walk to CFRB at Yonge and St. Clair. Ruth had her old job back with the Toronto Board of Education.

We now had been married singles for four years and the urge to start a family triggered our application to the Toronto Children's Aid in early 1966, to adopt. This would be our Centennial project. The good news came on December 23, 1966, while I was at an SBS Christmas party at co-worker

Mary Falconer's Rosedale house. Ruth's excited phone call said, "The baby has arrived and I have called the diaper service." Everyone was enthusiastic and elated and I rushed home to get Ruth.

We went to Grace Women's Hospital to meet our new baby boy. He had been born on December 16, 1966 and we were seeing him at seven days old. He was very handsome with ears nicely flat against his head, noted Ruth. We arranged to pick him up on Boxing Day and brought him home to the new nursery in our Montclair apartment. We couldn't get over our good fortune: what a child, what a boy! We named him George Andrew to fit my Daniels' male name lineage and we became very engrossed in new parenthood.

We could not escape Canada's Centennial celebrations of 1967. Everyone got involved. My father was the number one civil engineering superintendent at Expo 67 in Montréal. Centred on St. Helen's Island, it was the world's biggest fair of its kind. Pop kept us apprised of the many international pavilions connected by state-of-the-art monorails used to transport some 50 million visitors, many of whom had been motivated by the excellent advertising and promotional campaign steered by my good friend Larry Schachter, later to become my partner in our boutique Marketing Plus/ Signature Advertising.

All the radio stations we represented programmed promotional support for the Centennial year and Expo 67. Bobby Gimby's CAN-A-DA was very hummable and sing-along infectious. It became the Centennial Year anthem. Our Centennial was a rousing, national love-in embraced by everyone and every community. Millions of US citizens also discovered Canada via way of Expo 67.

The Daniels are now three and outgrowing our apartment. I am doing fairly well financially so it is an easy step to buy our first house on Glenrose Avenue, a typical square plan house with three bedrooms, a nice back yard in the desirable neighbourhood of upper Mount Pleasant Road, situated on the edge of North Toronto and convenient to my office at Yonge and St. Clair.

Andrew had a nice new nursery bedroom and the lovely back yard lawn and garden were ideal for his playpen in the summer months.

As a national sales representative, I soon learned the route to success was winning large shares of all available advertising media dollars from the major ad agencies. Their media departments administered hundreds of thousands of dollars and they ruled the roost. They looked unkindly on any rep who went behind their backs and directly to the client, but I became adept at straddling the agency and still was able to engage with a client's advertising and marketing management to generate dollars for our stations. Arnold Stinson came to rely on me for winning big dollars for our network.

The key to success was getting to know each station's programming and community-based sales promotion campaigns. Placing a client's product or service within this broadcast environment often resulted in the brand gaining increased awareness and subsequent sales results.

Western stations CKNW and CJOB had particularly effective sales promotion departments and packaged goods advertisers enjoyed buying segments of these station's supermarket campaigns. The audience tie-in with supermarket shelf displays worked. Presenting clients and their agencies with a detailed campaign brochure outlining these sales opportunities was essential. They were all typed by our secretaries long before computers and I became adept at writing such proposals. These campaigns were sales promotion gems.

I was in constant presentation mode due to my multiple station representation and many of my successful client campaign proposals were commended by management as outstanding media marketing tools. I soon rose to be the top SBS Toronto rep.

Centennial Year caused Ruth and I to juggle our life with baby Andrew on many fronts. We reconfigured the slim back seat of our Mustang convertible to accommodate a crib but we did not stop our diverse lifestyle.

Visiting parents in Montréal and Expo 67 was super and Pop got us special passes to the World's Fair where we enjoyed many pavilions. Buckminster Fuller's geodesic dome was space age. The 360-degree Chinese movie and exhibit put you in the heart of their country. The Expo Monorail, one of Pop's major projects, was unique.

We continued to enjoy our Lake of Bays cottage and our Montgomery, Ransom and Slatter neighbours welcomed baby Andrew. Work followed me to the cottage where I often used quiet time to write future business development presentations. Our friends asked what it was like to be associated with such prominent and famous broadcasters as Gordon Sinclair, Betty Kennedy, Pierre Berton and other notables who were seen on the highly popular CBC-TV show *Front Page Challenge*.

I got to know Gordon Sinclair after I had sold sponsorship of his daily *Let's Be Personal* broadcast from 10 to noon. The client was the Borden Milk Company. On the first day of the sponsorship, I tuned in and was aghast when Gordon proceeded to lambaste the Borden milk truck which had blocked his driveway that morning due to a snowstorm.

Inevitably the ad agency was irate about this sponsor treatment. When I confronted Gordon about his remarks, he said, "Well, George, I gave the client several more minutes of extra time over and above their commercial, so Borden milk should be thankful." As P. T. Barnum said, all publicity is good publicity as long as they spell your name right.

When I sold McLaren Advertising one of the largest buys for the new car year (the General Motors account), I rewarded myself. McLaren offices were above exclusive men's clothier Harry Rosen's store, and in the window were a very nice checkered ice-cream jacket, dark blue shirt and red tie. I bought them and thought I now looked like gambler Nathan Detroit from the Damon Runyan-inspired musical *Guys and Dolls*. I still have the jacket.

In 1968, I was promoted to vice-president and manager of the SBS Montréal office adjacent to our CJAD/CJFM Montreal flagship stations, replacing Dick Moody who returned to the Toronto office and had a staff of three.

We found a three-bedroom semi -detached house in the Town of Mount Royal, a block away from the railway station. Commuter trains travelled the tunnel under Mount Royal and unloaded at downtown Union Station, a convenient walk to our offices at Crescent and Ste. Catherine St. We kept our Toronto house and almost covered the mortgage with a rental.

Our son Timothy John was born in Toronto on the first day of summer, June 21, 1969 prior to our move. It was a blessed event and we now had our hands full of family joy. It was going to be an eventful transfer.

In 1969, the US Government passed the *Public Health Cigarette Smoking Act* banning cigarette advertising, and in 1971, Canada followed the lead by pressuring Canadian manufacturers to stop advertising, which they did. As 70 percent of our Montréal office billings came from Imperial Tobacco (Players), McDonald's Tobacco (Export "A"), Rothman's and Benson and Hedges, this big hole in our sales threatened the demise of our office and ability to represent our half dozen groups.

I quarterbacked a solution to this crisis. We targeted Canada's major banks, a very conservative sector in advertising terms, as up to this point, they primarily used print and billboards featuring car loans and savings.

My corporate colleague H.T. (Mac) McCurdy, general manager of CJAD, was a friend of W. Earle McLaughlin, President of The Royal Bank of Canada. Mac and I invited Mr. McLaughlin to lunch at the prestigious St. James Club, and using persuasive points about attentive audiences who relied on CJAD's news and information programming, we got his ear. We concluded with him agreeing to instruct his advertising department and the Royal Bank's advertising agency to sponsor CJAD Traffic Reports. We named our Bell Jet Ranger helicopter the Royal Bank Eye in the Sky.

Reporters Len Rowcliff and Rick Leckner covered Montréal Island traffic twice daily during breakfast and drive home commutes for the thousands of cars on the many roads and expressways in the listening area. This 52-week order, worth several hundred thousand dollars, was a huge breakthrough in bank advertising campaigns and we leveraged this success to make aggressive sales presentations to the other major banks.

Within months, we were able to count them as advertisers and had filled the hole in our billings made by the tobacco industry and had the financial sector on air. Our stations and senior management applauded our achievement, and was another feather in my broadcast leadership cap.

In 1970, Pat Hurley was transferred to CFRB as the new general sales manager, much to the consternation of my boss Dick Moody. Mac McCurdy enticed me to replace Pat and become general sales manager of CJAD/CJFM. Although SBS sales commissions were an important contribution to the Standard Corporation bottom line, the major dollars came from within the CFRB/CKFM and CJAD/CJFM dominant stations in Toronto and Montréal.

These stations and their sales forces drove the growth engine of the corporation with their respective rate cards and the general sales manager had a special executive position within management. A GSM was expected to deliver an 8-10 percent increase in net revenue per annum and working the rate card was essential in this process.

The Canadian Radio and Television Commission had legislated that AM stations could sell only 1,500 minutes of air time per week and FM stations no more than 900 minutes per week. For CJAD, this meant that we could sell only 214 minutes per day over a seven-day week. Our price list (the rate card) was geared to audience ratings. The broadcast day is usually divided into four-hour time blocks. AM radio's prime time breakfast audience (6-9 AM) was charged at a premium rate.

Drive home time (4-7 PM) is the second largest audience in the broadcast day and was also sold at a preferred rate. Other day blocks, being less expensive, were often packaged with prime time. Special program features such as news, business reports, sports, traffic reports and must-listen-to weathercasts, were sold separately at a premium. CJAD rate card prices were carefully determined by audience ratings in the respective breakfast, drive and mid-day program segments, and my job was to carefully coordinate all these factors into our published rate card. We would issue a new rate card several times per year following the release of the latest BBM Radio ratings.

CJAD is a Montreal English-language station in the heart of French Canada. The Anglophone population of 600,000 was a vibrant community among millions of Quebecers and our audience ratings were significant. In prime-time breakfast, we competed alongside French-language leaders CKVL and CJMS and outnumbered both English and French CBC stations.

Tuning into CJAD's *Super News Quiz* at lunchtime, one would often hear Francophone housewives phoning in to this contest as they often would to the early-morning *"Put a poem in the pot for Pinkerton's Flowers"* in the breakfast show. Cab drivers, many of them Francophones, were a large part of the Paul Reed evening show where he read poetry and interviewed prominent stars such as Ella Fitzgerald, Nat King Cole and other entertainment notables.

My CJAD retail sales force of 10 was an eclectic group of guys and gals responsible for achieving 60 percent of revenue, while SBS Montreal and Toronto offices contributed the other 40 percent.

Creative sales ideas often were generated by our local guys. John Spikerman had a Hovercraft, an airbag-supported amphibious vehicle that could travel over land, water, frozen lakes and snow. John's idea was to use the Hovercraft for special weekend Laurentian and Eastern Township on-air reports from chalet country with him as both driver and broadcast reporter. CJAD and CJFM programming accepted the idea for Saturday and Sunday winter coverage and I put together a December through April sponsorship package. We forecast this to be an audience builder. With a 60-second weekday schedule and sponsor identification on remote cut-ins, it was fairly priced and quickly purchased by Scotia Bank and its Toronto advertising agency.

While these negotiations were going on, our airwaves were saturated with news of the October 1970 FLQ crisis. The Front de Liberation du Quebec grew out of several Québec 1960s separatist cells and its objective was complete destruction of the influence and symbols of English colonialism.

The movement called for an independent Québec and began a series of violent attacks, bank robberies, over 200 bombings and kidnappings for ransom.

It all came to a head with the October 5 kidnapping of British Trade Commissioner James Cross from his Westmount home and on October 10, the kidnapping of Provincial Minister for Labour and Immigration Pierre Laporte who was then murdered by the FLQ. These were very serious Canadian and international terrorist events.

Canadian Prime Minister Pierre E. Trudeau, amidst a rancorous English and French language debate in the House of Commons said, "just watch me" and put a lid on the FLQ terrorist uprising by invoking the War Measures Act, eventually resulting in the arrest and jailing of 497 persons.

We felt the results of this close to home as Québec cabinet minister William Tetley lived near our Vivian Avenue house and his daughter was our babysitter. Being concerned about more potential kidnappings, we canceled this arrangement. Also, Québec premier Robert Bourassa had a sister who lived nearby.

As part of the War Measures Act, the Canadian Army deployed troops and tanks on our usually tranquil streets. The Federal Government's moves against the FLQ resulted in a decisive victory; capture and arrest of FLQ leaders Jacques Rose and Francis Simard.

While the authorities were trying to find Pierre Laporte and James Cross, we tried to live our normal lives. I continued keeping up my flying skills by renting a Cessna 172 from the Montréal Flying Club at Cedres and St. Hubert Airports. On October 4, I took my Ad and Sales club buddies Barry Schachter and Cliff Eckells on a flight out of St. Hubert airport. The following day, our CJAD newscasts and front pages of Montréal newspapers showed photographs of the murdered Pierre Laporte trussed up in the trunk of a car which I had parked right next to the previous day before our flight. Was this a close call with the FLQ?

The airwaves also broadcast disturbing news about conflicts in the mid-East. Arab hijackers forced a Boeing 747 jetliner to land in the desert, evacuated the passengers and then blew it up. Rod Dewar was our mid-morning personality who frequently announced his support of and in his view, the underdog Arabs, just as he had voiced sympathy for the FLQ. With a large Jewish listening audience and many who wanted the capture of the FLQ terrorists, Rod's sympathies for these folks was just too toxic. General manager Mac McCurdy gave Rod some Air Canada unlimited airfare tickets, told him to cool it for a month and took him off the air.

Rod was livid. He stomped out of the station and went to English language CBM radio and broadcast inflammatory words against CJAD, thus ending his high-profile career with our audience, and Andy Barrie, who had been recently hired as a swing shift announcer, was put into his slot.

It was a deft move. Andy became very popular and went on to success with sister station CFRB Toronto and subsequently as the CBL-FM highly-rated morning man.

In the midst of all this community disruption, I was selected by Standard Broadcasting to be one of three Canadians to take the National Association of Broadcasters Harvard Executive Management two-week seminar in mid-August 1971, shortly after our third son, Christopher Alexander, was born on August first. A very blessed event and Ruth was doing well. On to Harvard Grad School where only 50 broadcast sales executives from across the continent were enrolled.

We lived on the Harvard campus. Each day starting with 7:30 a.m. breakfast the faculty of Sterling Livingston and James Marshall grilled us on our overnight homework, usually a case history of a company business problem. We were divided into Syndicate groups of six and dissecting various companies from different business sectors was stimulating.

Broadcasting hardly came into the discussions. Rather the major Dr. Livingston thesis of the time *Marketing Myopia* really was the benchmark of how to understand companies and organizations. How to evaluate salespeople and their temperament also was an indelible learned skill. We worked all day and all evenings before hitting the sack at 11 pm.

It was an intense two weeks. For the first time, I was being educationally challenged and loved it. I walked out with some valuable management tools which have stood me in good stead to this day. My professional tool kit now included consultancy sales techniques and expertise in how to evaluate companies' organizational needs and strategies. I couldn't wait to get back to work and put my new business-building ideas to work, at home and in our radio stations.

In Montreal, the mood continued to be 'separatist sombre' in late summer 1971. Toronto advertising agencies reacted negatively to the FLQ situation as it pertained to English-language media in Montréal and seemed convinced newspaper readership and radio audiences would diminish in favour of Francophone media.

Fred Ursal of SBS National Sales Toronto phoned me in a panic with news that Scotia Bank's advertising agency wanted to cancel their several hundred-thousand-dollar sponsorship of our Hovercraft winter weekend broadcast reports. Apparently the only hope of saving the contract was if I could convince the Quebec general manager and his ad team to retain the contract.

I arranged a meeting with them and pulled out all the stops. My presentation to these Francophone executives was entirely in French. I demonstrated our CJAD audience leadership equal to several of the top French-language stations. I played audio excerpts of Francophones calling into our stations and our interactive program features. I was successful, saving the contract after two hours of speaking entirely in French. I was exhausted.

I returned to the station late Friday afternoon and waiting for me in my office was Mac McCurdy. He was all smiles and had the weekly sales report. It was good news. For the first time in several weeks we were above budget.

But after looking at me, he said "You look lousy, what's the matter?" I said, "I feel terrible." He grabbed the phone and called Sidney Margulies in the newsroom and told him to get his Ford News cruiser and get me to a doctor right away.

With the siren blaring, he took me to a specialist where I had an electrocardiogram. It blipped wrong. The doctor told me I had to have complete rest for the next several months.

I phoned Ruth and it now being Friday evening and with this concerning diagnosis, we went to Moishe's Steakhouse for what felt like perhaps a last supper. The glasses of red wine and filet mignons fuelled our strategizing of what our family would do next. We decided to get out of town and away from the cacophony of separatists, terrorists and stressful budget sales targets.

CJAD management was understanding of my need to comply with the doctor's order for two months of rest. Our retail sales manager would cover my responsibilities while I was away. We packed up our new Oldsmobile Vista cruiser station wagon and moved into our Lake of Bays cottage. It was Labour Day and the lake and surroundings were a blissful tonic. Nevertheless, we were very ready to be parents of our three boys five and under.

Andrew was now kindergarten age and Irwin Memorial Elementary School was just eight miles away in Dwight. We enrolled him and arranged for him to be picked up each morning by the school bus. This turned out to really be a large taxi driven by Elwood Campbell of his son's bus line. This small rural community service was really appreciated.

One of our cottage projects was to build stone steps down to our dock. Neighbour David Montgomery helped by lifting flagstone rocks from our property as Andrew held tools and I tried to carefully, without straining, help.

The new stairs were halfway done when Andrew, who was holding a very heavy crowbar, dropped it on my foot. OW, OW-- now I really had to rest up due a very sore limb. This project was completed prior to our returning to Montreal at the end of September.

Our Town of Mount Royal House was a super home for our family with lots of local conveniences, good neighbours and the commuter train to work. Back at CJAD, I was welcomed with a lot of concern for my health but my management authority did not seem, to me anyway, as effective as it had been prior to the health incident.

I felt neutered but plowed ahead anyway and applied some of my Harvard-obtained skills to improving our sales team. It worked, and we continued to achieve our sales growth budgets.

Marketing Magazine ~ February 14, 1983

RADIO REPORT

CFRB's George Daniels

It's all in the cards

The view from a 'comfortable pew'

GEORGE Daniels, vice-president of sales for CFRB, Toronto, believes that one of the fundamental reasons for the station's continuing success in its highly competitive market is that CFRB listeners not only listen attentively to the station, they also respond enthusiastically to the advertising.

Media buyers today, Daniels explains, have a tendency to take a segment of a station's audience and then only look at the 'relative efficiency' of the buy. "They maintain that this is the only relevant issue," he says, "but I maintain that there is another side of the coin and it's called the effectiveness of the medium—and that's what CFRB delivers. Effectiveness."

Daniels insists that CFRB's effectiveness is equally as important as its efficiency. "In the face of the toughest efficiency buying challenges that agencies and clients put in front of us, we are still able to demonstrate that with good commercials on this station, their efficiency guidelines don't have to be quite as precise. What happens is that we are so effective that we not only reach their specific audience within the larger audience, but we also help them pick up sales at either end of the target audience."

According to the most recent BBM survey, CFRB has an adult audience of over 1.1 million people—almost double the number two station CHUM-FM. As a result, it isn't difficult to understand why Daniels admits candidly and emphatically "right off the bat" that "we at

where is the rest of this?

Spring 1972: Assessing my stress levels and Making a Major Move

By the spring of 1972, I realized that my stressful broadcast executive profession potentially could cause another medical interruption. Ruth and I decided to go back to Ontario and I submitted my resignation to Mac McCurdy. He promptly said; "George you cannot do this, you are going to be the next President/GM."

I replied, "Mac, with all due respect, I am not hanging around for another ten years waiting for you to retire." He persuaded me to continue working for another several months in order to hire my successor and train and transition this person.

I agreed and began an eight-year settlement in Orillia in my new vocations in the automotive and foundry industries, a period which ended with my resignation from Galtaco due to the company impugning my integrity by cancelling a major General Motors commitment I had made in support of our delivery of pinion flanges.

GM Bill Hall had telephoned me asking if I had seen their notice advertising for a general sales manager. This had been publicized in March while I had taken the family to Snowmass, Colorado for a skiing holiday.

This came at an opportune time and CFRB wanted me to apply formally as they had several other highly-qualified candidates and some came from Western Broadcasting and the CHUM organization. Even though I had not sold one minute of radio airtime in the past eight years, Bill Hall assured me that my strong management skills would be, as he said, "a piece of cake".

CFRB wanted me to start right away. Ruth and the boys would have to stay in our Harmon Rd. house until the end of the school year while my Monday-to-Friday plan necessitated me renting a modest one-bedroom apartment at the intersection of Oriole Park and Eglinton Avenues.

When I had last worked at Standard Broadcast in the late 60s and early 70s, a Midland Osler Securities Equity comment said: "CFRB Toronto is the most successful AM station in Canada. It reaches 50.9 percent of the listening audience in its market, more than all other 10 Toronto stations combined."

But, oh how the airwaves had changed by the early 1980s. There were now nearly three dozen radio stations available in the megalopolis of Oshawa,

Toronto and Hamilton. Additional signals could be tuned from Southwest Ontario and Buffalo. New TV channels including cable TV now fragmented the total available audience.

While CFRB continued to have over one million listeners per week, they were mostly over 50 and the station's share had been eaten into by others. The Wally Crouter breakfast show (quarter-hour average of 161,000 adults) was about 25 percent of listeners in this demographic level---still very respectable but a far cry from the 60s and 70s.

CFRB continued to be a personality, news, information, talk and music powerhouse. Informative discussion and interview shows were headliners. High-profile stars from stage, screen and competitive TV were regular guests. Tony Bennett, the highly-popular crooner and good golfer, was buddies with breakfast man Wally Crouter. Front Page Challenge was CBC-TV's highest-rated prime time program where host Fred Davis quizzed an all-CFRB panel of Gordon Sinclair, Betty Kennedy and Pierre Berton.

Morning newscaster Jack Dennett was a fixture on Toronto Maple Leafs hockey broadcasts with the famous Foster Hewitt and we were the voice of the CFL Toronto Argonauts with Bill Stevenson and Bob Bratina calling the plays and interviewing coach Leo Cahill, Ralph Sazio, Jackie Parker and other CFL Hall of Famers. It was a blockbuster programming combination and an ideal environment for most advertisers to promote their products or services. This is what my team had to sell.

The problem I inherited with the retail sales team was complacency. Their attitude seemed to be *we have the must-buy ratings,* so several reps acted as if they were going to get a sale anyway instead of fighting for a large share of a client or ad agency budget. Some of this also permeated the national sales force, who also were enamoured with FM (now easier to sell) than those on CFRB AM.

In addition to a sales staff personnel challenge, the ad agencies enjoyed trying to knock CFRB off a radio buy. They would deem their client's target demographic as 18-25 or 18-29 (similar to television ad targets) to the neglect of our CFRB-preferred 25-54 demo and secondary 55 plus, both of which was where the monied audiences were found. We needed sales representatives who would aggressively sell our advantages in this very competitive environment.

Standard Broadcasting Corporation fully expected me to drive an 8-10 percent sales growth per annum. CRTC regulations still only allowed us to sell 1,500 minutes of airtime 5:30 am to midnight per week, forcing me to squeeze every angle to achieve ambitious budgets.

As a student of personnel sales management development thanks to my Harvard course and Dennis Waitley's *Psychology of Winning* seminars and tapes, I had learned that successful managers do and get done those uncomfortable things the average leader does not.

I tackled my apathetic retail sales force by using the McQuade Survey to gauge their individual temperaments, which resulted in me easing out three or four order takers and replacing them with sales pros from IBM and Pitney-Bowes, both companies which provided employees with strong sales training. Much to the consternation of some in the industry, I promoted female sales representatives. The makeover process took several months but turned out to be the correct recipe for moving forward.

CFRB programming formats were sacrosanct. As a sales manager and within reason, I could control the messages within the 60-second commercials we sold. However, opportunities presented themselves that benefited both, starting with our creation of weekend remote broadcasts from our Good News Reporters. The station hired graduates from Ryerson and sent them into the community with our news cruiser to gather stories.

We obtained sponsors and we were gratified to have Mary Ito and Valerie Pringle, who both went onto further broadcast prominence, as part of this team. CFRB's Monday to Friday traffic reports from the Bell Jet Ranger with Henry Shannon and Eddie Luther were highly-rated programming. The station also had a large weekend cottage country audience. I came up with the idea that we should have Friday and Sunday night traffic reports to and from the Muskokas. Newscaster John Enright provided these popular reports that were often sponsored by oil companies and car dealers.

While Andrew was at Ridley College in St. Catharines, Timothy and Christopher went to Couchiching Heights elementary near our Orillia home. In the summer, the boys went to Camp Kawabi in the Kawarthas.

We had to put our house on the market and it was taking a long time to sell. I continued to commute as the economy was hit with a recession. Interest rates went to 19 percent but then an opportunity came up to buy a house with just a 10 percent mortgage on Glenview Avenue in North Toronto across from Havergal College. With Standard Broadcast's assistance, we bought the house and I used it while we waited for the Orillia house to sell. It did, finally, and we moved back to Toronto in the spring of 1981. The boys would now be enrolled in well-known Toronto schools; John Ross Robertson and subsequently Lawrence Park Collegiate.

It was nice to be back in a friendly North Toronto neighbourhood. We had a number of friends nearby from Devil's Glen Ski Club and our Muskoka cottage. Ruth was back at the Toronto Board of Education supply teaching at John Ross Robertson School which was at the end of our block, very handy. She then went on permanent staff at Oriole Park School until retirement. Our boys participated in track and field, ski racing and cottaging in summer. Tiff and Chris played rugby at Lawrence Park and were selected for the 3 Nations Tour, as their coach called it, travelling to Ireland, England and Wales. They were billeted and survived beans on toast and their first visits to UK pubs.

Getting to know and sometimes work with some high-profile people was one of the side benefits of being VP Sales of Canada's most successful private broadcaster. Prime Minister Brian Mulroney had been on Standard's Board of Directors with E. P. Taylor, Bud McDougall and Conrad and Monte Black and I saw them frequently.

Some of our own personalities were famous, too. The 1977 Donald Jack book *Sinc, Betty, and the Morning Man: The Story of CFRB,* humorously recounted how popular they were. Toronto Star reporter Jocko Thomas became famous for his reporting from 'Police Headquarters'. Sports celebs such as Arnold Palmer, Ralph Sazio, Angelo Mosca, Dick Shatto and Allan Eagleson would pass my office door on the way to a studio interview and a quick chat often ensued.

Gordon Sinclair: Unplugged and off air.

Gordon Sinclair was Canada's most famous and irascible broadcaster, investigative reporter and to many, a loveable curmudgeon. Daily at 11:50 am on CFRB's five-minute feature, *Let's be Personal,* Gordon's stories were a delight or provoked concern and angst among his over 250,000 listeners. These ratings were nearly equal to Jack Dennett or Peter Dickens 8 am newscasts and they were dominant audience numbers far greater than competitive radio stations' prime-time breakfast shows.

Gordon's ratings were even larger than some TV station prime-time programs. At five minutes to noon, he broadcast the news of the day and retained a huge attentive listening audience. Gordon was CFRB's jewel in its crown.

In June of 1980, I helped celebrate Gordon's 80th birthday with the rest of Standard & Argus management with a surprise boardroom party just after his noon broadcast. Argus, our Corporate boss, owned Dominion Stores, a leading supermarket chain and Gordon had been made a Director of Dominion Stores several years previously. He was very proud of this position and how his business acumen had been accepted by his peers.

Dominion Stores Employee Pension Fund had been in the news lately as the Toronto Stock Exchange was investigating suspected illegal withdrawals. Gordon was very aware of this situation. I joined CFRB's president Don Hartford, VP and general manager Bill Hall, program director John Spragge and the Argus-Standard corporate bigwigs from their 10 Toronto Street HQ, most of them the Who's Who of Bay Street.

They included John Craig Eaton of the department store chain, Dixon Chant, chairman of Scotia Bank, our chairman C. W. (Winks) Cran, brothers Conrad and Monte Black and Gordon's friend and co-broadcaster Betty Kennedy.

Dominion Stores provided the birthday luncheon food and our boardroom table displayed the largest salami I had ever seen---eight feet long and eight inches in diameter. All the fixings included freshly baked rye bread, salads, pickles, sauerkraut and a chocolate cake with *Happy Birthday Gordon* along with a suitable number of candles. The salami was cut to our order and served by corporate secretary Brenda Burns. A spread fit for the broadcast star.

When Gordon came in, escorted by Don Insley who had not revealed why Gordon was wanted in the boardroom, our star looked like he had just come from the woodshed instead of a first-class broadcast studio; an old golf shirt, baggy pants with a hole in the back pocket from which a handkerchief protruded --- his classic casual attire for radio announcing as no TV cameras were ever present.

To our spontaneous singing of *Happy Birthday to You* Gordon looked nonplussed. Spying one of several Dominion Stores directors he went right up to him and with livid anger he said; “You! You’ve stolen the employee pension fund. It’s not acceptable!” We were all aghast at his angry outburst which put quite a damper on the celebratory mood. The programming executives went into action, got our star calmed down and defused this tense situation. Hey! It was just another example of Gordon being Gordon.

Generating dollars in the lull of the post-Christmas season required us to create ingenious sales promotion packages to generate incremental advertising dollars. Using barter/contra airtime credits, we negotiated some Caribbean travel packages, which involved offering a one-week March trip for two in return for a car dealer, furniture retailer, condo developer, camera jewelry store owner spending $20,000 in advertising in January and February. They would receive Caribbean trips with their spouses, including airfare to first-class, all-inclusive resorts. The clients assumed this taxable benefit and were escorted by me, other management executives and one of our popular on-air personalities.

One of our trips was on a cruise ship and included a stop in Bermuda where we saw a shabby Canadian submarine at our wharf. Another year, we toured St Lucia. Sailing Week in Antigua was the venue for one trip and it was here we saw a large chunk of the world wealth displayed in gorgeous yachts in Nelson’s Dockyard. One of them belonged to Elton John’s lyricist Bernie Taupin. These perks helped Ruth and I see sand and sun in a relaxing way amidst our busy family lifestyle.

CFRB had always done remote broadcasts from the Canadian International Exhibition and so I came up with a special sales promotion package including a package goods brand (coffee or cereal) to be featured on our remote. I pointed out to management that this sales driver would enable us to reach our August 31 year-end budget. I started to put this presentation out to the national sales team when to my surprise, GM Bill Hall stopped me and the campaign.

Unknown to me, Conrad Black, Standard’s Chairman, was secretly negotiating the sale of our Corporation. I was instructed to take a week’s vacation. On my return, Bill Hall fired me. I got severance enough to keep me and the family going before finding a new career path. So, by trying to generate more dollars, tied in with the station remotes, I was let go. I perceived this as being very unfair and determined I would never again work for another Corporation. And I have not. Shortly after, several other Standard executives were let go as Black cleared our management ranks to help sell the company (which he subsequently did) to Allan Slaight, formerly of CHUM-CFGM fame.

PART VIII

The author's sense of social responsibility grows, he takes on the challenges of the Boston Marathon, the World Masters Games and a Royal Commission on Violence in the Media

Part VIII

Completing the Boston Marathon and the first World Masters Games

My long-time love of competitive running throughout my school days and then in response to a medical issue continued when we moved to Orillia in 1972 and I joined the YMCA's Forty on the Run executive fitness group which focused on cardio-vascular fitness. Half marathons, about 10 miles, were common for us. Orillia was a twin city with Auburn, New York and we all competed in the Canada-USA Games, alternating between cities. The Auburn marathoners motivated us to form the Orillia Road Runners as a first step to us entering the world's best-known running event; the Boston Marathon.

The Boston Marathon represented to me the pinnacle of personal physical and mental achievement and it took me nearly seven years to put all the elements together; constant training, then qualifying by submitting a result from a recognized marathon (in my case, the Ottawa Marathon) along with a qualifying time for my age group that would meet their standards. I ran it in three hours, 12 minutes, 17 minutes faster than the criteria for the 40-50 years group, sent my results to Boston Marathon head organizer Jock Semple, and was officially invited to take part in the 1979 Boston Marathon on April 16.

Looking back, I feel a great sense of pride about Boston. At age 44, I finished 4,500th of 10,000 entrants in a time of three hours and 17 minutes, was cheered on by my family support group, and I got my employers to pay for it all because of my impressive and profitable sales achievements.

BROOKS
CANADA's
STEADY
GEORGE

Boston Marathon

The Ultimate Fitness Challenge

Chapter Boston Marathon P 2

It is December 1978. I am 43 years of age and a member of the Orillia (Ont) Road Runners club named after the cartoon Wily Coyote of beep- beep fame.

In May a group of us O.R.R. - with wives and children, had gone to Ottawa. I ran the Ottawa Marathon in 3Hours and 12 Mins..It is my first Marathon . My fellow club members point out that I've a very respectable time and being over 40yrs.old can apply to the Boston Marathon Committee to be an entrant for next April's venue.

My mind is racing with the events that led up to this critical point in road race training: The bet with myboss about the M.T.A. (Mass Transit Authority) contract, CANUSA games between Orillia and twined city Auburn N.Y. Read earlier chapter No. ? and being accepted by the Boston committee.

A Marathon race is run over a distance of 26 miles 385 yards where the Pros and the Amateurs are running together in a prestige event. Marathons still commemorate the epic feat of Pheidippides in the 490 B.C. Greco -Persian wars ,when he ran26 miles from Athenia to Marathon to enlist the aid of the Greek Spartans against the Persians.The modern Olympics started in Athens in 1896, then, as now, the event is considered the blue-ribbon event of the Olympic Games.

Today Dec.1978 running is considered an essential part of cardio vascular health and fitness. I certainly know its benefits after my coronary insufficiancy in 1971. I also know 12 to 20 miles per week is more than ample (4 - 5 mi./day over five days) to maintain a *positive stress relieving* fitness level.

Major cities around the world hold and host prestige Marathons where the world's elite distance runners compete in an event with the average fitness runner.

Aside from the Olympic Marathon, the Boston Marathon has become the runners Mecca. Its 26 mile course is unique, with various obstacles that challenge one physically and mentally. * What the Indiannapolis 500 is to auto racing, The Masters is to golf, the Grey Cup/Super Bowls are to football, The World Cup to soccer, the

GED 7.

Stanley Cup to hockey.........
The Boston Marathon is to running.
To be accepted as one of their competitors is an achievement in itself.

This Dec. day I'm now reviewing in my mind the parameters and disciplines I have to go through --- like I did for Ottawa this spring. Gauge myself - self discipline - timing - integrate family obligations - Ruth, Andrew, Tiff and Chris into my training regime. Also my Corporate leadership responsabilities to a large staff and millions of dollars to generate for our mutual well being.

Marathon running is far more strenuous than any form of track or cross country running, since it is all road work. A Marathoner who aspires to succeed must go through a period of at least three months of rigorous training. So ... here I am Dec. '78 and Boston is 3 and a half months away on April 16 1979.

I will be training in the middle of a typical sub zero Canadian winter. Ruth is marvelously supportive. She invests in a space age GORTEX track suit. It sweats and also helps my body heat maintain normal levels. Footwear is of paramount importance. I shop carefully for a pair the pros use.

I've studied - as have my fellow Orillia Road Runners, many elements of how to achieve Marathon success. ... So how to handle my training includes a realization that we runners can actually run 3 times our " average daily distance "- - compiled in one week of our three month training schedule. Allowing several days to rest and recover .. I know that I will be training at least 5 days per week.

It's now Christmas '78. I've been keeping up my 20 miles per week training. As decision time arrives I must more than double this distance. I know I've got to listen, read about and practice Positive Mental Attitude - today. My Guru's are Dennis Waitley and Jim Fixx. I discuss this project with Preet. (Dr. Preet Pallapson. marathoner and Rehab. Doctor for Cardio patients). The concern is training in sub zero temperatures in the snow.

Its Christmas day with the family. Howls of glee f rom the boys over their presents and

GED 8

stocking stuffers. I now have an opening to go for a run before the Christmas turkey dinner. Today's goal is to run 10 miles. It's slippery. I have to use my brain to prejudge pitfalls. I train all winter. Can you imagine juggling a 9 hour work day in an automotive factory and foundry environment. Home at 6 to 6.30..to then change into longy's and Gortex suite, neck warmer and toque, gardening gloves. Then a 8 to 10 mile run in the oh so forbidding darkof winter.. wearing red reflective tape front and back.

Hey here I am on theHwy 11 service road opposit the Orillia Square Mall. I'm just cruising along at a steady 7 mile per hour pace. I'm thinking only another 12 days to go and we'll be leaving for Boston at Doug McKays expense. (Refer prior Chapter about Galtaco career).

Suddenly after about 7 miles , I'm crippled. I can't believe it !. !! It's just like someone shot me with the most severe Laser Gun . My whole left rear side and buttock area are paralized. Obviously I'm at an extremely **painful stop.** After 4 months of preperation this disaster hits.

I'm inching my way approx. 200 yds. to the, still open car dealership to phone home. Ruth, God bless her. She comes to get me and takes me to Emerg. Dr. John Muller-one of our O.R. Runners group examines me. He says, " George,I'm not comfortable saying this - but you need a Chiropractor". Knowing my Boston goal he sends me to Dr Jim Gillespie who has the hands and strength of two football players in one. One minute I'm on his table.. the next being lifted like a bag of bones. After an hour I'm feeling almost intact. Recovery commenced and was achieved about 3 days later. I am advised to do a gingerly and not too fast 5 mile run. I tentativily do on April 3 '79. Eureka! I am now O.K. again. Little did I think that after this injury I would be able to get to Boston'let alone run the Marathon.

Today is Mon.April 9th. Ruth and I have negotiated with Andrew, Tiff and Christopher's Principal that we can take them out of school for this special family trip. The '72 Oldsmobile Vista Cruiser station wagon is loaded for the day and a half drive to Boston. We will travel via way of Auburn N.Y. and stay over night.

It's two days later and we are now in Boston checking into our downtown hotel near

GED 9

the Prudential Center. The **Pru** is Boston Marathon H.Q. We become typical tourists, visiting Fanuel Hall, The Boston Common, Harvard and the restaurants at the harbour. The old MTA Subway reminds us of the Kingston Trio's well known hit record " Beneath the steets of Boston -- etc." The mood in Boston is all anticipation for next Monday's Marathon. When I say to a cabby or restaurant waiter that I will be running on Patriots' Day-- I'm treated like a Star. - Free cab rides and no charge desserts are the norm.

" Dad when are we going to see the course ??" the kids say. So here we are in the quaint little village of Hopkinton 26 miles outside Boston. It's 3 days before the race. We drive slowly back through other beautiful Massachusetts small towns like Framingham and passed the well known Wellesley girls' college. At the 20 mile mark we come to " Heart break Hill" . Three quarter of a mile of 30 degree grade.. every runners mental and physical challenge. Yet it looks doable to me.

It's Sunday evening and we are in Luigi's Italian Restaurant. We are here for the almost manditory carbo load feast of pasta. The place is packed with other runners. I have starved myself of all meat for the past five days and no running -just rest. The carbo load of pasta will go into my muscles for the extra strength I'll need for tomorrow's performance.

' Day April 16 in Massachusetts. 7 a.m. and only time for some toast and coffee. 8a.m. and I at the PRU boarding one of the hundreds of busses that are going to take the 7800 official entrants to Hopkinton.It's perfect Marathon weather; overcast, slight drizzle and 50 degrees F. I willnot have to worry about getting over-heated. I've already changed into my running singlet and shorts. Several months ago my Auburn NY marathon running friends told me to have my Boston shirt customized with words that the animated spectators can pick up on. My outfit is royal blue with stencilled white lettering. On the front is; **CANADA's** and on the back **STEADY GEORGE**. I'm wearing my track suit and have a duffle bag that is specialy tagged. It will be returned on the bus to be picked up at the baggage depot in the Pru. In Hopkinton we are lined up and seeded based on our qualifying time (mine 3hrs 12 mins from Ottawa) This puts me about three quarters of the way in the back of the pack. We know the famous Bill Rogers is ahead of us on the starting line.

GED 10

It's 10 am. Like many I am also wearing a garbage bag to keep out the drizzle. I intend to discard it when I've warmed up after several miles. The starting gun goes off. We all just stand in position. It's impossible to move with the mob in front . Now there is shuffling . I check my watch. Finally I can get some traction. It takes nearly two and half minutes to cross the starting line.

We are now starting to run and all is uneventful for the first half hour. The streets are lined with spectators - quiet for the most part. I've settled into my seven and half mile per hour pace. I ditch the garbage bag. I am now at about the 5 mile mark. Coming around a corner I can see up ahead of me a flat roofed convenience store. On the roof under large umbrellas is a 4 to 5 piece Dixie Land Jazz Band with an MC on a microphone and binoculars. All of a sudden Mr. Binoculars spies me and announces " Here comes CANADA'S" Hey he's talking about me. As I run past the the store Mr. Binoculars eyes me again and announces over the PA. " He's Canada's Steady George -- lets hear it for Steady George with the Dark Town Strutters Ball" - and they start to play. Wow! Am I feeling special or what. What a motivator. I like this feeling.

An hour or so later we are entering the town of Wellesley and here are all the girls in their neat uniforms lining the road. They are cheering for all the female runners and booing the males. One of the girls steps out of the crowd and starts to run along beside me. In a cheeky aggressive way she yells at me " You spindly, little, skinny runt. You couldn' t run down your own Grandmother." I'm laughing. It's another form of motivation. I keep up my pace.

There are more spectators now. One old Lady runs along beside me for a few paces and offers me some ice cubes she has in a bowl. Every 5 miles there is a water station and we grab the 10oz. cup - - slow down a bit and guzzle. One or two men are offering us beer. Larger crowds now. Boston population is 650,000 but on this (Patriots Day) holiday over one million people will line the route.

We are getting close to the 20 mile mark. The drizzle has stopped. I am now passing runners who have slowed down or dropped out. Marathon veterans have previously explained that when one sees this situation " other runners slowing down (weary and

GED 11.

exhausted) or dropping out". There are two things that go through your mind. The first is ; I'm exhausted, too .. aand it would feel so good to stop now and rest " .. or the second is; .. I have not trained all those months to give up now and what the H--- ! I am passing them. I am doing it . I can handle this challenge. **PMA All the way to the PRU.** It's a good feeling .. **I can do it.!!**

Heart Break Hill... is just ahead and now the crowd lined up about 5 rows deep becomes eerily quiet They know that this is the point that a runners body resouces $after 20 to 21 miles, are just about depleted. It's called **Hitting the wall.**

As i start up the hill. The quiet crowd is almost GOULISH as they see runners dropping like flies.

I have not " Hit the wall yet " I am mentally concentrating, with **Mind over matter**... I can do it. I am running it. The **Boston Marathon..** One of the world of Athleticism , Fitness and Self Dicipline (for the partisipant) Events that challenges one to be at the pinnacle of understanding ones self worth. I cannot let myself down now. I will not let down my supporters. Ruth and the Children. The ORRC and our Aurburn running buddies. Galtaco management and staff who have lent encouragament every " training run .. over a lot of weeks ".

So this is it !!! I am half way up **Heart Break Hill** and for the second time in my life (Ottawa being the first) **I Hit the wall.**

The crowd has surged inward. The normal road width is narrowed down to approx 12 feet. More runners are dropping out.. Concentate George ... Concentrate George .. is my mantra !! Just keep lifting those aching legs, the screaming feet, and gasping for more lungs full of air. Remember George it is easier to run uphill , than it is to run downhill.

Oh Oh whats this??? It is an Ambulance andit is heading straight at me. Oh my God ,let him not hit me!! With nervous tension I just miss staggering into the vehicle. Out of the crowd a voice yells " You can do it CANADA " Many thanks, **Yes I can.**

GED 12.

Running is now part agony and obstinent determination.**Wow** I am over the top of **Heartbrake Hill** and running toward a
large Policeman who is controlling the crowd. He is wearing white gloves. Now he is stepping towards me. He says " " CONGRATULATIONS CANADA " He shakes my hand-- - saying " It's only five and a half miles downhill from here". He gives me a slap on the back that nearly knocks me over. I stagger on, regain my pace and concentrate.. concentrate..

Running downhill after 21 to 22 miles on the one hand is refreshing.. no pushing up hill, your'e floating downhill (not exactly the wings of a butterfly). Underfoot on the road way can be treacherous. A four inch pothole is a crater. Police barriers for crowd control are as intimidating to we runners as they are to the spectators. Speed bump burms are other obstacles. Georges head says .. Pretty close now .. You can do it ..

I start running with a new group. To this point **We are the survivors**, after 21 miles. One of our running pack is a woman. And then the Interlopers invade. Oh you know those folks who charge into the now thinned out group of Officially Numbered Bostonn Marathon Entrants and with no shirted numbers decide to run the past 3 miles of the event so they can say that they where in the Boston Marathon. For we who have played by the rules they are ANATHEMA. They have no understanding of who we runners are , at the 22 to 23 mile mark. Push .. shove .. get in the way.. total disregard for the Boston Marathon institution or it's participants. They now become another obstacle , with their aggressive interruption of the orderly flow and pace of the last few miles of our run.... when we really need every clear line to the finish.. .without uncouth cheats.

The crowds keep cheering. We runners talk to each other and offer encouragement. We visualize our Goal .. Crossing the FINISH LINE. We are now on the outskirts of Boston in an industrial area, with old railway tracks down the center of a cobble stone raod. I am paying attention to every step.. to avoid pot holes, tracks and heaved stones ...it's very bumpy.

Only a mile or so to go now. About 8 minutes at my pace. The road is now lined with tenament house on each side. The crowds are thick and clapping. Despite the 50

GED 13.

degree temperature every window in these apartment buildings is open. The occupants are clapping and cheering too! We can hear their Radio's tuned to WBZ whose overhead Traffic Helicopter is broadcasting coverage of todays event.

With this super crowd support I now know how Guy Lafleur, Jack Nicklaus, Daly Thompson, or Boston's own premier marathon runner Bill Rogers.. must feel with tremendous crowd encouragement. It's motivating me with less than half a mile to go.

And then rounding a corner .. there it is --- the statuesque **Prudential Centre Skyscraper ... ... Our Goal ! ! !**

It is really noisy now with lots of cheering and clapping for all of us. I can see the **Finish Line** with it's big overhead Digital Time Display. It indicates that it is now 3 hours and 12 miins. since the race started. (close to my Ottawa qualifying time).

Then I hear it-- - "Go Dad Go.. Go Dad Go " It's coming from the top of a tree just near the finish line. I see our oldest son Andrew in his tree top perch, cheering me on. What an inspiring feeling.

Eagerly I run and lunge for The **Finish Line** amidst a narrowed down road with cameras popping all around.

I cross the the Finish Line in **Three hours and fourteen and a half minutes.** This means I've averaged a seven and a half minute per mile pace throughout the Marathon. I dont know it yet but I will find out later that I finished 4150'th (out of the 7800 official entrants) an improvement of approx. 1000 positions better than my 5200 seeded starting spot. Not bad for a 43 year old eh !

Right after we cross the finish line I stop approx 20 feet into the finish chute. Now the woman with whom I have been running collapses over me with a tearfull hug. I feel exhausted and emotionally drained too, and reciprocate.

We are now being herded down the garage ramp under **The Pru.** There are many volunteers with distinctive Dayglo Vests. The whole garage is converted into a mini hospital, with para medics, doctors, cots and various medical apparatus. Each runner is given a space blanket. This is a lightweight aliminum cellophane type blanket. A Marathon runner generates considerable body heat. Rapid cooling at the finish can precipitate hypothermia thus this special and practical souvenir blanket. It's now time to recover, celebrate and party with family and friends.

40 Wynford Drive, Suite 104,
Don Mills, Ontario M3C 1J5
(416) 441-6113

September 4th., 1985

Page: 238-2491 Code 2 ~~(613) 746-5876~~

JIM MERRITHEW
PHOTOGRAPHER/PHOTOGRAPHE

295 BEECHGROVE
~~316 QUEEN MARY ST.~~, OTTAWA, ONT.

Ms. Donna Wood
Supply & Services Branch
Canadian Governmnet Film
and Video Centre
Personal Records Annex Building
Golden Rod Street
Tunney Pasture
Ottawa, Ontario
K1A OM9

Dear Miss Wood:

RE: World Masters Games Marathon
Toronto, August 11, 1985

I was a participant with bib number 629 in this Masters Games.

Your photographer, Mr. Jim Merrithew took quite a few photos of myself during this 26 mile marathon.

I can only presume he took quite a few shots of myself because I was consistantly in the front of the pack during the run. Or maybe it was due to the colourful blue polka dot hat I wore. It could have been because of the words I wear on my running shirt - "Canada" on the front with number 629 and "Steady George" on the reverse.

If you would have one or two colour prints, say 5" x 7" of myself that you can provide me with, it will be appreciated.

Incidently, I finished 6th in my 50-54 age category and 37th overall in three hours and twelve minutes.

Thank you for your help in advance.

Yours very truly,

George E. Daniels,
Executive Vice President.

GED/cb

NATIONAL CAPITAL MARATHON

CANADIAN COMMONWEALTH GAMES TRIALS

This is to certify that GEORGE E. DANIELS

finished 465 in 3:12:40.5 in the 4th Annual

National Capital Marathon.

May 14, 1978
Date

John Foster
for NATIONAL CAPITAL MARATHON COMMITTEE

BOSTON '79

CANADA's
STEADY
GEORGE

MASTERS GAMES
JUEGOS VETERANOS
JEUX DES MAÎTRES
TORONTO CANADA
AUGUST 1985

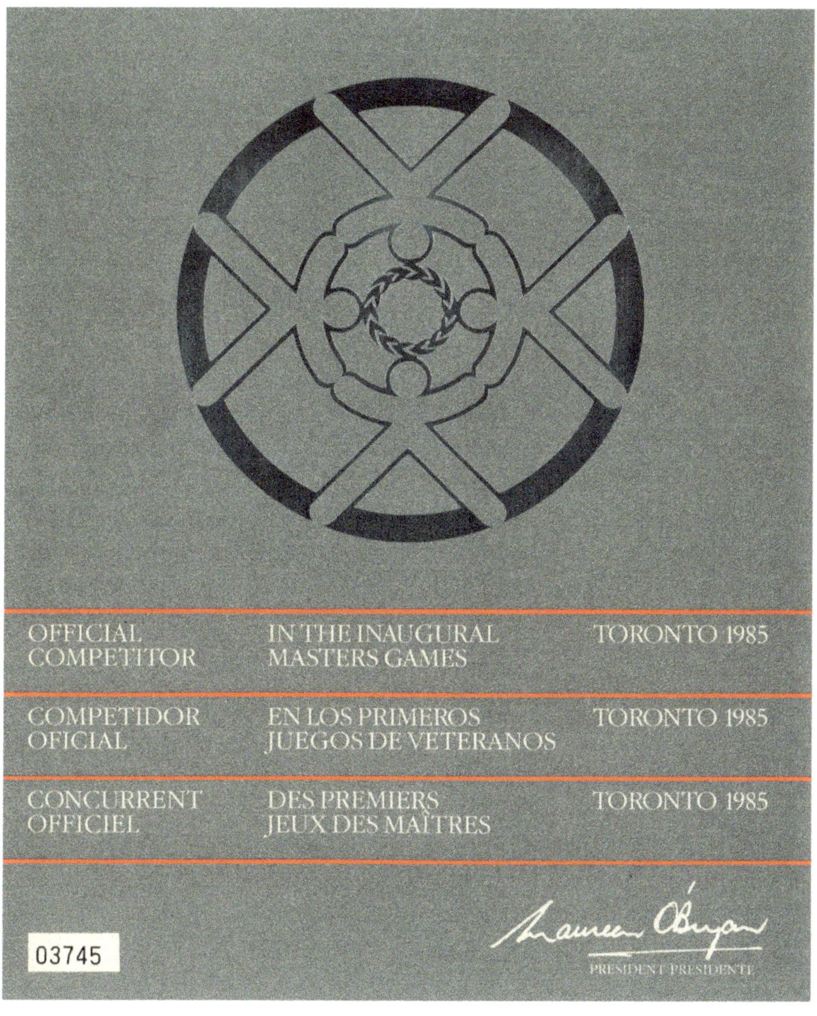
OFFICIAL COMPETITOR
IN THE INAUGURAL MASTERS GAMES
TORONTO 1985
COMPETIDOR OFICIAL
EN LOS PRIMEROS JUEGOS DE VETERANOS
TORONTO 1985
CONCURRENT OFFICIEL
DES PREMIERS JEUX DES MAÎTRES
TORONTO 1985
03745
PRESIDENT PRESIDENTE

Concerned Parents: Presentation to the Royal Commission on Violence in the Media--March 1976.

With three boys ages 5, 7 and 9 becoming increasingly media savvy, their TV included the positive Sesame Street, Mr. Rogers and various children's cartoons.

As parents, we became increasingly concerned about stories making the headlines, many which have violence vividly portrayed. The Northern Ireland guerrilla activities with horrible street scenes were disturbing. Headlines such as *"Rhodesia faces war with Islamic troops as riots break out." "Muslims open attack in the heart of the Lebanese capital on December 9, 1975".* All too many of these broadcasts seem to be adjacent to children's programming. Couple this with a significant number of promotional commercials featuring violent movies and other stories, it all became overwhelmingly disturbing and certainly not appropriate for young eyes.

What could we do about it? Probably not much, but we could try. So when the Ontario government announced the Royal Commission on Violence in the Communications Industry, we thought we could make a contribution to these hearings. The following pages are our submission. It was well received and widely reported. In particular, CTV videoed our presentation and it made the National News. We received many congratulatory phone calls on our presentation. Here is what we had to say:

The Royal Commission on Violence in the Communications Industry.

On May 7th, 1975, Her Honour Pauline McGibbon, Lieutenant-Governor of the Province of Ontario, approved an order in council which gives us the following task:

To study the effects on society of the increasing exhibition of violence in the communications industry.

To determine whether there is any connection between it and the incidence of violent crime in society.

To hold public hearings so that groups, individuals, members of the communications industry can make their views known.

To make necessary and appropriate recommendations on what measures could be taken by the Province of Ontario, by other levels of Government, by the general public and by the communications industry.

VT INCEPIT FIDELIS SIC PERMANET

Ontario

The Royal Commission on Violence in the Communications Industry.

TO: The Ontario Royal Commission
on Violence in the Media

Orillia Hearing
March 31, 1976

PRESENTED BY:
Mr. & Mrs. Geo. E. Daniels,
374 Harmon Rd..
Orillia, Ontario.

DATE PREPARED: March 5, 1976

The Purpose of this Submission...is to demonstrate the "concerns" - contributing situations - and some solutions to "violence in the media and society.

We are a middle class family as follows:

George E. Daniels - age 40 - Business Executive
Ruth E. Daniels - age 38 - Household Executive and Supply Teacher
Andrew - age 9
Timothy - age 6½
Christopher - age 4½

... and, no doubt represent a fair number of people who feel and think as we do.

What are the Daniels' family concerns?

On T.V. : Inspite of "self regulation" in childrens' programming of sponsoring manufacturers to reduce - repeated appeals to children to purchase inane products and violence oriented toys, we find, in general, that these commercials have been discontinued.

however...

Far too frequently, childrens' T.V. programming on private channels now insert dramatically visual "crime" oriented promo's for upcoming programs which feature - shooting - chasing death and anxiety -- result -- directing childrens' minds to the "Starsky and Hutch and Mannix" type of murder oriented shows.

The greater number of channels now available to our household not only on the VHF but also UHF and cable seems to indicate more dramatic and explosive programming through sensationalism type shows to win audiences. These shows can be regular programs or movies.

...but, entertainment programming on T.V. is not the only violent culprit...

T.V. News - whether its the constant repetition of Ulster Guerilla Warfare, Ware in Vietnam or Angola - shootouts in the urban Ghettos of the U.S.A. or other world spots, we are deluged with a constant barrage of disorder, riot and turbulance.

In the Movies : Personally, having experienced the movietone news clips of Belsen & Buchenwald and Nazi and Allied War coverage at the end of World War II, and its nightmare producing impact on my mind as a child, I find a shattering similarity and little difference between the impact on my mind of these World War II movie clips and the:

Page 2

In the Movies (cont'd)

Sensational...Shocking...Explosive...Turbulent movies such as:

Jaws
Towering Inferno
Godfather
Clockwork Orange, etc.

In the Newspapers : These publications are not immune to the proliferation of violent stories! See samples attached with this presentation.

Sensational headlines lead story headlines and photos of a Societies at War, e.g. Angola, Northern Ireland or repeated car crashes add to the constant barrage of "disorder and ferocity" abroad today.

Another Concern: Many friends have said: "Why bother submitting to the Commission on Violence...it's just a political thing and nothing will happen at the end of it anyway, it will just get pushed under the rug".

We don't want this to happen--although it is obvious much of Broadcast Media comes under Federal Control and therefore, how is this Commission going to not only make its findings felt--but also achieve implementation??

Other Points of Concern: Who produces violence oriented T.V. and Movie shows? Hollywood studios?? Independant Producers? What Canadian Companies?

Watching the credits and sources of most of this material indicates that much of it comes predomenantly from foreign sources with highly "urban story themes" not necessarily Canadian.

Who distributes these shows? The companies doing this function are selling a "show" service that should be monitored and have a "code of ethics" attached to it--oh yes, we know that movies have a "censor board" but it would appear to us that it cannot be much more than a rubber stamp if it lets - all the gangland murders happen -- such as you see in the "Godfather" for instance.

Page 3

Now, we are all for Freedom of Speech and the Press, but it would seem to us that greater effort should be placed on prompting such organizations and member groups as:

1) Canadian Association of Broadcasters
2) Media Directors Council
3) Canadian Daily Newspaper Publishers Association
4) The Magazine Association
5) Movie Distributors Association

To have stronger "code of ethics standards" when it comes to their product having stories, shows or newsevents that are involved with ferment, vehemence, disorder, turbulence, infuriating situations and all aspects that make up violence... exams could be set up--courses on morals--good taste and human objectives should lead up to a certificate.

******

Audiences continue to buy violence: Obviously films like the Godfather are very successful at the box office.

The March 8 newspaper headlines about the unfortunate seven youths killed in a car accident in Acton undoubtedly sold many copies or aroused many listeners.

On T.V., aside from the many crime detective shows which are highly rated--even our National game, Hockey, is sold and audiences love it with violence overtones.

We can only assume that writers, creators, programmers, publishers and all who contribute to and control media, find the violent story, or show, an essential part of their product mix--to win audiences.

With the increasing number of T.V. signals, whether imported on cable or via extra networks or private stations, our Country is still fairly small and the population or audience potential is only growing slowly. So people who control the media will still be competing for this small audience with quite frequently a sensational product that wins readership or audiences from violence.

Therefore, to achieve a leavening effect, we recommend that you reduce or do not fragment the available audience any more than it already has been.

In general, we urge that you try to reduce some signal availability so it is not necessary to schedule violence to gain audiences.

Page4 .

CONCERNS ABOUT VULGARITY

Vulgarity is a state of lowness which can be horrid, shocking and as tantamount to violence as are other forms of incitement.

We are concerned about vulgar pornography in todays media.

This type of pornography, whether it be the news-stand Penthouse variety, Blue Movies, or in other media forms creates bad taste and an infuriating position for many of us.

Pornographics appeal to the prurient point of view via stimulating eroticism is a missbehaviour closely related to violence in the media. It is another sad commentary on the breakdown in the social responsability of our society.

Page 5

Concerns about Published Surveys: There seems to be a considerable amount of substantiated documentation that proves "violence in the media" is not good.

"18,000 murders and other violent acts that the average North American child will see on T.V. before he is an adult".

Dr. Michael B. Rothenberg as reported in Dec. 18/75 Globe and Mail.

The serveys that point to children who are raised in a constant state of geurilla battle such as in Northern Ireland do not understand or know the more temperate, compassionate and "lets get along with our fellow man" side of life.

Some other Solutions: All T.V. shows which are of violent nature should have a "physciatrist general" super imposed message that would flash every minute: "This show is violent and injureous to the brain and is not recommended for your health".

Final Point and Recommendation: The mass aircraft highjackings of several years ago were in large measure attributable to the "latent psychy" of supposed average (sometimes "hoods" or action seekers) citizens being triggered by violent movies, T.V. news and shows.

In this case, society did something when it was pressured and in danger.

Today: - Airport Security,
- Airline Personnel Training
- Airline Traveller Awareness and co-operation

...have resulted in the near elimination of this violent blot on our society.

If society can co-operate on "high jackers" and recognize a common enemy, then it is equally capable of understanding the debilitating effect violence has on the everyday social fabric of our society....
and....
doing something about it.

/lc

EXHIBIT

At Ronalds-Reynolds Jane Rae is director of consumer affairs which involves her in:

Demographics out, Psychographics in

New Consumers have made a shambles of typical demographic analysis because the psychological needs of the 1970s cross all barriers of age, sex, and family structure. Lifestyle measurements are beginning to discover the "why" reasons which shape buying needs. Example of values rather than demographics defining an audience: "youthfulness" (as opposed to "youth") is a personality rather than an age characteristic.

Quantity out, Quality in

Notice the demise of the Protestant work ethic? We crossed a new frontier of the "psychology of affluence" as the struggle for daily substinence eased in the 1960s and 1970s. Affluence, education, and cynicism increased and our needs changed. Our values are no longer the traditional ones of job achievement, social status, gaining material goods, but of quality of life involving intangible values that are entirely personal and often not demonstrable. In the post-affluent society we seek a compatible personal environment; we're selfish; and if we don't like it here, we'll raise goats in the south of France.

CYNICISM INCREASED:

GOES HAND IN HAND WITH THE VIOLENCE-BEHAVIOUR & LOW ESTEEM for MORALS ALL of WHICH are COMPOUNDED BY the MEDIA.

THE GLOBE AND MAIL, THURSDAY, DECEMBER 18, 1975 15

Child sees 18,000 TV murders, doctor says

© New York Times Service

NEW YORK — By the time the average American child graduates from high school, he has seen on television "some 18,000 murders and countless highly detailed incidents of robbery, arson, bombing, forgery, smuggling, beating and torture," according to a Seattle physician who wants the medical profession to protest against televised violence.

Calling the amount of violence depicted on television "a national scandal," Dr. Michael B. Rothenberg noted that 146 research articles based on 50 studies involving 10,000 children had all shown that viewing violence produced increased aggressive behavior in the young.

"No study I could find in reviewing the entire literature on the subject showed that violence did not have such an effect," said Dr. Rothenberg, who is a pediatrician and child psychiatrist at Children's Orthopedic Hospital and Medical Centre in Seattle.

In an article in the Dec. 8 issue of the Journal of the American Medical Association, Dr. Rothenberg said that one violent act was depicted every minute in television cartoons for children under age 10 and there was, on the average, six times more violence during one hour of children's television than there was in one hour of adult programming.

Although network tabulations for this fall's television season indicate a decline in violence during prime-time programming, Dr. Rothenberg said that a survey by Action for Children's Television had not shown any significant change.

He added that reducing violence during family viewing time—between 7 and 9 p.m.—did nothing to protect children from the "enormous amount of violence" depicted between 3 p.m. and 7 p.m. and 13 million children are still watching television after 9 p.m. when there is heavy violence content," he said.

This year's study conducted by CBS Inc. showed that children's programs with "pro-social" content produced the desired positive effect among those who watched them. By the same token, Dr. Rothenberg said, "children pick up anti-social messages from television."

Dr. George Gerbner, professor of communications at the University of Pennsylvania and long a student of television violence, said that his preliminary findings showed that violence content was up in 1974 so that a purported decrease this year "is meaningless."

Dr. Gerbner's research has shown that heavy viewers of television are inordinately fearful—"they think the world is even more dangerous than it really is." Television violence, he said, "creates victims. It teaches people what they can get away with against other kinds of people. In order to have social violence, it's not enough to train people to be aggressive, you must also train people to be afraid, to act like victims."

Arthur R. Taylor, president of CBS Inc., acknowledged in a recent speech before the Hollywood Radio and Television Society that "the public feels there is too much violence on television."

Calling this a warning signal, he said the networks were acting responsively to "the needs of our society." Taylor cited a study by CBS for the first part of the fall season which showed a 30 per cent decrease in violence for all the networks and a 39 per cent decrease for CBS alone.

The National Broadcasting Company expects to complete a three-year study on the effects of television upon teenaged boys next year.

THE GLOBE AND MAIL, SATURDAY, FEBRUARY 28, 1976 11

...reement to rush passage of e bill, which expires on Dec. ... because Mr. Andras said ... needed its powers as part ... the Government's security ...ecautions in preparation for ... Olympic Games this sum...er.

—The act gives the minister ...d his officials power to turn ...ck at the border any visitor ...ho, they believe, might en...age in acts of violence. ...here is no appeal from the ...der and no reasons have to ...e given for the decision.

...ct applies ...nly to visitors

...The temporary act gives the ...inister the power to deport ...nyone likely to engage in ter...rorist activities should they ... allowed into the country.

It applies only to visitors. ...anadians, landed immi...rants, people who applied for ...eir visitors' visas abroad ...nd political refugees are not

...acilities la... for surveill...

But through... the person th... considers unde... country, he sa... ernment doe... manpower or

...oophole the immigration Se...urity Act was intended to ...lug.

He said he is also looking ...r ways to allow at least ...me limited independent as...ssment of intelligence infor...ation that is used to stop a ...rson from coming into the ...ntry.

Orillia crime rate doubles

'Leacock's Sunshine Town no longer'

ORILLIA (CP) — The Orillia made famous by the late Stephen Leacock's fictional tales of sunny Mariposa no longer exists, police commissioner T. Jackson Purvis says.

"The horrible truth of it is that Orillia is no longer the sunshine town of Stephen Leacock's dreams. What we have today is a breakdown of basic principles, principles of life people of my generation were taught to respect."

He told a local group on Thursday that from 1974 to 1975, the crime rate rose substantially: Break-and-enters into private homes were up by 100 per cent, drug incidents by 108 per cent and bomb threats by 234 per cent.

"There is an ever-increasing need for adequate policing in this city. The church, the home and the school have abrogated their responsibilities. The last resort is the police."

Daily Packet and Times

City News Page

MORE THEFTS, DRUG OFFENCES, BOMB THREATS. . .

The grim reality of crime in Orillia

By JACK CHIANG
Packet Staff Reporter

Crime in Orillia is becoming a serious concern for officials here as indicated by Orillia Police Commission chairman T. Jackson Purvis in his speech to the Orillia Social Services Bureau last week.

The question is: How serious?

Well, here's the grim reality: There were more thefts and break-ins in 1975 than in 1974. And more robberies. More frauds. More drug offences, indecent acts, arsons, bomb threats and bail violations. And more.

A report on the 1975 operation of the Orillia Police Force obtained by the Packet and Times, indicates that there was a substantial increase in most crimes in 1975 over 1974.

Here are some highlights of the report:

— break-in and enters increased to 345 in 1975 from 206 in 1974;

— arsons increased to 32 from 22;

— drug offences increased to 48 from 23;

— indecent acts increased to 19 from six;

— bomb threats increased to 22 from five;

— thefts of more than $200 increased to 102 from 80;

— thefts of less than $200, such as shoplifting and thefts of bicycles, increased to 848 from 772;

— bail violations increased to 73 from 58;

— possession of offensive weapon charges increased to 16 from nine.

— robberies increased to 12 from two.

FEWER SEXUAL OFFENCES

While crimes increased in most areas, there were some decreases, too. In 1975, only three indecent assaults were reported, compared to 15 in 1974. Other sexual offences also decreased to three from 10 in 1974.

Another major decrease was in traffic offences. Though more traffic accidents were reported (976 in 1975 and 871 in 1974), fewer charges were laid.

Highway Traffic Act offences decreased to 2460 in 1975 from 3238 in 1974; only 168 impaired driving charges were laid in 1975, compared to 186 in 1974. Parking violations decreased to 1113 from 1909 and dangerous driving charges decreased to 55 from 67.

Deputy Police Chief Ken Boyd said that in all, Orillia was not better or worse than any other place in Ontario.

Provincially, there were "shocking increases" in violent crime in the OPP's jurisdiction. Fred Blucher, chief inspector of the OPP's community services branch, reported earlier that there was a 30.9 per cent increase in homicides, to 93 in 1975 from 71 in 1974. Robberies increased by 23 per cent to 240 in 1975 from 195 in 1974. There were 3269 frauds in 1975, up 22.9 per cent. There were 3127 car thefts, an increase of 20.2 per cent and 18834 break-ins, an increase of 18.5 per cent.

The report, submitted to the Orillia Police Commission by Police Chief William Blanche, will be made available to the public on request in the near future.

In his introduction, Mr. Blanche described the past year as "a very active one for the members of the Orillia Police Force".

The chief also spoke of the ever-increasing demands for better policing and the need for better facilities.

"It is inevitable that our police forece as a whole and the investigation department, in particular, will have to expand to cope with the ever-increasing demands and complex situations of today," said the chief.

"Efficient police communications are becoming increasingly necessary as police responsibilities grow more complex and, while at the moment, our radios are not proving adequate, steps are being taken to upgrade the system and the Ontario Police Commission assures us that this situation will be remedied in the near future."

Mr. Blanche, who is on vacation now, was not available for further comment.

CRIMINAL INVESTIGATIONS

The report says that 71.2 per cent of the cases assigned to the department's criminal investigation branch in 1975 were cleared. In 1975, 546 cases were assigned to the branch, 389 of them were cleared and 429 charges were laid.

The branch consists of Sgt. John Ennis, constables Gordon Pye, Ralph Hough, Ray Williams and Dennis Ball.

"The criminal investigation branch has become a very important part of the police force. The days when a simple and quick investigation would suffice are past. Crimes and criminals are becoming more sophisticated," the report says.

The report also voices another area of concern such as with juvenile offenders. It indicates that in 1975, a total of 157 juveniles — 118 male and 39 females between the ages of seven and 15 — were charged. In 1974, only 112 juveniles were interviewed. No figures were released as to charges laid against juveniles in 1974.

DIFFERENT REASONS

Different reasons contributed to Orillia's rising crime rates. Mr. Purvis said last week that Orillia's increase in crimes has been caused by "a breakdown of basic principles, principles of life people of my generation were taught to respect." But he did not specify what the "basic principles" are.

Deputy Chief Boyd said one of the reasons for the increase is better policing and better detection of crimes.

Other police officers, however, simply said that 1975 was "a bad year."

Though there was only one incident of attempted murder in the city, four murders were reported in the surrounding areas.

In 1975, five persons were killed in fires, while Orillia had not had fire deaths for many, many years.

There were two kidnappings, one fatal accident and two drownings in the city in 1975.

Brechin OPP report increase in some crimes

In Brechin OPP's patrolling area, from Washago to Cannington, the number of robberies, break-ins, thefts of more than $200, frauds and possession of offensive weapons charges, increased in 1975 over 1974. Possession of offensive weapons charges increased to 12 from five. Break-ins increased to 241 from 183. Thefts of more than $200 increased to 34 from 30 in 1974.

But other offences such as sex offences, assaults and drug offences decreased. In 1975, there were only 80 assaults, compared to 88 in 1974. Only two sex offences were reported in 1975, while five were reported in 1974. Thefts of less than $200 decreased to 155 in 1975 from 188 in 1974. Drug offences decreased to nine in 1975 from 18 in 1974. Only 30 car thefts were reported in 1975, compared to 34 in 1974.

No homicides were reported in 1975 and 1974.

OPP report 4 murders

As far as violent crimes were concerned, 1975 was a bad year for the Orillia detachment of the OPP, as four murders were reported.

Two persons have been

Traffic accidents decline but injuries reported increase

There were more traffic ac-

to 1113 from 1909 in 1974. There

But the number of persons

The World's First Masters Games, Toronto/Barrie 1985

It was the launch of the world's largest multi-sports event for mature athletes. Unlike the Olympics, athletes represent themselves, not their countries, so there is no selection process.

The Masters Games, which are held every four years, are open to mature athletes in various disciplines with categories from ages 45 and up. My partner Larry Schachter and I decide that being a Games' entrant will be a good boost for our agency, Marketing Plus, and our representation of Sport Ontario and Track and Field Canada.

Over the two weeks of the Games, I competed in a 10km run on the first day and a 5km cross-country in Barrie, capping it off with a 42km Marathon on the last day of competition. The Sports Medicine community was very interested in the participants, so I volunteered to be part of a special medical evaluation study after the Games with follow-up for the next 10 years. I was supported and cheered on by Ruth, Andrew, Tiff and Chris. It was an exhilarating time for significant achievements.

MASTERS GAMES/TORONTO REHABILITATION CENTRE

MEDICAL RESEARCH PROJECT

NAME: Daniels MR. George (Surname / First Name) Date of Birth: 06/23/35 (Month / Day / Year)

The following are the results of your Level V test carried out as part of the Masters Games/Toronto Rehab. Centre Medical Research Project into the effects of physical activity and aging.

[✓] Your heart rate and blood pressure responded normally to the increase in workloads.

[✓] Your exercise electrocardiogram was within normal limits.

[ ] Your pulmonary function test was within normal limits.

Your actual body weight was:

Kg	Lbs.
64.7	142.25

According to actuarial tables, your ideal body weight should be:

Kg	Lbs.
70	154

Your percentage (%) body fat was 14.5.

Normal upper limit for men: 16% - 19%

Normal upper limit for women: 22% - 25%

Analysis of expired air shows that your maximum oxygen consumption was 55.0 ml/kg/min.

To compare yourself with normals in the same age group, please see below:

NORMS BY AGE GROUPS FOR PREDICTED MAXIMAL OXYGEN CONSUMPTION (ml/kg/min)

MALES

Age (yr)	17-19	20-29	30-39	40-49	50-59	60-65
Excellent	≥ 62	≥ 57	≥ 49	≥ 43	≥ 40	≥36
Good	55-61	51-56	45-48	40-42	36-39	32-35
Minimum	49-54	45-50	40-44	36-39	32-35	28-31
Below Minimum	43-48	39-44	35-39	32-35	28-31	24-27
Poor	≤ 42	≤ 38	≤ 34	≤ 31	≤ 27	≤ 23

FEMALES

Age (yr.)	17-19	20-29	30-39	40-49	50-59	60-65
Excellent	≥ 43	≥ 41	≥ 38	≥ 35	≥ 32	≥ 28
Good	40-42	38-40	35-37	31-34	27-31	25-27
Minimum	37-39	34-37	31-34	28-30	23-26	21-24
Below Minimum	34-36	31-33	28-30	24-27	18-22	17-20
Poor	≤ 33	≤ 30	≤ 27	≤ 23	≤ 17	≤ 16

Thank you for your co-operation, and we hope you enjoyed the Games. Keep up the good work and stay fit and healthy.

T. Kavanagh, M.D.
Medical Director

/ac

Sports

10—The Packet, Thurs. Sept. 13, 1979

DANIELS RECALLS BOSTON ADVENTURE

Finishing marathon takes stamina, discipline

By JIM HARRIS
Packet Staff Reporter

George Daniels, 44, finished behind some 4,300 other runners in last April's Boston Marthon, but the fact that he finished at all as a first-time entry was notable.

Daniels, general sales manager of casting for Otaco and Galtaco Inc., and a Kiwanis Club member, told his fellow Kiwanians Monday what it was like to be in the classic of modern marathons.

Daniels told his club he started out from Orillia with the idea he might not finish at all, because of trouble he had nine days before with a bruised bone. That was caused from sitting on his wallet when he drove his car, he said, and aggravated by the 70-mile-per-week training program he was putting himself through to prepare for the race.

"I did not run for eight days before the Boston Marathon," he said.

But at Auburn, where he and his family stopped on the way to Boston, he met Lee Michaels, a marathoner who was in Orillia for the CANUS Games last year. Michaels took him along to a session at the Auburn YMCA, where he heard a pep talk on motivation, control, and taking a positive outlook on what is to be achieved.

That struck the very centre of Daniels' Achilles Tendon, which he had also nursed back to action after it became weakened the year before.

Fitness, Daniels maintains, not only keeps the body in good health, but also the mental, spiritual, social, business and family areas of life.

Daniels started the 26-mile run, one of nearly 8,000 registered entries, with another 5,000 left standing behind the starting line wishing they were running.

So great was the crowd of runners, "It took me five minutes to cross the starting line," he said.

The beginning of the course is downhill, and the weather was a marathoner's ideal — cool and drizzly. He passed the five mile mark 37 minutes into the run and found his body had settled nicely into the rhythm of running.

ORILLIA FUN RUNS ARE HELD EVERY SECOND SUNDAY, STARTING AT YMCA

Many of these runners are set for Skylon Marathon next month.

"You've got to be careful you don't get stampeded."

Another thing he had to take on the run were the many offers of water, juices and, in the case of one elderly lady, an ice cube in a bowl, along with a blessing. The words on his sweatshirt also attracted much attention from the crowds lining the route.

"The crowd was marvellous. They handed you oranges, juice, anything. They were there three deep and it was drizzling."

He said the race really got serious after the twentieth mile, where a series of four hills culled all but the steadiest runners. A loud-speaker on a police cruiser announced his official time as he passed (2 hours, 38 minutes).

7½-MINUTE MILE

"It dawned on me that I was running about a seven-and-a-half minute mile."

The last few miles, he said became the most difficult. But he overcame any difficulty by setting a series of short-distance goals until he came within sight of the finish line.

Daniels' finish time was three hours, 18 minutes, 39 seconds. He will receive a certificate for that.

Early in his talk, Daniels described his experience in the Ottawa marathon in May, 1978, which he finished in three hours, 12 minutes, among about 4,000 entries.

With that one under his belt he learned, he was qualified to enter the Boston run. Two requirements for the Boston run are that the runner must have completed one other marathon and must be over age 40.

UNDERSRSTAND BODY

He said there are a number of other things to take into consideration as well — a program, discipline and diet among them.

"You've got to understand your body is craving more food than you normally eat," he said. He also said runners must be prepared to drink more water than usual, and do it while running.

Water, and juices are important to the body, he said, to replace a component called glycogen, which becomes depleted after about 20 miles of running.

Daniels said he is now preparing, with several other Orillia runners, to enter the annual Skylon international marathon from Buffalo to Niagara Falls in October.

GEORGE DANIELS

Miller High Life

CERTIFICATE OF COMPLETION

This is to certify that

GEORGE DANIELS

has competed in the

1983 MILLER HIGH LIFE TORONTO MARATHON

and finished in a time of

3:10.38/442nd

Carling O'Keefe Breweries — Race Director — Ontario Track & Field Association

PART IX

George joins a new world of automotive parts manufacturing and sales as Director of Marketing for North America---but learns once again about the pitfalls of corporate takeovers.

Part IX

Success in the Auto Parts industry

By the spring of 1972, I made up my mind to resign from CJAD as VP of sales. Ruth and I decided to move back to Ontario. Our game plan involved her driving to Collingwood with the kids, staying with her mother and armed with my resume for exploring opportunities in Orillia. Having learned to fly on the floats at the foot of Main Street on the Bay and being knowledgeable about the area was a logical choice. Ruth was my sales management ambassador. She met with real estate agents and dropped off my credentials to several leading companies.

On a Sunday morning several weeks after Ruth had returned from her trip, the doorbell rang at our Town of Mount Royal Vivian Avenue home. I was in my PJs and dressing gown writing another CJAD radio business plan while Ruth was looking after Andrew, Timothy and Christopher.

I answered the door to a gentleman who introduced himself as Howard McRae, comptroller of the Orillia Bartaco-Otaco Foundry and manufacturing plants. Over coffee, he explained that company president Brian Barr and he had reviewed my resume and flown to Montréal this morning to interview me and negotiate an offer to join their company as marketing sales manager.

Apparently the two company executives had done their research on my various career skills. In particular, Howard McRae understood the role of a radio general sales manager, which is to generate dollars out of a finite intangible such as air time. Howard is also a director and shareholder of Orillia's CFOR radio station. Probing his broadcast industry executive friends, he says I have a good reputation for generating growing dollars out of the limited number of 1,500 airtime minutes a station is permitted to sell per week. This is a Canadian Radio and Television Commission regulation for AM stations. By comparison, FM stations are only allowed to sell 900.

Howard goes on to explain that he and Brian Barr think that I could apply my business building sales-per-unit pricing strategy to their foundry Disamatic. I was embarrassed to ask what a Disamatic is but Howard laughs and explains that it is a highly-efficient horizontal mold machine that cycles 1,500 times in an eight-hour shift. He likens it to our radio station vertical transmission tower broadcasting 1,500 60-second announcements each week. They are confident my sales and pricing skills that are efficient and effective in broadcast terms can be applied to their Disamatic and its cast-iron parts output.

Howard further explains the basic workings of their ductile iron foundry. Otaco has two large electric induction furnaces. They are clean, with no environmentally-unfriendly coal gases being spewed out. Ductile iron is almost pure steel. By comparison, grey iron has a softer tensile strength. At the end of the Disamatic horizontal piston is a 2-1/2 foot-square sand mold with 3-4 cavities. The 2,500-degree Fahrenheit ductile iron melt is poured into the mold in under a minute. Solidification starts to take a place as the molds are further pushed down a production line. The molds are then broken apart to reveal such automotive parts as pulley Hubs, brake calipers, and such diverse products as farm equipment plough shears.

The company has identified that it needs to accommodate more parts coming off each mold, parts that will have to be sold at a profitable price--an on-going challenge for the sales department. Hundreds of parts are produced each eight-hour shift. What an intriguing sales challenge this would be for me in a whole new automotive business sector.

Howard seems pleased with this interview. He thinks I would also be able and suited for their factory. It is adjacent to the foundry and produces a range of products such as wheels, axles and hubs for the camper-trailer manufacturers, Lionel, Coleman and Bonaire being their main customers. Otaco transit seating division is Canada's main supplier of bus seats to General Motors and Flyer Industries. Their scoreboard division is a leading supplier for school gymnasiums and arenas and they also make basketball backstops, gym mats and bleacher seating.

I indicate that I am up to the challenge, ready to relocate from Montréal to Orillia and on the spot, Howard offers me an executive position as Director of Marketing. This comes with an attractive salary. Although not as lucrative as a broadcast sales manager, there will be important compensating factors by living in a small town. Affordable housing and four-season lifestyle with nearby schools will be easy to adjust to. They offer to pay all our moving expenses. We have a few days to consider and after careful thought, Ruth and I agree to the offer. Now comes the hard part; extracting myself from CJAD and Standard Broadcasting.

My broadcast executive responsibilities have pushed my boundaries to near exhaustion. It was the height of the FLQ crisis when Quebec separatists went on a terrorist rampage, forcing Prime Minister Trudeau to invoke the War Measures Act. This put a strain on our English-language CJAD station in the mostly French-language Montreal market. "Oh, you guys won't be able to sell any English time now," said the doubters, thus putting pressure on us to reach large, aggressive sales targets which I had set. I worked the sales force to persevere. In addition, we had an active young family to look after, plus the company had sent me to Harvard for the prestigious Broadcast Sales Exec's management course where I was one of only three Canadians.

It was all too much and I had a minor coronary blip. It was a warning. Time to change from the stressful mile-a-minute pace to something more manageable and after careful self-appraisal, I went to General Manager Mac McCurdy and announced my resignation. Surprised, he said, "George, you cannot do that, you are destined to be our next president." I replied, "Mac, with all due respect, I am not hanging around here for another 10 years waiting for you to retire." He understood and persuaded me to stay on for another several months to find my successor, which I did--John Bartram from Foster Advertising.

In the summer of 1972, we moved to our Lake of Bays cottage. I continued my last few months at CJAD and commuted via Algonquin Park and Ottawa to Montreal. By the end of summer, I had sold our Town of Mount Royal home and bought a fairly-new back split in Orillia.

We stayed at the cottage with Andrew going to the Irwin Memorial School in Dwight for the month of September. The Campbell school bus/taxi even came directly to our door to pick up Andrew for which we were grateful. We finally moved in October. A warm Mariposa (Stephen Leacock's name for Orillia) welcome was orchestrated for us by the Bartaco management and we found new friends on our spiffy Harmon Road Street. Larry Temple, our real estate agent, toured us around and got me enrolled in Kiwanis. We then networked into Beavers for Timothy and Cubs for Andrew who also became a goalie in CYO hockey. The one-hour car ride to Collingwood, visiting Ruth's mom Doris, and skiing at Devil's Glen became part of our family routine.

Bartaco Industries Limited

George E. Daniels

Brian W. Barr, President of Bartaco Industries Limited of Orillia, has announced the appointment of George E. Daniels as Director of Marketing for the Corporation.

Mr. Daniels joins Bartaco with an extensive background in marketing and communications. He is well known across Canada. For the past six years he has been with Standard Broadcasting Corporation, latterly as Vice President and General Sales Manager of CJAD Limited, Montreal.

In his new appointment, Mr. Daniels will be fully responsible for marketing counselling and co-ordination of Bartaco's eight Canadian subsidiary companies.

My new job at Bartaco Industries is for me propitious. I have a desire to climb the corporate ladder and now, the courses in marketing, sales and business management seem to be paying off. Notwithstanding our family's need for a stable income in a good community environment is also an on-going motivator. You can imagine my exhilaration in realizing that I am going from being a media sales representative to working in a manufacturing industry that supplies automotive parts to the backbone of our Canadian economy.

When an early edition of the Globe and Mail's October Report on Business section prints my appointment notice, seen here, I am, as they say in England, chuffed. It feels good. Wow! I am Director of Marketing for the Bartaco Corporation. Now I have to get to work.

President Brian Barr and comptroller Howard McRae are marvelous in introducing me to division managers and groups of employees at the Otaco foundry and factory divisions. Companies that were further afield such as Vic Tanny's health spas and the highly-specialized aluminum foundry, Haley Industries near Ottawa would come later. It is human nature to resist change. Therefore, I could detect some reluctance to accept the advertising sales guy to their world of factory whistles, noisy machinery, scrap metal, induction furnaces, unions and shiftwork.

Managers, engineers, purchasing agents and shop stewards let alone the shipping departments have been working their systems long before I come along. I have a lot to learn. Probing and assembling all the information for each division, let alone individual departments, is going to take me some time.

Using the basic tenets of marketing---getting to know the product, its pricing structure and distribution channels---will require careful analysis and perhaps a period of time not quite in keeping with the "let's get it done now" philosophy of the entrepreneurial Barrs, as I will soon find out. Bartaco's corporate headquarters is on the second floor of a two-storey 1940s brick structure that had been added to the 1920s three-storey, quarter-mile long factory building. President and executive offices are closed off from the large open-concept space for Accounting and various administration staff.

The first floor has several small offices for division sales managers and a large factory manager's office which becomes mine and the previous tenant, the factory chief, is relocated within the plant. I sense some concern about me displacing this guy. The situation will soon be exacerbated. Within a month of my arrival, Bartaco sells a lot of its publicly-traded shares to Alco Standard Corporation of Cleveland, Ohio. They proceed to exercise considerable management control as follows; Alco sends in an evaluation team of executives. They determine the Otaco foundry division is doing fine. Haley Industries, which specializes in aluminum structural parts for the aircraft industry, enjoys a positive balance sheet so no marketing counsel from me is necessary.

Of more pressing need is the Otaco factory division, so I am reassigned, pushed sideways, to be general sales manager of the factory division. I immediately inherit Bill Simpson, sales manager of all factory products with the exception of the public transit bus seat line spearheaded by sales manager Dick Lauer. There is a sales supervisor for scoreboard installations and another for farm parts. Paul Foster is the farm guy and also a commercial pilot who I am going to work with on the company's charter aviation needs.

My first task is to get to know the staff and a particular challenge is to be working with two very experienced sales managers 20 years my senior. Bill Simpson has an intimate knowledge of the factory product output, coupled with good relationships with many customers. Working in tandem with casting salesman Paul Foster, they make a good team. I spend some time with them on the road, mostly in Ontario, meeting customers, including small manufacturers of trailers for Canadian Tire. In Quebec, Otaco sells a wheel-and-axle package to several large camper/trailer manufacturers.

Dick Lauer was Mr. Public Transportation Seating. He had come over to the company from Hayward Wakefield, the Orillia bus seating manufacturer, when it had been taken over by Otaco. I worked closely with Dick getting to know the bus seat customers who are really transit authorities such as the Toronto Transit Commission. I learned that the key to success was getting one's product specified. Translation: the Otaco 220T had to be inserted into the bus manufacturer's overall model specifications. This resulted in a lot of sales development work and getting pre-approval of our products. For example, Dick Lauer, our staff and I had to work closely with the TTC maintenance engineering and purchasing department to get our bus seats specified. This took a lot of time.

Small gymnasium and arena scoreboards were one of the factory special product lines. Part of an athletic division for gym mats and various apparatus, the scoreboards were driven by electro-mechanical stepper relay switches similar to the standard traffic light.

In early 1973, chairman Bob Barr met Montréal's Peter Ritzenthaler at his solid-state electronics factory, which made the new state-of-the-art electronic indicators for race tracks. Bob bought the company with the idea of converting our standard scoreboards to this new technology. I was assigned to make it work.

I now spent several days a month in Montréal at the Ritz plant. The new engineering required analyzing reducing time scoreboards for basketball and hockey. After several months, we developed a 5-foot wide by 3-foot high by 10-inch electronic scoreboard in a lightweight fibreglass casing. There was nothing like it on the market and we could sense we had a winner. At the same time, we set our sights on larger scoreboards for the 1976 Summer Olympics and the new Edmonton Coliseum.

My marketing assessment of scoreboard sales potential concluded that our economies of scale and pricing meant we could not make a profit in Canada and could achieved only in the United States. Management agreed and I targeted the Porter educational supplier headquarters in Chicago. I was successful. Their VP of marketing agreed to take on our electronic scoreboards. We decided to launch the scoreboard line in June 1973 in Atlanta at the annual US educational purchasing agents' convention and suppliers' exhibition.

We designed a compelling display and exhibit, shipped it to the Atlanta Coliseum and I arrived on the Thursday to set up before the start of the convention scheduled for Friday at midday. Dick Priebe, Porter's VP of Marketing, was well prepared with pricing and sales literature.

We set up our joint Porter/Otaco booth on Thursday morning. Our company policy mandated that any in-the-field expenditure over $10,000, even though pre-approved, had to have the president's last-minute signoff.

So, waiting for the Otaco factory lunch hour to be over, I used the nearby Coliseum payphone. It was 1:15 pm. The receptionist answered and I asked to speak to Jim Morrisey. She said he was not there. I asked to speak to the comptroller and was told he was out. The next in the chain of command was the plant manager and apparently he was not there either. I was surprised. Our plant would always have one or two of these managers at work. I asked what is going on and where they were. The receptionist said, "George, I am not supposed to tell you this but we have been bought out by a corporation and the people you asked for are no longer with the company."

I was shocked. I soon realized that in the management hierarchy I would probably next to be let go. I certainly did not have approvals to move forward. I immediately went back to our booth and informed the Porter company that I was immediately canceling this marketing thrust and taking down the display. Porter was extremely angry and I was called out for reneging on our arrangement.

By the time I got back to Orillia, it was Friday night. Fully expecting to be terminated by the new owners on Monday morning, Ruth and I speculated on what I might do next to earn a living. One option was to start another hamburger stand like Weber's on Highway 11.

On Monday morning, I arrived at my office and things seemed almost normal. My two trusty sales managers Bill Simpson and Dick Lauer and our executive secretary Linda Clark were still in place. What is going to happen next was the buzz.

After lunch I was called upstairs to the corporate offices and introduced to the new president Doug McKay and VP of operations Mel Element. It was a curt meeting. Apparently they had reviewed my file and said they would like me to come back the following morning and justify my existence. Analyzing what it all might mean, I prepared myself for what would turn out to be one of my best presentations.

McKay and Element were attentive as I told them I had no intention of justifying my existence. Furthermore, that if they looked closely at my resume and what I had uncovered and achieved in a brief year or so, they would understand its importance. I asked them to look at the Otaco-Bartaco corporate jumble of excessive diversification and questionable profitability, after which they would realize that in me they had one of the best sales management assets going. Looking at each other, they asked me to step out of the room.

Twenty minutes later and with a smile, Doug McKay said, "Okay, George, you are now on board as special assistant to the president. We are going to spend the next several months exhaustively analyzing the various corporate divisions and setting up the new Galtaco Corporation. In addition, we are giving you an immediate $5,000 dollars a year raise, a company car and expect you to operate between Orillia and our other Company headquarters at the Galt Malleable Iron Co. in Cambridge." I was ecstatic. Wait until Ruth hears this news. We are solid.

I now embark on learning about our new corporate leaders. Doug McKay had joined Galt Malleable Iron from a leading sales engineering position with General Motors. Galt Malleable was a grey-iron foundry with a stamping facility that made stainless steel sink strainers. Doug had built a ductile iron foundry in Brantford with a Disamatic similar to the one in the Otaco foundry. He also persuaded one of GM's young dynamic executives, Doug Major, to join the company. For the next year, I worked closely with both these men. It was an impressionable learning experience.

With the objective of streamlining the new combined companies into primarily automotive-parts foundry and factory manufacturing, we did the following; I shared responsibility for divesting the Bartaco-owned Vic Tanny's, a plastic mold parts company and Haley Industries.

Sales of ductile iron castings from the Orillia and Brantford Disamatic Lines were flourishing. Detroit was producing 14 million cars per year and the foundries of the big car companies could not keep up with the demand for pulley hubs, brake calipers and other engine and drive train parts.

Outside suppliers such as ourselves were an important part of Ford, General Motors, and Chrysler's manufacturing mix. Servicing a steady stream of orders from Bendix, Kelsey Hayes and Simpson industries, companies who machined our raw castings to assembly-line specifications, was part of the ongoing key account relationships one must develop with these companies to ensure continuing sales of tons of high-quality product each month.

With the foundry divisions running smoothly, it was determined that I would now spend a lot of time working the factory divisions. Two big opportunities loomed large and the Otaco electronic scoreboard division was one.

The 1976 Montréal Summer Olympics will require four or five state-of-the-art electronic scoreboards so we targeted this opportunity. American and Swiss Timing companies were already pre-approved over many years at Olympic venues and going up against them was tough. Nevertheless, we won a significant order to supply the main scoreboard in the Olympic rowing basin.

This success was noted by other large stadium groups that were on the horizon. Coliseums in Edmonton, Québec City and Philadelphia presented good opportunities. In particular, I worked hard on the huge NHL-accredited scoreboard installation for the Edmonton Coliseum. It took months of work and many trips getting to know high-profile Oilers' president Peter Pocklington and the Mutart contracting company.

We gained their confidence when their main consultant in electronics, the Alberta Telephone Company, verified our technology. We were up against a major competitor, Swiss Timing. Putting on my best sharpening-the-pencil pricing strategy with Doug's approval, we won the order. This was a pivotal achievement and helped us win similar scoreboard sales to the Québec Coliseum and York University.

The Toronto Transit Commission has a notable reputation as being one of the best public transit authorities in North America. Otaco and the basic 220T transit bus seat was in nearly 90 percent of the hundreds of buses and subway trains serving Toronto and suburbs.

Major changes in public transit growth were being fueled by the needs for safety and lower maintenance costs while moving the growing population in Southern Ontario. The Ontario government formed the Urban Transportation Development Corporation (UTDC) and Ontario Minister of Transportation Jim Snow appointed his top bureaucrat, Kirk Foley, to head this new Crown Corporation.

Their prime task was to come up with a new streetcar, as the old, iconic streetcars operated by the TTC since the 1940s were getting costly to operate. UTDC engineers worked with TTC engineering and maintenance to come up with a new state-of-the-art Light Rail Vehicle (LRV) and the modern streetcar was born.

Its interior seating specifications were also engineered to be applicable to buses. This called for cantilevered seats mounted on the vehicle walls with no supporting pedestal underneath. After much testing, it was proven that a cantilevered seat would be far safer than a traditional pedestal seat and would have the added cost saving maintenance benefit of an unobstructed floor cleaning space.

UTDC and their prime customer TTC let it be known that they expected our OTACO Transportation Seating Division to come up with a new seat and bid for the business. It was a tough challenge. Our competitors' fibreglass and tubular steel-supported transit seats could be mounted from the LRV or transit coach walls but still required a pedestal for support.

Sometimes the better mouse trap appears right in front of you. One day we visited Kindred Industries in Midland, which made stainless-steel kitchen sinks. While we were delivering another shipment of sink strainers, Dick Lauer and our plant engineer noted the 15-ton presses Kindred used to form the deep draw of a sink. Someone remarked that the bottom of the sink looked like a seat and that's how we started down the road to design, engineer and produce a stainless-steel transit seat.

Our journey included applying to the Federal Government for a design engineering repayable loan so we could bring on board Thomas Faul, a noted industrial design engineer. We got the funds and Tom moved into our engineering department several days per week. In his own Mississauga headquarters, he produced artistic renderings of a proposed stainless-steel seat with a padded comfortable insert. I was pleased to be part of the Otaco-Thomas Faul team that presented our concept to UTDC and the TTC. We got a very positive response.

Ordering high-quality, stainless-steel sheeting, we made special tooling for our 20-ton Cincinnati press to punch out the first prototype samples for the seat and separate back. Welded together, it was a fit. Our upholstery department had lots of transportation grade foam fillers and long-lasting vinyl and we created prototype padded inserts for the seat and back.

The Ontario Government's public transportation department funded 100 percent of UTDC and nearly 90 percent of TTC. Working towards our new transit seat being specified, we arranged a special demonstration at Queen's

Park with Jim Snow. All the stakeholders were in attendance and our mockup was well received. Now, we had to prove it could work when installed in the vehicles. Minister Snow arranged for us to put our seat through rigorous testing at the Oakville Government of Ontario test facility.

This was an extensive stress test under all kinds of possible crash scenarios and designed to ensure passengers would survive unhurt. Fire tests on the padded foam insert and transportation grade vinyl were rigorous. Dick Lauer and I spent countless hours during these tests and were rewarded when our new prototype seat and its components finally received the seal of approval.

We had done our homework well in developing this product. I came up with the name Innovator 1 and everyone seemed to like it. Federal Government audit inspectors who had advanced us the funds also endorsed Innovator 1. The Ontario Government, both directly through Minister Snow and UTDC, placed their confidence in this new seating concept for the LRV streetcars. Len Bardsley, TTC's head of engineering and maintenance, gave his OK.

This was exciting; we had won our first customer for the innovative public transportation seating line.

Toronto Transit LRV Street Car with Stainless Steel Innovator 1 seat , with red comfort pad insert advertised in Where magazine 2005...featuring Art Gallery of Ontario. Otaco's Innovator 1 Transit Seat went into service in mid '70's.

Innovator 1 850 typical rail and street car installation.

Pictured above is the Los Angeles County rail car installation by American Seating.

THE GLOBE AND MAIL

Innovator 850 Seating

Riding the rocket with the TTC boss Confirmed Monday as the new chief executive, the dynamic Englishman is determined to put some snap back in the faded red banner **NEWS, PAGE A7**

Buzzing in my head is the popular song, *"On The Road Again"*. One has to go where the real customer is and many are in the United States. The Otaco Transportation Seating Division belongs to various industry trade associations and the American Public Transit Authority is the premier organization affecting motor coach and rail transit. Otaco is a member. Our goal, and a crucial link in the marketing and sales of Innovator 1, will be to target the transit authorities who belonged to APTA. In turn, it will also be necessary to sell to the bus and rail car manufacturers. One choice opportunity to do this is to be an exhibitor at the annual APTA convention.

Our opening sales salvo comes in June of 1977 in New York at the APTA convention in Manhattan Hilton. Recently-elected President Jimmy Carter is the keynote speaker. He announces that his government will now fund 80 percent of public transit in major United States cities. This is widely acclaimed and gives us lots of encouragement. Now, transit authorities in these cities will have the dollars to buy new buses, streetcars and subway trains and these new vehicles will have to have new features and benefits. We see this as a huge potential market for Innovator 1.

With our US sales representative Peter Reading working out of Chicago, we schedule a plan to demonstrate Innovator 1 to the major North American transit authorities, aiming to get our product specified in all new transit vehicles. Thus, when the vehicle manufacturer goes to tender, they would have to include Innovator 1 as specified by the transit authority. Doug McKay assigned me to work with Peter Reading in the United States market while Dick Lauer would continue his excellent rapport with Canadian public transit authorities.

Over the next year, I travel extensively in the United States. Peter Reading opens many doors for us to get acceptance. Pricing in any public tender is always critical. Although more expensive than traditional bus or streetcar seats, Innovator 1 earns its way because it is largely vandal-proof with hard to damage stainless steel. It offers comfortable cantilevered seat safety with ease of floor maintenance.

The Massachusetts Transit Authority puts out a tender to refurbish 600 rail cars with new seats and I recommend to president Doug that we go after this business. He asks, "What would it take to get the order? " I tell him, "probably meetings with purchasing and engineering people at least four or five times over the year to get specified. "He says, "that seems like a lot of travel expense." I say, "Yes and well worth it". He challenges me, "Do you really think you can get the order?" I say, 'yes and furthermore when I do, I will run the Boston Marathon and you will pay for the family to come and watch me as part of a holiday'. "You're on, George." And so begins a series of MTA/Boston meetings. We get specified and in April 1979, I run the 79th Boston Marathon. The family has a blast with lots of memorable moments. There is much more to the Innovator 1 story. Some time after I had left the company, American Seating bought Otaco Seating and melded the products into their offerings. I had spearheaded successful Innovator 1 sales in Toronto, Vancouver, Boston, Philadelphia and more. Checking with Douglas Oswald, Director of Marketing for American Seating in March 2017, he reports that they continue to service and sometimes sell Innovator 1 to nine transit rail authorities and 12 major-market bus operators. Doug tells me we were successful and certainly no planned obsolescence was built into our line.

Bruce Gowan, our comptroller and a neighbour in Muskoka, tells me: "George, you are the company's dynamic marketing executive who shared responsibility for the Innovator line of transportation seating which today (2017) is still the class of the industry".

Volunteerism is another excellent way of getting away from the pressures of my business life, and in Orillia, the home of celebrated Canadian humorist Stephen Leacock ("Sunshine Sketches of a Little Town"), I found an exciting opportunity.

Orillia was in the process of creating the Leacock Festival of Humor to celebrate their favorite author and staging it at the newly-refurbished Orillia Opera House. I was asked to become one of the founding directors and delighted to contribute to the growth and development of the event, which became as important to Orillia as Shakespeare was to Stratford.

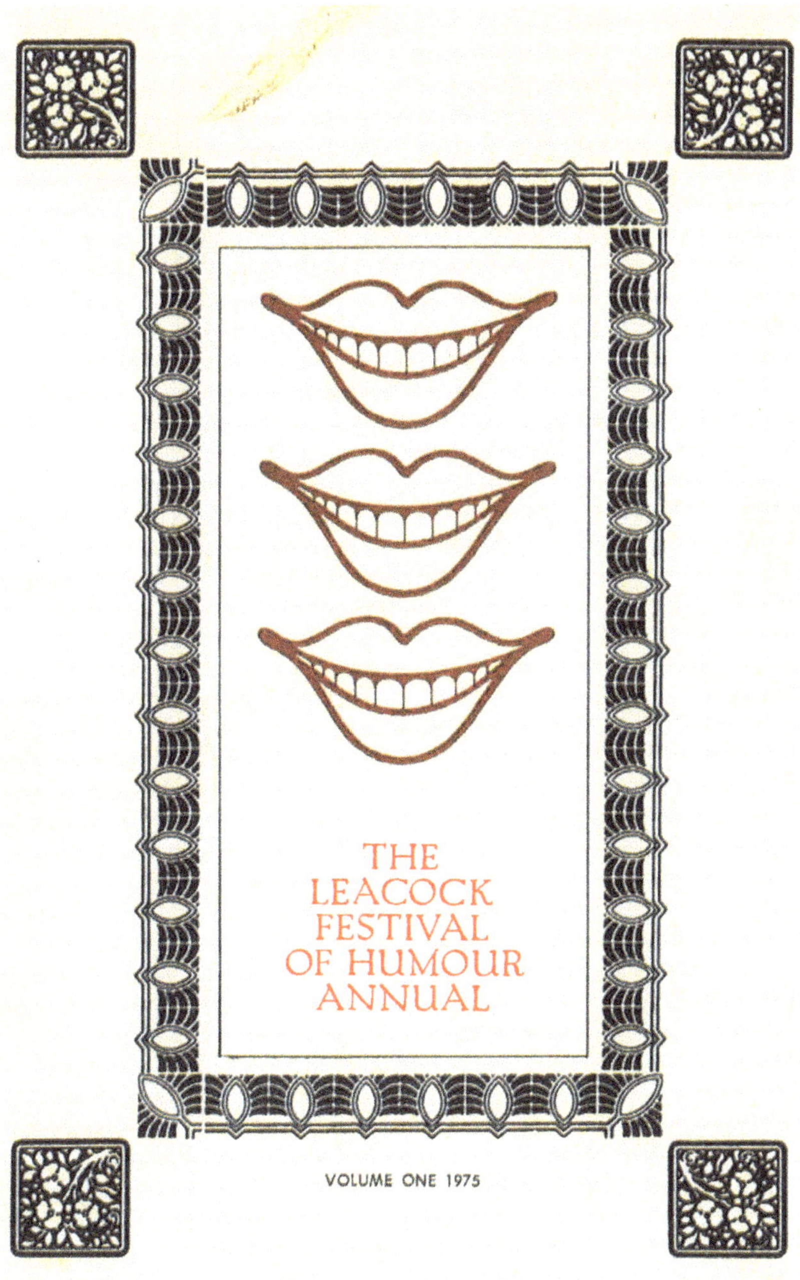
THE
LEACOCK
FESTIVAL
OF HUMOUR
ANNUAL
VOLUME ONE 1975

Galtaco
Foundry Fickle Finger of Fate Award

Presented to George E. Daniels 1978 on the occasion of being made sales & marketing manager for North America.

George Works Part VIII
Chevrolet - GMC - Oldsmobile Automotive Manual

Make: Light Truck Year: 1977 Model: Pickup (2WD)

Pickup (2WD) > BRAKES-REAR AXLE AND DRIVE > (T5-23) 1973-1978 CGP3 REAR AXLE ASSEMBLY(7,500 LB CAPACITY)(DANA) >

OTACO - Galtaco Foundry Pinion Flange

Chapter 8 Clutch and drivetrain

AXLE SHAFT "C" LOCK

PINION SHAFT
LOCK BOLT HOLE

13.3 Locations of the pinion shaft lockbolt and axleshaft C-ring lock

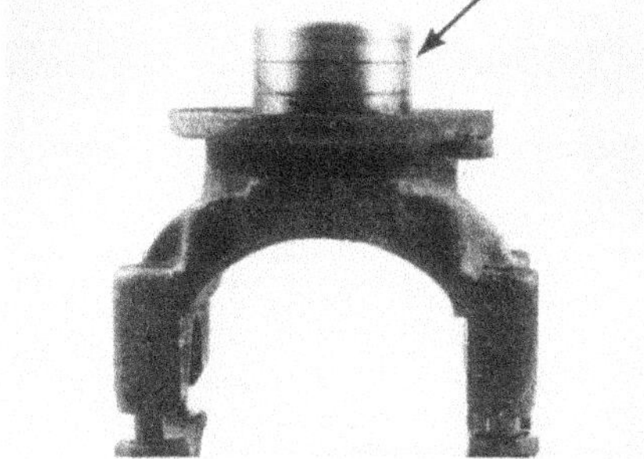

17.11 The sealing surface of the pinion flange should be free of nicks and gouges

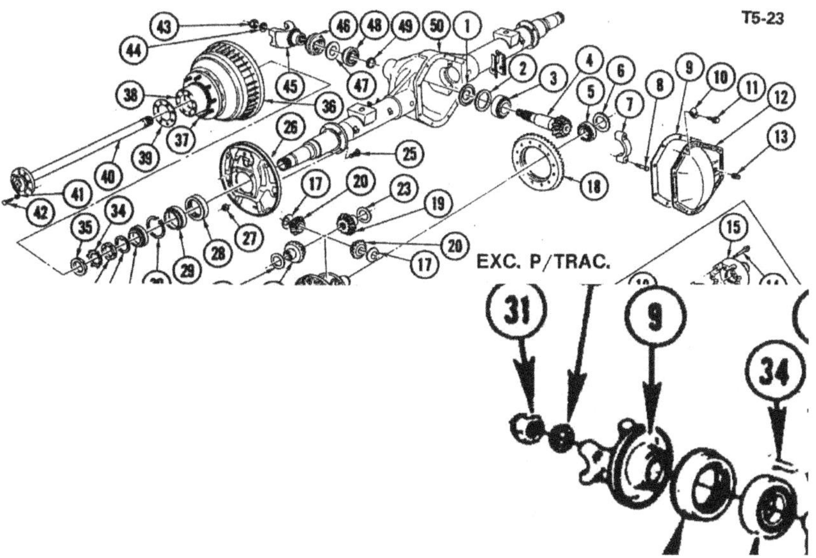

Chevrolet GMC Automotive Part

PART X

Vowing never to work for any corporation again, George partners with advertising friend Larry Schachter to form their own successful advertising agency.

Part X

Marketing Plus Inc. and Signature Advertising

I had returned to Standard Broadcasting/CFRB in the spring of 1980. Achieving many successes as Vice President of Sales, I learned the inside dynamics of radio programming. The creative process, including writing and voice was basic to the on-air personalities as well as the sales staff. In the spring of 1984, Chairman Conrad Black cleared out the executive ranks in order to sell the company. I was let go. It was an abrupt axe. The higher you go in a corporation, the slipperier the carpet. I determined never to work for another big company.

When long-time friend Larry Schachter, who had just left an executive marketing position with the Canadian National Exhibition, asked me "What do you think of advertising agencies? I replied that having battled them many times as a media sales representative, I was not impressed. Larry then said, "What would you think if you owned one?" That would be different, I replied.

Larry had already formed Marketing Plus and was working out of his Don Mills house. Needing a partner, I decided to join him. He would be the President and I the Executive Vice-President, thus giving our clients the confidence of working with senior executives.

We rented a small VIP services office at Lawrence Avenue and Don Mills Road with a partner's desk so we sat opposite each other. There was one phone, a coat rack and a filing cabinet. We rented typing services as required. Plan your work and work your plan became our business development strategy and only one partner in the office at any one time was the norm. The other partner had to be on the road hustling business and after all, we had only one phone.

The advertising and marketing sector is a rough, competitive field. The big agencies had large staffs and resources to acquire clients spending hundreds of thousands of dollars in media expenditures. We set our goals to not compete with them but rather to target small-to-medium companies who needed big agency services but only had $250,000 or more advertising and promotion budgets.

One of these was the Mayfair Racket Club where Larry was a member. They had two large tennis facilities in north Toronto and were about to expand to several more. Marketing Plus became their first advertising agency and we went after the tennis community to promote membership in these new facilities.

I got lucky when Ruth's cousin Barb and her husband Ted Dallimore inquired about my new venture. After explaining, Ted said, "Now that you are no longer involved with CFRB, let's sit down and work out how you can help our Sandy Cove Marine." This was quite a break. Ted had no advertising agency but had access to co-op advertising dollars from Mercury Marine and other suppliers of outboard engines and boats. Marketing Plus became their agency of record.

Larry and I collaborated on the clients' creative and media selection needs. This process would start after interviewing the client and getting an interpretation of the features and benefits of the product or service to be sold. We researched the clients' geographic and population demographics to select best customer needs. We would determine the product or service advertising or promotion strategy within a budget. It was presented to the client for approval and then we went about implementing this plan.

Our recommendation to Sandy Cove Marine included the one-two punch, mostly successful for retailers, of using newspapers and radio.

Larry created a newspaper advertisement for a name-brand runabout boat powered by a Mercury Marine outboard engine. My job was to write one or two 30-second radio commercials. In my media and manufacturing experience, I had written many proposals and often they included a creative idea and direction. So here I was with a blank piece of paper to write a compelling radio spot that would have synergy with the print ad Larry had created. I was well versed in what to do by ad tycoon David Ogilvy, and had read his book, *The Ultimate Guide to Writing Powerful Advertising.* Using a call to action such as, "Hey, boating fans," I used short words and sentences, got the client's name and his boat in the copy two or three times with a closing call to action, e.g. 'Test drive it now at Sandy Cove Marine.'

We submitted our ideas and the campaign to Ted Dallimore and explained that having added, 'powered by a Mercury Marine Engine' information, this campaign was eligible for 50 percent Mercury co-op funding. Ted liked this and we went on to do many campaigns using co-op funding. Sandy Cove Marine came to rely on our proof-of-advertising tear sheets and scripts before releasing the dollars. We had started to carve a niche in the marine dealer retail sphere that would be part of our client roster for years to come. And we got it.

"I'm sorry we couldn't convince you, but as someone once said—'doing business without advertising is like winking at a girl in the dark. You know what you're doing, but nobody else does!'"

Developing new clients and growing our business was often done by leads passed along by media sales representatives. Good ones know the client landscape and have a wealth of knowledge and can also provide Nielsen, BBM and other free research data. Having been a sales rep and now the company's resident media buyer, I knew these representatives would be helpful in passing along prospective client information.

The consumer isn't a moron; she is your wife, explained guru David Ogilvy. Understanding this, we were successful in creating advertising and promotion for a range of clients where the woman was the key decision-maker. They were shopping-centre merchants' associations, fashion retailers, EnviroGreen brands, Cup-A-Noodles soup, Humpty Dumpty Foods and Santa's Village to name a few.

Number 76 of a series to promote creative print advertising sponsore
The Globe and Mail

Annual Report (our first)

"Hello. We're from Marketing Plus." "Never heard of you."

How many times did we have that little dialogue this past year! But it's not surprising when you've been in business less than a year.

So we're using the Globe and Mail's Report on Business to introduce ourselves. Finally. And coincidently with our first anniversary, our "annual report."

Our principals combine over 75 years of experience in marketing communications—on both sides of the desk—and bring a successful track record from our individual careers to our clients' problem solving. While we're modest in size, we're Top Ten in enthusiasm and energy… and our size translates into continuing involvement by the principals.

Our "newness" also extracts from us the vigor required to prove ourselves to the business community and communications fraternity.

Our expertise enables us to bridge product/service advertising with retailing knowhow, in the extra dimensions of POP, trade programs, consumer promotions, etc.

We can refer you to some of our birthyear clients to support this.

1984 ANNUAL REPORT 1985
MARKETINGPLUS INC. …looking bright

We have already…

- ☐ Created and executed a first-time advertising campaign for one of Canada's largest recreation facilities.
- ☐ Created and produced an incentive program for 6000 travel agents on behalf of a major tour operator.
- ☐ Created and produced an instant-win promotion, nationally, for Canada's largest non-food convenience chain.
- ☐ Created and produced a successful radio promotion for a major national packaged powdered bleach.
- ☐ Acted as marketing consultants to several sports-oriented national amateur associations.
- ☐ Designed an incentive program for a 60 outlet chain of Ontario lumber dealers.
- ☐ Planned and produced an ad campaign that moved several million dollars worth of boats and accessories in 11 days.
- ☐ Created and produced TV commercials for a national Outboard Motor Company.
- ☐ plus a dozen other projects.

A satisfying result is that we've already been invited back on a number of occasions …all in our first year.

We invite you to be part of our 2nd annual report.

respectfully submitted by

Larry Schachter, President — George E. Daniels, Executive Vice President

MARKETINGPLUS INC.
40 Wynford Drive, Suite 104, Don Mills, Ontario M3C 1J5 (416) 441-6113

Number 76 of a series to promote creative print advertising sponsored by The Globe and Mail

R. Bruce Montgomery, creative director and Madison Avenue friend helps George win the Landscape Ontario advertising account with these visuals from the presentation;

"AN IDEA IS LIKE A SEED. IF YOU PLANT IT IN A FERTILE FIELD, AND WATER IT ENOUGH, YOU'D BE SURPRISED AT WHAT WILL GROW."

Ben Franklin

"AS YE SOW, SO SHALL YE REAP."

MATTHEW, III:17

"IT WAS JUST A LITTLE SEED, BUT I WATERED IT WELL."

Jack (re: his beanstalk)

"BULLSHIT HELPS A LOT OF THINGS GROW. IT WORKS JUST AS WELL IN ADVERTISING!"

Charles Saatchi

"MONEY HELPS, TOO!"

Maurice Saatchi

Left to right: George and Ruth Daniels with Helen and Alan Guttman with Mitzi and Larry Schachter

Ode to George E.

While your life turns to apple pie
and you fly across the Muskokan sky
I'm sure you'll find lots
of pleasurable thoughts,
'bout leaving us all high and dry

We've enjoyed many wins, but blew some
At times, things looked quite gruesome.
What made it more queer
is that we'd often hear,
That we made a really odd twosome.

But somehow we survived all these years
with many laughs and occasional tears.
I'm feeling paranoid
As I now face the void
of your daily dose of good cheers.

That you're loyal needs no further proof,
the old frame bears the heart of youth
Semi retirement's your way
to finally say
"I'm going home to my beloved Foof."

Now as we hear your swan song
you know that you'll always belong.
Take it from me old friend,
while this seems like the end,
It's really just saying so-long.

Larry

What a Year!

☆Gretzky ☆Jordan☆Elway...

and now ☆ Daniels☆

Drop in at the retirement celebration for George E. Daniels

TUESDAY MAY 18TH 1999

(5PM TO 7PM)

AT

THE ROCK "N" DINER

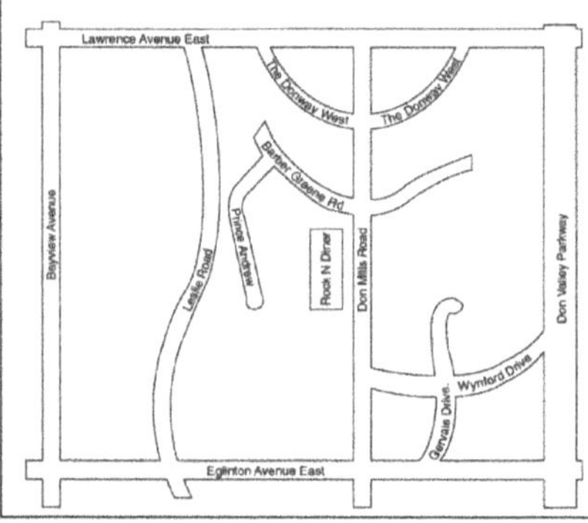

Rock "N" Diner
900 Don Mills Road
North of Eglinton Ave. E.

"Cash bar available."

PART XI

In retirement, George immerses himself in flying, community advocacy, charitable fund-raising projects and family life---and takes an interest in the family history of the Daniels.

Part XI

The Golden Years

The Collingwood Flying Club, its Cessna 177 Cardinal and Young Eagles-COPA for Kids program

Coming up to retirement at Christmas 1999 in Collingwood, I joined the Collingwood Flying Club, a group of a dozen pilots at Collingwood Regional Airport. They had recently bought a 1968 Cessna 177 Cardinal, incorporated as not-for-profit and offered fractional ownership at a reasonable price. A monthly fee of $240 entitled me to two hours flying per month, including fuel, insurance and all expenses. The aircraft was stored in a Quonset hut hanger operated by Collingwood Classic Aircraft Foundation.

Through the years, I had retained my Commercial Pilot license. Maintaining this credential involved an extensive medical by a Transport Canada-approved doctor every six months, attending DOT seminars and various work with an instructor. The club welcomed me, in part, because my commercial license helped keep the group's insurance reasonable.

The CCAF annual *Gathering of the Classics* was an opportunity to put my marketing skills to work. Hundreds of aircraft were joined by classic cars for the early-August event at the Collingwood Regional Airport. Spectators came from far and wide and enjoyed ex-CKEY Radio broadcaster Keith Rich providing delightful public-address commentary about everything on display. I received accolades for generating a huge crowd with my publicity campaign.

In the mid-90s, the number of pilots coming into the industry was declining and the airline industry was concerned about where it was going to get future cockpit crews.

The Experimental Aircraft Association of Oshkosh, Wisconsin came up with a pilot recruitment solution called Young Eagles. The idea was to get general aviation pilots to donate some of their time to take young people for test flights. This was to take place following a brief ground-school session and explanation of aircraft engines and communications.

They formed Young Eagles chapters and a leadership headed up by the first man to break the speed of sound, test pilot Chuck Yeager. EAA/Young Eagles chapters would run events for a dozen or so teenagers with several donated aircraft. At the conclusion, each participant received a Young Eagles certificate signed by the pilot and Chuck Yeager.

I became a Young Eagles volunteer pilot. The North American objective was to fly over one million kids by year 2000. It was far exceeded. Due to insurance reasons, the program in Canada was renamed *COPA for Kids*. I believe you get out of life what you put in and I enjoyed flying these young people several times per year. I'm now considered a Flight Leader in the program.

Aviation is exciting and vital to our nation's future. We demonstrate in the program that flight is a vital part of transportation and communication, the same as cars, buses and trains, computers and the Internet. We show them the advantages of hard work required to achieve a pilot's license to de-mystify the art and science of aviation.

I use the Cessna Cardinal to donate flights for several persons as prizes in fundraising, in particular with our Andrew Daniels' Fish Stewardship Foundation auction. Another use has been to raise dollars for historic restoration projects, rewarding flights with generous donors to raise money for various causes.

The Canadian Owners and Pilots Association recently gave me a diamond-studded wings lapel pin commemorating more than 60 years of membership. I have my US pilot's license and fly out of the Naples Flight Centre in Florida. They recently nominated me for the *Orville Wright 50 Years of Safe Flying Certificate*. I continue to enjoy being aviation current as I fly around central Ontario.

Against the Wind: The battle against wind turbines proposed for Collingwood Regional Airport airspace. George represents the Collingwood Flying Club and general aviation pilots at the Environment and Land Tribunal, a court of justice.

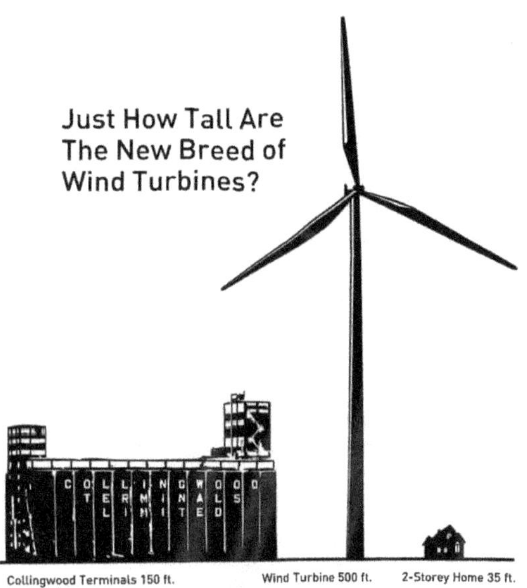

My basic pilot training as a bush and ferry pilot ingrained in me the essential role general aviation plays in the economic well-being of communities. As such, the Collingwood Regional Airport provides vital services and benefits to four municipalities in Southern Georgian Bay. A 14-mile stretch of beach located halfway between Stayner and Collingwood and three miles south of Wasaga Beach, it was used by Amelia Earhart and other early 1930s pilots as a training runway.

I am a member of the Collingwood Flying Club, flying a Cessna Cardinal with a hangar at the airport. We fly COPA for Kids' introductory donated flights. Our flight operations include an interface with airport workers and pilot users. Several maintenance companies, two flight schools and the headquarters of four major corporations' aviation needs account for the three dozen employees at this aviation hub, which is almost a satellite of Toronto's airports.

When one of the largest wind turbine companies announced in 2010 it had contracted with Beatty Brothers Farms, immediately next to the airport lands and main runway, we were appalled. They proposed eight industrial-size turbines 500 feet in height, which would create a disastrous safety hazard to airport flight operations. It did not make sense.

WPD, the wind turbine contractor, orchestrated the project under the Ontario government's Green Energy Act which provided substantial dollars to farmers who would host the placement of wind turbines on their property. This taxpayer-funded largess was like candy to a non-caring farmer.

My Collingwood aviation colleagues and I were disgusted by the apparent total disregard for flight safety. Did they not realize by putting up these structures and compromising the airport's operation, they were going to damage business commerce for their community?

The aviation community was not against alternative sources of green energy, whether solar or wind sourced, but we could not approve of the erection of giant wind turbines which would encroach on flying zones of from 6-15 miles around airports.

Three prominent business people with significant investment tied to the airport galvanized me and a core group to fight the turbine plan. Applications were made to the Ontario Government to rescind the WPD/Beatty Brothers contracts.

This turned out to be a five-year cumbersome legal process costing over $1 million. Evidence-based objections were made to the Environment and Land Tribunal which operates as a court of justice. Three municipalities and their lawyers fought WPD.

I was one of three additional appellants from the private general aviation sector, presenting on behalf of the Collingwood Flying Club and the Andrew Daniels Fish Stewardship Foundation. The Tribunal was particularly diligent in examining the credentials they required for "acknowledgment of expert duty" before permitting me to be accepted as a presenter. Jeff Parton, President of the Collingwood Flying Club, wrote to the Tribunal as follows;

"Mr. Daniels is eminently qualified to advocate our significant concerns about why the building of these eight massive structures should be denied and revoked." He then quoted my commercial pilot license qualifications and the Tribunal quickly agreed that I was an aviation expert. But it took about another hour of legal challenges before they also agreed that I was a qualified Fish Habitat Steward under our Foundation.

The Tribunal dictated that petitioners against the wind turbines must centre their arguments on two aspects; impact on human health and impact on the environment.

I stated that the Collingwood General and Marine Hospital is chartered to protect and provide Simcoe County-area health needs with many services including ambulances both on the ground and in the air. I was adamant that I, as a professional pilot, as well as MedEvac Ontario air ambulance pilots, would be unable to fly around these wind turbines. To fly in and out of the Collingwood Hospital, the MedEvac helicopters have to vector off GPS navigation aids. Inclement and marginal flying weather sweeps in off Georgian Bay during winter months. The hazard represented by wind turbines is just too big a safety risk for pilots and their patients and passengers. I showed this via actual NavCan weather charts and my technical map showing wind shear turbulence caused by wind turbines also reinforced my evidence.

The Batteaux River and its series of headwaters streams come from underneath the proposed turbine construction sites and is a vital spawning habitat for trout and their habitats. On a field trip with the Tribunal chair and legal counsel, we were able to show trout swimming in this stream, another important piece of our environmental evidence.

The Clearview Airport was enhanced by owner and town councillor Kevin Elwood and Chuck Magwood, the latter of SkyDome repute. With John Wiggins, founder of Creemore Springs Brewery, and the Canadian Owners and Pilots Association, they brought over $1 million of legal muscle to counter WPD. Betty Schneider crowd-sourced a 1,200-signature petition. We attended many supplementary hearings to reinforce our case.

The community was very concerned about the proposed blot on the landscape, best summarized by a front page and editorial in *On the Bay Magazine.* It read: 'We are against the wind and the looming onslaught of these industrial turbines in our community. That's why we take an advocacy position to protect what we hold dear.'

We won this court battle. Amidst the celebration, Kevin Elwood said this ruling has national significance for aerodromes.

Alex Besse QC, speaking for the Collingwood legal community said, "George, we were all impressed by your well-researched and articulate presentation to the Tribunal. Well done!"

(As a footnote, in March 2018, MPP Jim Wilson (Simcoe-Grey) rose in the Ontario Legislature and demanded that the Liberal government reimburse the private citizens for expenses caused by the failed project. "These citizens did you a favor. You owe them $1.6 million. Will you not do the right thing and pay them back?").

Memorable Travel

Over the years Ruth and I have been blessed with many opportunities to travel. Whether visiting family in the UK, friends in France or exploring Morocco, the Caribbean and the former Yugoslavia, we have experienced a wealth of understanding through these travel destinations.

We will always remember and feel the history of many places, including these highlights:

- Seeing St. John's, a 300-year-old Anglican Church high on the east coast of the Barbados cliffs in the 1970s, enjoying the Barbados beaches, sugar cane plantations and getting a Barbados' pilot license endorsement.
- Visiting Fortress Louisburg ruins in 1962 in our new Chevy II and then returning in the 1980s to see it had been rebuilt as the largest historic reenactment fortress city in North America.
- Flying to Casablanca on Royal Air Maroc in the early 80s and being in the cockpit of the DC-10 to welcome the dawn prior to landing. Wow! Staying in Agadir with side trips to Rabat and Marrakesh was special, including our coffee and cake stop in a Bedouin tent where we sat on large, plush carpets. We visited the Mamounia Hotel in Marrakesh where we could feel the Churchillian presence from his painting visits. Ruth will never forget her ride on a camel.

The long-lasting friendships we made in the Montreal Advertising and Sales Club in the 1960s were rekindled in 1992 at a reunion of the Club leadership. A dozen of us met for a three-day weekend at our Lake of Bays cottage. It was a lot of fun and the consensus was to have more reunions at the homes and or cities of our alumni.

We were able to do this over the next dozen years and had marvelous times visiting the various homes and destinations of our pals. Our trips were well organized. Our Maritimes and Peggy's Cove visits were enjoyable. Closer to home, we assembled in Barrie, the Thousand Islands, Ottawa and Montreal. California beckoned us three times. In Hawaii in 2000, we celebrated the new century. We cruised the Caribbean and got a taste of Florida, discovering Naples where we have rented a condo in-mid winter for over a dozen years.

My several business vocations have also provided various travel opportunities and Ruth was able to join me on most of the convention trips. My broadcast responsibilities took me to Dallas, Los Angeles, and to St. Lucia, Antigua and Barbados with clients. While with Otaco Transit Seating, we attended the American Public Transit Authority annual conventions in New Orleans, New York, Dallas and San Francisco. In Canada, it was events in Quebec City and Edmonton.

These travels have provided us with priceless experiences.

COPA Flight 85

Collingwood's Community Chapter

"Flying Youth" for Tomorrow

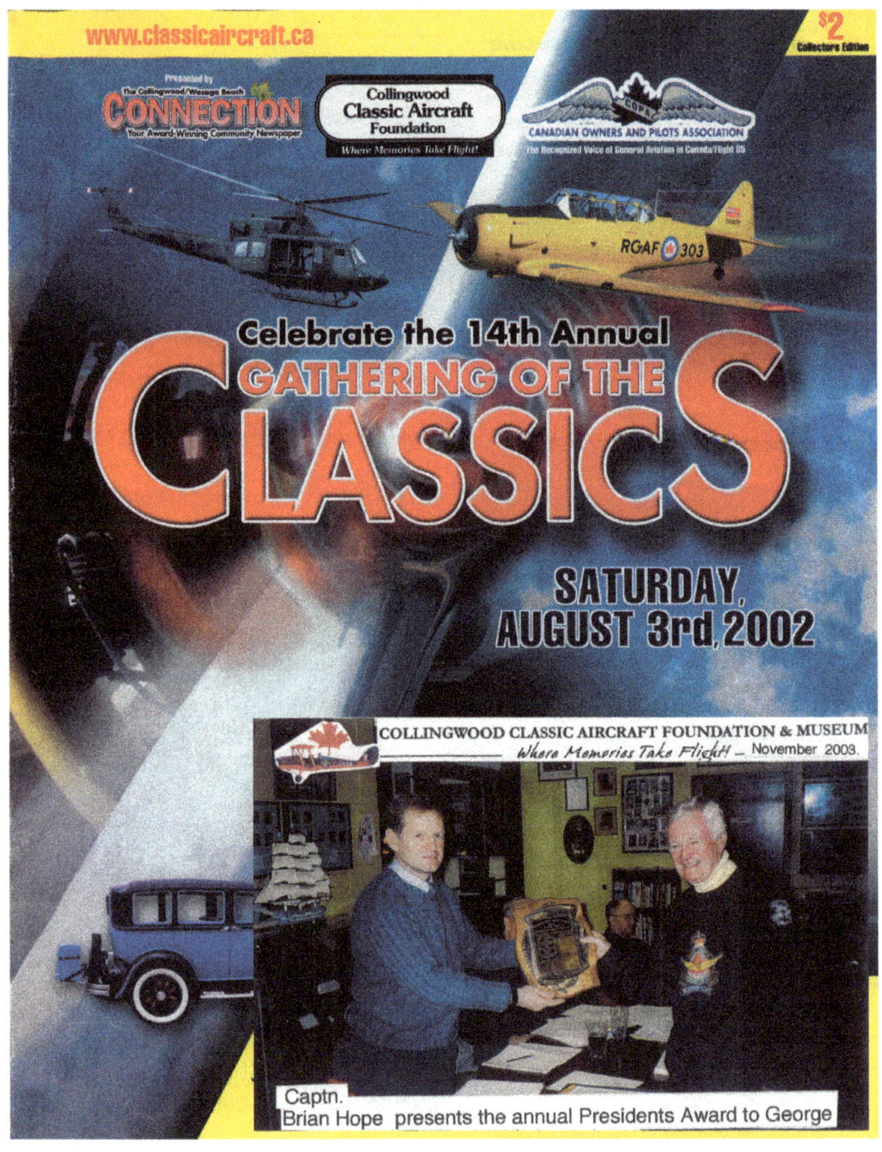

Captn.
Brian Hope presents the annual Presidents Award to George

COPA Flight Captain George Daniels (left)presents Norm Porter with his personalized Founders Members plaque.

L to R - New Young "Boy Scout" Eagles
Warren Young, Blair and Drew Werbitsky

SEE
Lo' Bays - Muskoka
from the air
Fly with Comm. Pilot George Daniels
2 people 1-1¼ hrs. Value $325.00
Diane Crews Co-Pilot, Navg'tr
assists pilot George Daniels Fly
C-FOEK
Member
Year Joined: 1957
Expires: 30 APR 16
COPA
CANADIAN OWNERS AND PILOTS ASSOCIATION
AIR CREW
GEORGE E. DANIELS
MUSKOKA
AIRPORT
LITTLE NORWAY MEMORIAL

CAPTAIN
GEORGE
CARDINAL

George Daniels, Lake of Bays Association executive Brian Simpson and Fraser Govan, also of the Lake of Bays Association, move a log from the path of the weir they recently built at Norway Point as part of a rehabilitation project to enhance fish spawning.

Tragedy spawns a living legacy

Article by Cathy Cahill Kuntz / Photographs by Kelly Holinshead

Andrew Daniels loved to fish, especially on Lake of Bays. He was a respected angler in the area and was known for his catch and release practices. He knew all the best places to fish and was the one others relied on to find out where to go for the best catches.

"When he was three he learned how to turn over rocks and grab crayfish as they tried to scurry away," says his father, George Daniels. "It didn't bother him that they bit. At four or five he'd catch those crayfish and sell them to local fishermen. He went on to become a passionate fisherman."

When Andrew died suddenly in his 38th year on Feb. 5, 2004, family and friends knew they wanted to honour him by doing something that would benefit future generations. What better way than to help protect two things Andrew cared for very much: fishing and Lake of Bays.

"Andrew was passionate about fishing. We'd go out water-skiing; Andrew would be fishing. We'd go out in the boat; Andrew would be fishing," says Bob Ransom, Andrew's neighbour, friend and president of the Andrew Daniels Memorial Fish Stewardship Program. "We wanted to do something that would improve fishing in Lake of Bays – donate something in his name. We discovered there wasn't a fish stewardship program in the area, so, we started one."

The Andrew Daniels Memorial Fish Stewardship

Photographs courtesy of the Daniels Family

Andrew Daniels proudly holds up a fish he caught during a trip to Scotland in 2000 (left). George Daniels, Jackie Godard and Chris Daniels hold up the conservation ruler and fish poster launched by the fish stewardship (below).

Program works to improve fish habitat in Lake of Bays. Family and friends have gone far beyond just donating funds in Andrew's name. The committee consists of numerous individuals who gather once a year to plan.

Five years after the program began, they continue to donate time and effort toward rejuvenating streams and spawning habitat as well as advocating for clean lakes and sustainable shoreline habitat around Lake of Bays.

"When we came up with this idea, we phoned the Ministry of Natural Resources," says Ransom. "They agreed there was a lot to be done. Fisheries biologist Steve Scholten suggested we go out onto the lake and have a look at the conditions before we did anything. We hired someone to survey the tributaries, rivers and lake and determined that the tributaries were in desperately bad shape."

Ransom adds, "People know about the three main rivers but it's the little ones, the tributaries that produce the fish. I'm shocked how important these creeks are to fish habitat. They are a yard wide and a foot deep but they are cold and they are flowing."

The health of smaller streams has deteriorated over the years for a variety of reasons. Deforestation right down to water has caused siltation. Culverts have been installed too high to be used by fish as they migrate upstream. Development has taken place without the consideration of its impact on fish habitat. As a result, brook trout (also known as speckled trout) numbers have decreased because they depend on small tributaries for their habitat.

"Like a canary in a coal mine, brook trout provide

an early warning sign that there is a problem with the condition of a stream for breeding as brook trout are very sensitive to temperature and cannot breed if the water is too warm," explains Bruce Montgomery in a Lake of Bays Association newsletter. Montgomery, a friend and neighbour of Andrew's, is also vice-president of the Andrew Daniels Memorial Fish Stewardship Program. His grandfather, Royal Montgomery, was a founding member of the Lake of Bays Association whose original mandate was to protect the fish of Lake of Bays. He was also the person who taught Andrew Daniels the art of crayfish catching at age three.

Around the time they approached the Ministry of Natural Resources, George Daniels, Andrew's father, explained to Ben Boivin, councillor with the Township of Lake of Bays, what they wanted to do in memory of his son. Boivin told the group about the $25,000 Bigwin Fish Reserve Fund.

"The fund was earmarked for the restoration and rehabilitation of fish habitat on the Lake of Bays," Boivin says. "The council recognized the fit with what the friends and family of Andrew Daniels were trying to do. The Andrew Daniels Memorial Fish Stewardship Fund grew from there."

The program depends on individual donations, municipal contributions and support from the Lake of Bays Association and the Lake of Bays Heritage Foundation. The Township of Lake of Bays, as well as providing funding through the Bigwin Fish Reserve Fund, issues tax receipts for donations to the program. The stewardship has also received grants from the Ministry of Natural Resources.

The finishing touches are put on a new specially engineered culvert at Norway Point designed to facilitate fish as they go from Lake of Bays into Braemore Pond to spawn.

The initial project of the Andrew Daniels Memorial Fish Stewardship Program involved contracting a fish biologist in 2005 to identify and evaluate all the streams flowing into the Lake of Bays and look for evidence of use by brook trout.

"Stream health is crucial to the migration and spawning of brook trout," says Daniels, co-ordinator of the program. "The biologist indicated those streams that were practical to rehabilitate and those that were not."

Jackie Godard and her family have a small stream that runs through their property. In 2005 they were

George Daniels is proud of what the stewardship has accomplished, such as the weir and culvert seen in the distance behind him.

Nick Godard cleans out this small, natural weir on his family's property.

asked if their stream could be part of the study and her sons, Adam and Nicholas, got involved.

"Steve Scholten instructed the boys how to pull back fallen trees and debris that were blocking the brook trout from migrating upstream. Since then, the water has been thick with smelt," Godard says. "Our stream is a good, healthy stream now. We didn't have much to clear this spring and we've seen quite a few fish. It's really very beautiful."

"Seepage areas are important for young fish," explains Scholten. "The channel from the seepage area was blocked by sand so the Godard family opened it up which allowed the young trout to enter. It seemed to be an immediate success because while clearing the channel, they caught a little trout. Jackie's sons continue to keep watch over the area."

That same year the Godard family got involved with the work of the program, Daniels asked Jackie to become involved as secretary of the program.

"Becoming secretary for Andrew Daniels Fish Sponsorship Program was an easy decision for me because it reinforces what I and the other members are passionate about – having a clean, healthy lake and free flowing streams for the survival of our fish habitat," she says.

In 2006, the group, through a partnership with the MNR and financial assistance from the Bigwin Fish Reserve Fund, also launched a new fishing tool: a conservation ruler that contains information about local fish and can be placed on the inside of a fishing boat gunwale. The ruler assists anglers in determining whether to keep or release a fish.

"The MNR used to produce a ruler," Daniels says. "They gave us their artwork, networked us into the MNR printer and gave us a special price. Then we raised $4,000 from local retailers. All the marinas, retailers and the post office have been behind this from the start. It's been marvelous."

In addition, 300 copies of an 11" x 17" Lake of Bays fish poster were paid for by local businesses, lodges and resorts. Both ruler and poster are available for $10 at many retailers and marinas in the Lake of Bays area.

In October 2008 major culvert replacements were completed to help rejuvenate tributary streams and a spawning pool habitat at Norway Point Road and Old Highway 117.

"The tributary at Norway Point used to be full of fish," says Ransom. "We discovered the culverts weren't allowing for the proper fish migration."

The work was a culmination of three years of efforts and was completed under a Township of Lake of Bays contract with consultants.

Scholten explains, "The culverts were identified by the township as in need of replacement. We wanted them replaced in a way that was best for the stream."

The Department of Fisheries and Oceans worked with Scholten to lay out the appropriate engineering required for the project. As a result of the culvert replacement, the water will always be deep enough to allow fish to run up the creek to their natural breeding grounds.

"We were out there, watching the work on the culverts," says Daniels. "It was quite nerve-racking, like having a baby, but, we did it."

The township has now committed to installing fish-friendly culverts all around the lake as replacements and upgrades are made.

"Any one of these tributaries are not particularly significant but, collectively, they are important to the health of the lake," says Scholten. "This group of people are increasing awareness on the lake about the importance of protecting fish habitat, particularly small streams. Lake of Bays, as one of the larger lakes in Muskoka, is unique because it still has brook trout. This is a growing project that's moving from doing inventories to doing more hands-on projects."

This year the Andrew Daniels Memorial Fish Stewardship Program has its sights set on the Boyne and Oxtongue Rivers and Rabbit's Bay stream.

"First, we'll study them to see if they need rehabilitation. We'll look at the Oxtongue River at Marsh's Falls to see if a fish ladder is needed to allow the fish to go up stream to spawn and if there is anything else we need to do to enhance spawning in that area," says Boivin

Scholten adds, "We hope to do some hands-on protection work on the Rabbit River where the expansion of the boat launch and parking lot are starting to have an impact on the stream."

Water temperature data loggers will also be temporarily installed on the Boyne River this summer so temperature data information from the season can be studied.

"We've learned about the dynamics of the lake and the changes that occur," says Ransom. "It's a fish eat fish world and we are figuring out what we can and can't do to help turn things around. There are a hundred things we could be doing but we're being diligent. We keep slowly moving ahead. It took time to get into this mess and it will take time to fix it."

This year the group is also hoping to continue working at Norway Point in order to deepen an area that provides over wintering and nursery habitat for brook trout.

Thomas Ransom, Bob's son, and a number of other young people will assist in the rehabilitation efforts this year.

"We'll recruit 10 or so kids to walk up and down the river to remove leaves and rocks and clear silt and garbage," Ransom says. "We want lower and deeper waters."

The Andrew Daniels Memorial Fish Stewardship Program has also made several applications on various fish stewardship initiatives for G8 funding.

"None of this would have been possible if not for people like Bob Ransom, Bruce Montgomery, Ben Boivin, Jackie Godard, Steve Scholten and families like the Robinsons and Woodsides who understand what they as landowners can do to help improve the lake," says Daniels.

Daniels has been a link to many of the organizations that have worked together for the good of the lake. He participated on the board of the Lake of Bays Association from 1968 until 1994 and was founding co-chair of the Lake of Bays Heritage Foundation in 1985.

"It's good to know there are people concerned about fish in our lakes," says Boivin. "We're at a critical time. Once these fish disappear, they won't come back. It's important to preserve these indigenous species for future generations. We want to do it now for our grandchildren."

Daniels hopes other areas take note of the work done in memory of his son and adopt similar practices to protect the fish in their area.

"We have to protect what's left," Daniels says. "There used to be 70 tributaries. Now there are only two dozen left that are really important. It's rewarding to see people come on board and understand it is now a community-based organization. This will be going on long after I'm gone. It really is a living legacy to Andrew."

For More Information
Andrew Daniels Fish Stewardship Foundation
c/o 1002-1, Montgomery Point Rd. Dwight, ON P0A 1H0

Chris & George Daniels 705-635-3224
Jacquie Godard 705-787-1675
Steve Scholten MNR Fisheries - Biologist 705-646-5523

Antigua 1981.
With CFRB 1010 Radio station personnel,
Sales Reward week for staff and clients.

Greece 2007,
In the footsteps of Saint Paul, Athens,
Ephesus, Turkey.

Greece 2007, (cont'd)
In the footsteps of Saint Paul, including
Corinth, George in a roman bathtub.

England 2004
Saint Neots
Sleyburn, Lancashire, near Scorton.

England 2004 (cont'd)

The Titled Wig - our hotel

Warwick Castle

Yugoslavia, Dubrovnik 1987.
Familiarization trip courtesy of client JAT Yugoslav Airlines.

On the hotel balcony which is Tito's former villa overlooking the Port of Dubrovnik.

Prince Edward Island Ferry, 1962

April 1979 Returning from Boston Marathon at Sturbridge, Massachusetts.

Daniels
The Family Of
George and Keren-Happuch Daniels
H.Norman Daniels, George E. Daniels
& Family Contributors October 2011

The U.K. - Canada - U.S.A. Book of Daniels

This unique Daniels' family Heritage and History has been 10 years in development. It all started in July 1986 at the Biggleswade Chronicle Archives search ..to a Toronto reunion in 2000 at Elizabeth(Daniels) & Nigel Taylor's home , that the Authors have been working towards this book. A very interesting adventure to experience.

We have had enthusiastic support from many relatives. Of note Myrtle(Toni) & Harold Batcheldor supplied the original 1914 photo of the " Grand " George and Keren - Happuch with their 9 children. Mary (Peck) Smith, Julie Smith,& Margaret (Daniels) Newson wrote interesting family stories. Norman and George, in addition to writing, did considerable research. We received supportive photos out of many family albums,- for this we thank you.

The Book is bound with a Cirlox spine which allows one to add more pages as time goes on (Most Print Shops have a Cirlox bindery machine so you can easily re-assemble.) It is printed on recycled paper.

Understanding our family tree and legacy is a benchmark for the future. Enjoy !

H. Norman Daniels and George E. Daniels, 2011.

AUNT MAY'S WEDDING DAY APRIL 15th 1914

Standing from left CONNIE, HERBERT ARTHUR, DAISY, MAY, GLEN, LILIAN.
Sitting " " VIOLET, GEORGE, KEREN-HAPPUCH, ALBERT GEORGE, GERTRUDE.

CERTIFIED COPY OF AN ENTRY OF MARRIAGE

GIVEN AT THE GENERAL REGISTER OFFICE

Application Number G 011031.

1873. Marriage solemnized at the Old Baptist Chapel in the District of Biggleswade in the County of Bedford

No.	When Married	Name and Surname	Age	Condition	Rank or Profession	Residence at the time of Marriage	Father's Name and Surname	Rank or Profession of Father
12	Sixteenth October 1873	George Daniels the younger	21 years	Bachelor	Garden Laborer	Biggleswade	George Daniels the younger	Market Gardener
		Keren Happuch Chambers	20 years	Spinster	—	Broom	George Chambers the younger	Market Gardener

Married in the Baptist meeting according to the Rites and Ceremonies of the Baptists by Certificate by me,

This Marriage was solemnized between us, George Daniels Junr, Keren Happuch Chambers

in the Presence of us, Thomas Wagstaff, Priscilla Daniels

Joseph Simpson, Minister

Gilbert Hoppus, Registrar

Biggleswade 22nd March 1993

MX 633204

CAUTION.—It is an offence to falsify a certificate or to make or knowingly use a false certificate or a copy of a false certificate intending it to be accepted as genuine to the prejudice of any person, or to possess a certificate knowing it to be false without lawful authority.

WARNING: THIS CERTIFICATE IS NOT EVIDENCE OF THE IDENTITY OF THE PERSON PRESENTING IT.

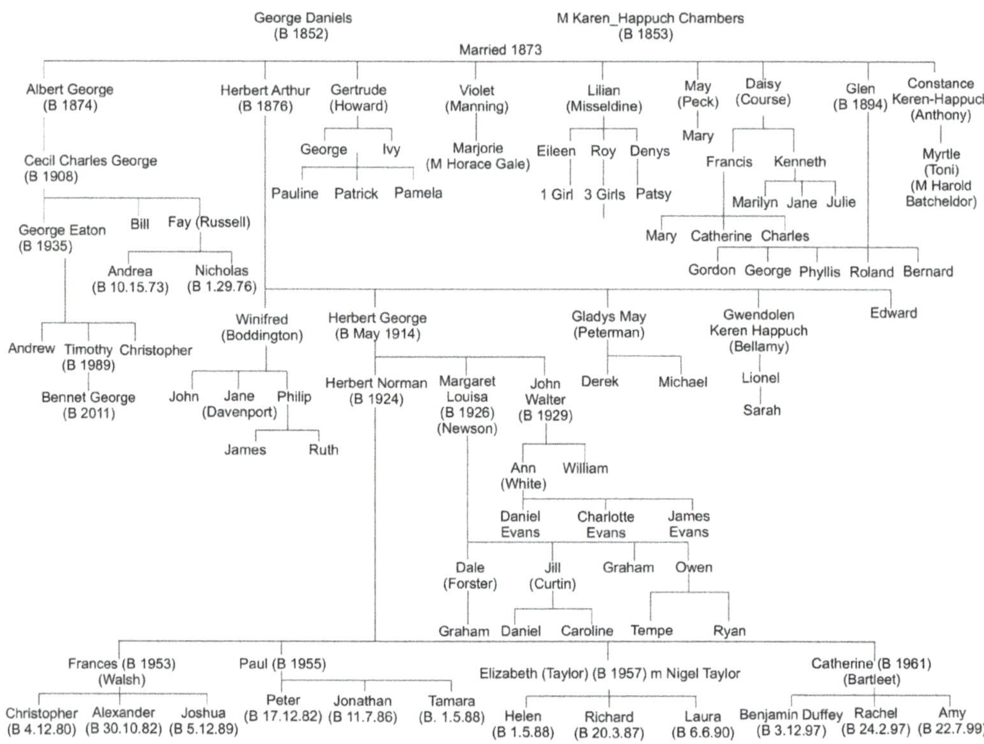

Daisy Louisa Daniels
b.6.3.1889
d.15.12.1966

m

Charles Henry Course
b.6.4.1884
d.6.3.1961

Francis George
b. 11.2.1916
d. 3.1.2007

m
25.5.1960

Meryl Elizabeth Lower
(Known as Betty)
b. 7.7.1928

Charles Paul
b. 17.9.1961
m (19.10.1995)

Siobhan Duff
(now separated)

Mary Elizabeth
b. 2.11.1962
m (20.6.1937)

Neil Rothwell Hughes

Frances Aiys
b. 15.3.1993

Hari Griffydd
b. 29.11.1999

Catherine Meryl
b. 17.2.1965
m (2.10.1993)

Alan Keily

Sam Alexaner
b. 30.5.1999

Kenneth Charles
b. 13.10.1919

m
7.9.1946

June Mary Chandler
b. 27.7.1920
d. 14.11.2005

Marilyn Ron
b. 13.11.1947
m (10.4.1971)

John Lingings
b. 2.4.1948

Emma Kathryn
b. 11.11.1975
lives with partner

Maxime Carasmel

Jules William Henry
b. 14.10.2002

Charlotte Anna Elizabeth
b. 15.3.2005

Amy Elizabeth
b. 12.3.1973
m (29.14.2006)

Matthew Mager

Mary Elizabeth
b. 2.11.1962
m (20.6.1937)

Lewis Derek Harvey
b. 3.3.1931
d. 24.5.1996

married for 2nd time
to
Melvin Garlick
on 7.9.2004
b. 27.2.1945

Rosemarie Julie
(Known as Julie)
b. 23.6.1958
m (1.8.1931)

Alan Leonard Smith

Michael Leonard
b. 23.3.1988

Alexander Charles
b. 3.17.1990

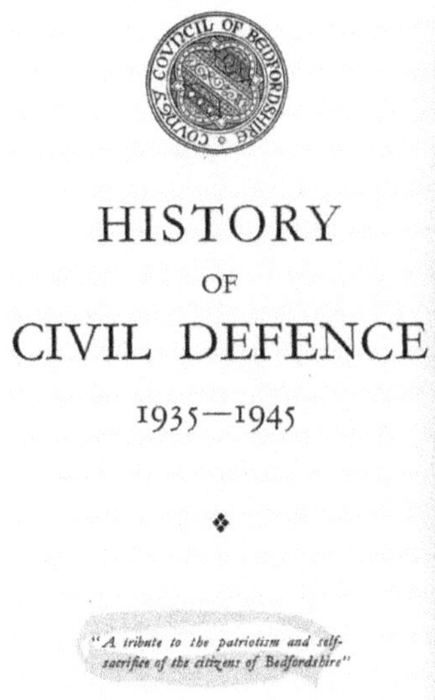

HISTORY
OF
CIVIL DEFENCE
1935—1945

❖

"A tribute to the patriotism and self-sacrifice of the citizens of Bedfordshire"

DAYLIGHT RAID ON BEDFORD

Photograph by "The Bedfordshire Times"

DAMAGE TO THE GROSVENOR HOTEL, ASHBURNHAM ROAD, ON 23RD JULY, 1942

WEST BEDS. AREA.
Police Station, Ampthill.
Marston Valley Brick Co., Ridgmont.
Police House, Aspley Heath.

CODE WORDS USED IN THE N
SYST

"Air Raid Message Yellow" =
"Air Raid Message White" =
"Air Raid Warning Red" =
"Air Raid Message Green" =

Subsequently the "Yellow and G "Message White" substituted in "Message Purple" replaced "Mes extinguishing of certain lights.

WARDEN

BEDFORD BOROUGH.
Garage, 8 Rothsay Road.
Training Centre, "Gordon Arms," 129a Castle Road.
Newnham Avenue (formerly Beresford Road).
Newnham Avenue, Corner of Wendover Drive (formerly 10 Wendover Drive).
Garage, "Fox and Hounds" Public House, Goldington Road.
362 Goldington Road.
Goldington Green.
51 De Parys Avenue (formerly Park Avenue).
Garage, 2 Pemberley Avenue.
162 Kimbolton Road.
2 Richmond Road.
64 Harpur Street.
Union Street (formerly 173 Tavistock Street).
65 Chaucer Road.
Greyfriars' Mission Hall, Greyfriars Walk.

Uncle Harry Manning's office and workshop where dad worked.

This poster widely distributed in the UK during WWII

241991 12th August 1946.

Sir,

Now that the time has come for your release from active military duty, I am commanded by the Army Council to express to you their thanks for the valuable services which you have rendered in the service of your country at a time of grave national emergency.

At the end of the emergency you will relinquish your commission, and at that time a notification will appear in the London Gazette (Supplement), granting you also the honorary rank of Captain. Meanwhile, you have permission to use that rank with effect from the date of your release.

I am, Sir,

Your obedient Servant,

Captain C.C.G. Daniels,
Royal Engineers.

THE GLOBE AND MAIL,
SATURDAY, JANUARY 31, 1987

DANIELS, Cecil Charles George — At Peel Memorial Hospital, Brampton, on Thursday, January 29, 1987, Cecil Charles George Daniels, in his 80th year. Dearly loved husband of 53 years to Bunty (Margaret Muriel). Dear father to sons George Eaton Daniels of Toronto and his wife Ruth, and Cecil William Daniels of London and Brampton, and daughter, Faith (Russell) and husband, Phillip of Victoria, B.C. Loving grandfather of Andrew, Timothy and Christopher Daniels of Toronto and Andrea and Nicholas Russell of Victoria, B.C. A varied career started in East Africa on the Kenya Uganda Railway followed by serving with distinction in the Eighth Army as Captain, Royal Engineers and in the Middle East on the Tel-Aviv-Haifa Pipeline. In Canada, his significant contributions included shared responsibiltiy of building some of Canada's prominent landmarks such as Port Churchill, the Trans Canada Microwave System, The Calgary Bow River Project, Expo '67 and Canada's first subway system in Toronto. Funeral arrangements are entrusted to the Ward Funeral Home, Brampton. A private family service will take place at Meadowvale Cemetery. If desired, donations to the Peel Memorial Hospital Foundation, Brampton would be gratefully appreciated.

St. Peter's Church
Scorton
Vestry Memorial Plaque
Note: Captian CC George Daniels
Royal Engineers
4th from the top left.

Some Daniels moved West to Canada & The United States

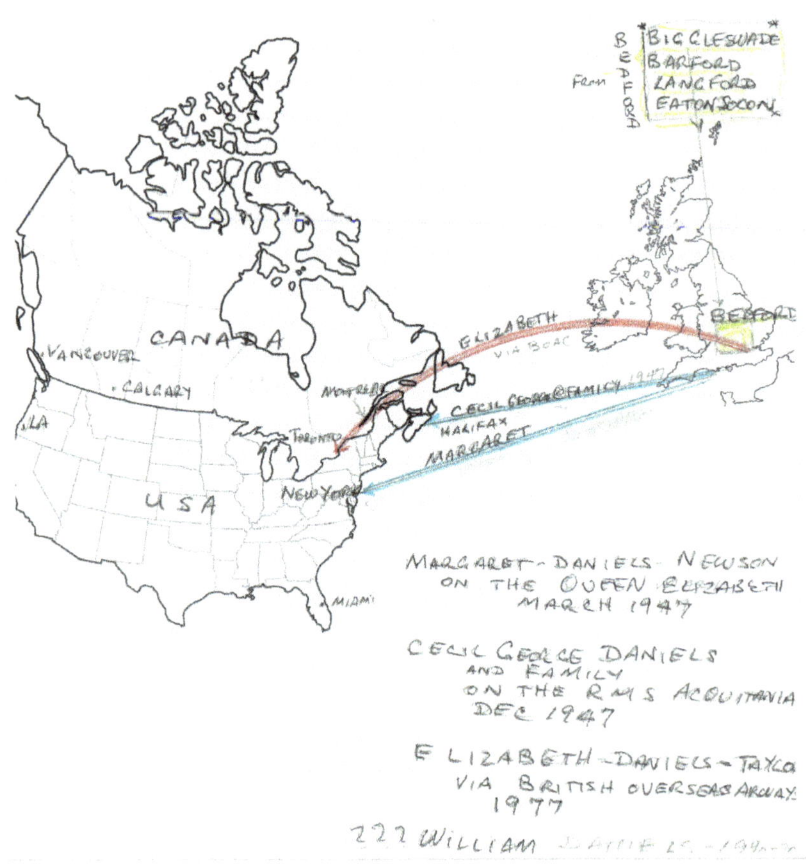

Margaret "Bunty" Daniels
Grandma Jessie Amelia Burton Daniels
(Cecil's Mother)
George and Bill
Scorton Lancashire
Circa 1942 to 1943

THE DANIELS FAMILY ARRIVE IN CANADA
ON THE R.M.S. AQUITANIA
PIER 21 DECEMBER 20, 1947

Our arrival in Canada 1947

SEEN HERE ON THE
DECK OF THE
R.M.S. AQUITANIA
HALIFAX PIER 21
DEC. 20 1947

FRONT ROW - LEFT TO RIGHT
BILL DANIELS AGE 9½
FAITH DANIELS AGE 5
GEORGE DANIELS AGE 12½

BACK ROW - LEFT TO RIGHT
SHIPBOARD NANNIE (NAME UNKNOWN)
MARGARET MURIEL (BUNTY) DANIELS (MOTHER)
CECIL CHARLES GEORGE DANIELS (FATHER)

FATHER, WHO HAVING BEEN IN CANADA FOR NINE MONTHS CAME FROM MONTREAL TO WELCOME HIS FAMILY.

Biggleswade Chronicle
Friday, September 23, 2011 www.biggleswadetoday.co.uk

From Canada to Chronicle

Ruth & George Daniels Sept. 20, 2011

A MAN whose grandfather was born in Biggleswade but whose family never knew of his background has returned to the town.

George Daniels, who was born in Bedford and his wife Ruth have lived in Ontario, Canada for most of their lives but still make occasional trips to Chronicle Country.

George's father Cecil was estranged from his father George and the two never discussed where George senior was born and brought up.

It was only when Cecil was in his hospital bed in Canada in the mid 1980s that he revealed his birthplace to the family.

George, 76, who attended the Bedfordshire Steam and Country Fayre at Shuttleworth while on holiday with Ruth on Sunday, said: "My father and grandfather were estranged and so my grandfather's background and childhood were never really discussed.

"I was with my father at his hospital bed before he died and he told me that my grandfather was actually born in Biggleswade."

George, who runs a communications and marketing consultancy business wanted to find out more so he travelled to Biggleswade in the late 1980s to research his family history.

He added: "There was an issue of the Biggleswade Chronicle which had his death notice in it but of course there were not many other details about where he had lived or what he did.

"I actually came into the office one day and looked through the archives, and in those days they actually published a list of the mourners who had attended the funeral.

"I managed to track one of them down and took things from there."

George still has a strong connection with Chronicle Country and is also in touch with acquaintances he has made in Bedford.

He was born in Harper Street and still returns to the area when he is in the UK.

Sam Vernon
Reporter

Descendants of George and Keren-Happuch Daniels' reunion
at Shuttleworth / Old Warden Aerodrome, Sunday Sept. 18, 2011
Front., L to R; Mary (Peck) Smith, descendant of May Daniels,
Ruth Daniels, Marilyn Lingings & sister Julie Smith
descendants of Daisy Daniels. Rear; Alan Smith,
George E. Daniels' grandson of Albert George Daniels,& John Lingings.

Excerpt from the 2012
Lake of Bays Assoc. Yearbook

"Tragedy Spawns Living Legacy"

...said Muskoka Magazine July '09

It has been 8 years since Lake of Bays avid angler (catch and release) Andrew Daniels died. Since then the Andrew Daniels Fish (Memorial) Stewardship Program has earned a prominent place in the good governance of Fish Habitat Resources around Lake of Bays.

Partnering with the Ministry of Natural Resources- Fisheries Biologists,The Dept. of Fisheries & Oceans and the Township of Lake of Bays we have shared responsibility for rejuvenating various Streams, Shoreline and Spawning Beds around the Lake. Of course, we also appreciate the very valued support of LOBA and the Lake of Bays Heritage Foundation in this work.

The Andrew Daniels Fish Stewardship has conducted Brooke Trout, Bass, Smelt and Northern Pike Fish Studies.. and more are in the planning stages for 2012 in conjunction with Fleming College (Lindsay) Fisheries Technology third year students. Our Management Group of a dozen keen Volunteers include seasonal and permanent residents. The Stream and Shoreline property owners such as the Godards, Edgars, Robertsons and Hatkoskis - to mention a few, are active drivers of this initiative.

To fine tune our name & brand we have retained Thoms & Currie, a Huntsville law firm to incorporate. They are in the process of helping us become a Charitable (Tax receiptable) Foundation..watch for the news soon.

Andrew's Catch
(Then released)
Bass at Brittania
Lake of Bays
Mid 1990's

Fish Stewardship Program
Lake of Bays
E-mail: adfsp@live.com

Tiff & Leah Daniels
& Baby Bennett (10 months)
Oct. 2011

International Ski Coach Chris on the Zermatt Glacier, Sept. 2011.
Note the Matterhorn in the background.

Harpur Street
Bedford

64. Uncle Harry Manning's design and decorating shop.
Harry married Violet Daniels and his craftsman skills were significant. His firm;H.S.Manning & Son were well known throughout England. One example is they decorated over 150 English Churches.

Following WWII he sold his building to his Methodist Church friend lawyer Ken Ewart Martel. Ken Martel was then joined by Harold Batcheldor (Myrtle) and they continued the Law firm until the late 1980's when Harold & Toni retired to Illminster.

Friday July 4, 1986

64 Harpur St. Bedford
Martel & Batcheldor Law Firm
Shown: Harold & Ruth Daniels

#65. George E. Daniels was born on June 23 1935 at this address. Parents Margaret (Bunty) & Cecil Daniels operated a beauty/ hairdressing salon shop called Titian at this location. Bunty, with red hair, named her shop after the famous Venetian Painter Titian who often used bright golden auburn colours in his paintings. Today the retailer in this store is a flower shop called Fleurette.

George's Birthplace.
Upstairs apartment, 65 Harpur St.
Mummy & Pops
Street Level
Beauty Shop Called "Titian"
Seen here: George visits on his 69th birthday, June 23, 2004

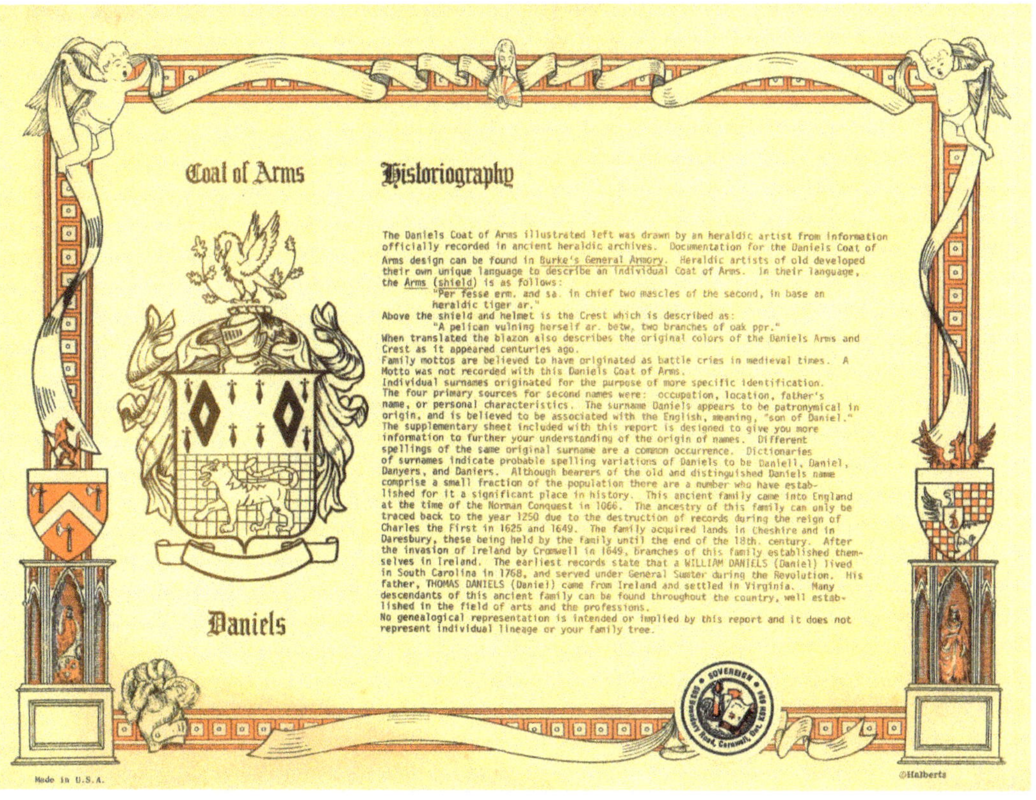

Coat of Arms

Daniels

Historiography

The Daniels Coat of Arms illustrated left was drawn by an heraldic artist from information officially recorded in ancient heraldic archives. Documentation for the Daniels Coat of Arms design can be found in Burke's General Armory. Heraldic artists of old developed their own unique language to describe an individual Coat of Arms. In their language, the Arms (shield) is as follows:

"Per fesse erm. and sa. in chief two mascles of the second, in base an heraldic tiger ar."

Above the shield and helmet is the Crest which is described as:

"A pelican vulning herself ar. betw, two branches of oak ppr."

When translated the blazon also describes the original colors of the Daniels Arms and Crest as it appeared centuries ago.

Family mottos are believed to have originated as battle cries in medieval times. A Motto was not recorded with this Daniels Coat of Arms.

Individual surnames originated for the purpose of more specific identification. The four primary sources for second names were: occupation, location, father's name, or personal characteristics. The surname Daniels appears to be patronymical in origin, and is believed to be associated with the English, meaning, "son of Daniel." The supplementary sheet included with this report is designed to give you more information to further your understanding of the origin of names. Different spellings of the same original surname are a common occurrence. Dictionaries of surnames indicate probable spelling variations of Daniels to be Daniell, Daniel, Danyers, and Daniers. Although bearers of the old and distinguished Daniels name comprise a small fraction of the population there are a number who have established for it a significant place in history. This ancient family came into England at the time of the Norman Conquest in 1066. The ancestry of this family can only be traced back to the year 1250 due to the destruction of records during the reign of Charles the First in 1625 and 1649. The family acquired lands in Cheshire and in Daresbury, these being held by the family until the end of the 18th. century. After the invasion of Ireland by Cromwell in 1649, branches of this family established themselves in Ireland. The earliest records state that a WILLIAM DANIELS (Daniel) lived in South Carolina in 1768, and served under General Sumter during the Revolution. His father, THOMAS DANIELS (Daniel) came from Ireland and settled in Virginia. Many descendants of this ancient family can be found throughout the country, well established in the field of arts and the professions.

No genealogical representation is intended or implied by this report and it does not represent individual lineage or your family tree.

Made in U.S.A.

©Halberts

The Cottage Scorton
Owners: Moss Family
Son: Jeff Moss a.k.a. Father Christmas
George and Son
Chris visit in Summer 2004

PART XII
EPILOGUE

The shot clock is counting down and the author has some thoughts as he looks back at his life.

Part XII

The Last Paragraphs

My life has certainly been a remarkable adventure; not without its attendant difficulties, but certainly with an abundance of joys and rewards.

I am reminded of Dr. Denis Waitley's analogy:

"Look on life as four quarters in a football game—two 15-minute periods in the first half of play, a 15-minute intermission, followed by the last two 15-minute periods."

I agree. I am now well into the fourth quarter of my life game, and to carry on Dr. Waitley's theme, some of the replay highlights from the first three quarters involve success, well-being and self-satisfaction. All have been my life-long teammates.

Many years ago, Ruth presented me with a small note which I cherish to this day. It simply says;

Happiness:

- Something to do
- Someone to love
- Something to hope and look forward to

As I write this in 2018, I am acutely aware that my game clock is winding down, and yet there is so much left to contribute to my family, my community and my country. I invite you to keep watching as I head for the finish line.

What makes George tick? The answers are within some of these truths. Persistence works for one to get ahead. Education will not; the world is full of educated derelicts. Heritage and money will not. The one thing that propels you ahead is persistence. It is omnipotent. (Author unknown.)

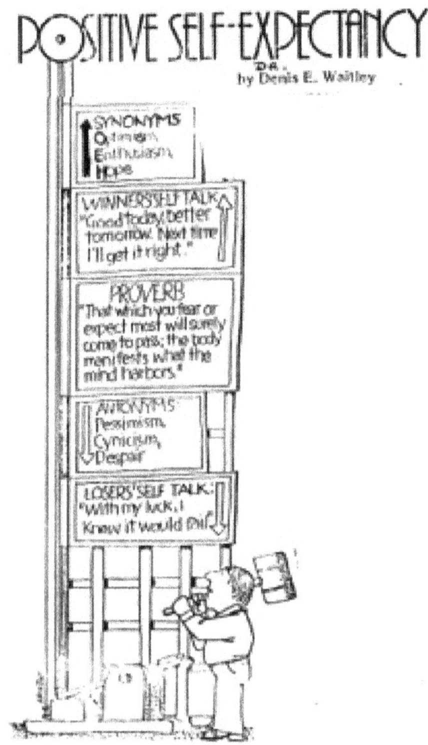

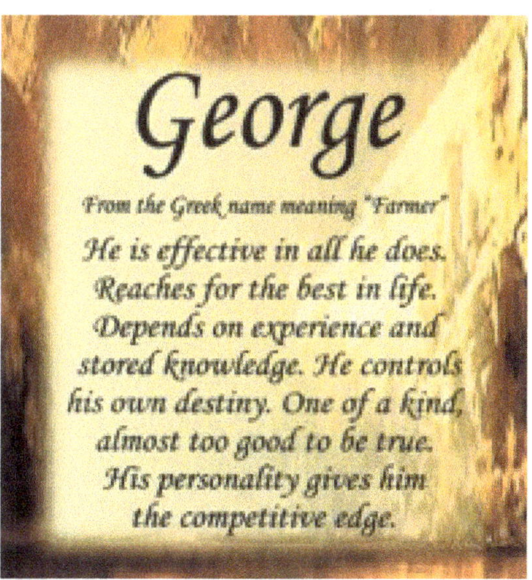

My eidetic memory was identified by close friend John Luke and has been important in helping me write my life story. The dictionary explains eidetic is the extraordinary ability to vividly recall images from memory after only a few instances of exposure and with high precision.

11 COMMANDMENTS FOR AN ENTHUSIASTIC TEAM

1. HELP EACH OTHER BE RIGHT — NOT WRONG.
2. LOOK FOR WAYS TO MAKE NEW IDEAS WORK — NOT FOR REASONS THEY WON'T.
3. IF IN DOUBT — CHECK IT OUT! DON'T MAKE NEGATIVE ASSUMPTIONS ABOUT EACH OTHER.
4. HELP EACH OTHER WIN AND TAKE PRIDE IN EACH OTHER'S VICTORIES.
5. SPEAK POSITIVELY ABOUT EACH OTHER AND ABOUT YOUR ORGANIZATION AT EVERY OPPORTUNITY.
6. MAINTAIN A POSITIVE MENTAL ATTITUDE NO MATTER WHAT THE CIRCUMSTANCES.
7. ACT WITH INITIATIVE AND COURAGE AS IF IT ALL DEPENDS ON YOU.
8. DO EVERYTHING WITH ENTHUSIASM — IT'S CONTAGIOUS.
9. WHATEVER YOU WANT — GIVE IT AWAY.
10. DON'T LOSE FAITH — NEVER GIVE UP.
11. HAVE FUN!!

IAN PERCY

PART XIII

Honours and awards

Part XIII

Honours and Awards

- Governor General's Sovereign Medal
- Ontario Senior of the Year medal
- Queen's Diamond Jubilee citation
- Diamond Anniversary Wings pin by the Canadian Owners and Pilots Association
- Board of Governors' Award for his contributions to education at Georgian College
- Betty Day Award by the Board of the Lake of Bays Association
- Life Membership (#M340045) in the Canadian Professional Sales Association for his contributions to the Association with respect to marketing, motivational and keynote presentations since 1974
- Collingwood Classic Aircraft President's Plaque for a marketing and promotional campaign that generated the highest-ever attendance
- Harvard Graduate School of Business Plaque recognizing his selection as one of 50 graduates from North America (one of three Canadians)
- The last Canadian to be named a King's Scout, preceding the death of King George VI two months later, when the honor was renamed Queen's Scout

Epilogue - Natural Environment

Natural Environment

This award recognizes those who have shown how to lessen human impact on the environment and made a long-term commitment to preserving Muskoka's well-being while encouraging others to practice good stewardship in the future.

Tamsen Tilson from Lake of Bays Brewing presents the Natural Environment Muskoka Award to George Daniels for his work protecting the environment.

George Daniels

George Daniels got his pilot's license in 1956. He takes people flying over Muskoka in his Cessna 177 Cardinal, to help raise funds for local charities through silent auctions.

But that's not all this energetic 78-year-old former broadcast executive does to contribute. His chief passion is Lake of Bays – both the community in which he cottages and the lake itself.

"Brook trout are highly sensitive to the environment: the water they swim in, the air that is around the water and all the junk that mankind throws at them," says Daniels. "Lake of Bays is one of the few lakes, and maybe the only lake outside of Algonquin Park that has brook trout. The fact that we have them means we have a good lake . . . so let's keep it that way."

As well as volunteering for the Lake of Bays association for 25 years including two years as president, Daniels helped found the Andrew Daniels Fish Stewardship Foundation, named after his late son, in 2004. He also co-founded the Lake of Bays Heritage Foundation, helped raise funds for a fireboat on the lake, and helps run the annual Lake of Bays Anglican Church Regatta. He was a recipient of the Queen's Diamond Jubilee Medal last year.

Being around Lake of Bays since his 20s means Daniels has seen big changes. "The condo-ization of Muskoka and fractional ownership has been a significant change," he says.

Daniels has been working hard to meld the interests of the permanent residents with the interests of the seasonal resident. "They're really the same interests," he says.

"Selecting a beneficial project, having the judgment to anticipate its success, selecting a willing volunteer team, and having the ability to mobilize and inspire them to go with the plan," says Daniel, defining his idea of leadership.

"I have no magic halo, I just try to make things happen," he says. "You get more out of life than you put in, so you might as well put in a lot."

George Daniels is the recipient of the Muskoka Award for Natural Environment.

The 11 recipients of the 2013 Muskoka Awards gather together after a night of celebrating the notable achievements of all the nominees.

reflected in those branches and you can never underestimate the talents of individual people," says Brock. "Tonight just brings to the forefront what I've always thought about people and I have a positive feeling about people generally."

All nominees are recognized and honoured not only at the gala dinner, but in print and on TV Cogeco, which plays a taping of the event throughout the year. All recipients received a mounted piece of pottery artwork from Jon Partridge and all nominees receive a lapel pin made of pewter.

Don Smith, publisher of *Muskoka Magazine*, led the evening by saying a few words and introducing Leah Leslie. sen-

Froude. His treatments are not covered, plus extra money will be necessary for renovations to his home to ensure Froude has the proper equipment when he returns.

"Last year at this time I had the privilege of presenting the Muskoka Award for citizen of the year to Gary Froude," she

she was quite honoured to be offered this tremendous opportunity. After the show, while signing CDs, she took time out to discuss the experience.

"Doing an awards show like this really brings home how many people there are who are working for the betterment of our community in Muskoka," she

"I had no idea the size of the event and how many people were being celebrated."

was really inspiring."

Now living in Nashville, Banks joked about needing 48 hours in Muskoka for her Southern drawl to dissipate and played a handful of tunes showcasing her vocal and guitar abilities.

"There are certain songs that were really influenced by growing up in Muskoka," she says. "It was kind of neat to have the opportunity to play them in a show like this where it is more meaningful."

The evening as a whole touched Banks but it was while reading the accomplishments of the nominees and recipients which drove home to her how truly amazing each individual and organization is.

"I had no idea the size of the event and

CANADIAN OWNERS AND PILOTS ASSOCIATION

Thank you

GEORGE E. DANIELS

For 60 years as a COPA member

Bernard Gervais APRIL 2016.
COPA President

On the left: George's Canadian tie from the 1984 Olympic Gala.
Above are his Diamond Anniversary COPA Wings.
The left medal is the Queen's Diamond Jubilee, 2012 and on the right is the Sovereign Medal for Volunteerism 2016.

The Governor General's Caring Canadian Award

Le Prix du Gouverneur général pour l'entraide

is awarded to est décerné à

George E. Daniels

In recognition of your outstanding and selfless contribution to your community and to Canada.

En reconnaissance de votre remarquable et généreuse contribution envers votre communauté et le Canada.

Governor General of Canada

Gouverneur général du Canada

2014

Certificat d'enregistrement du
Droit d'auteur

Certificate of Registration of
Copyright

Ce certificat d'enregistrement est émis conformément aux articles 49 et 53 de la Loi sur le droit d'auteur. Le droit d'auteur sur l'oeuvre décrite ci-dessous, a été enregistré à la date d'enregistrement comme suit :

This Certificate of Registration is issued pursuant to sections 49 and 53 of the Copyright Act. The copyright in the work described below was registered on the date of registration as follows:

Date d'enregistrement - Date of Registration : **January 5, 2017**

Numéro d'enregistrement - Registration No. : **1136508**

Première publication - First Publication : **Unpublished**

Titre - Title : **George Works ! Lad to Leadership, The Making of a New Canadian , George E. Daniels.**

Catégorie - Category : **Literary**

Titulaire(s) - Owner(s) : **George Daniels**
47 Fourth St. East
Collingwood, Ontario
Canada, L9Y 1T2

Auteur(s) - Author(s) : **George Daniels**

CANADA 150

Date d'émission du certificat - Date of Issuance of Certificate : **January 5, 2017**

Commissaire aux brevets Commissioner of Patents

(CIPO - 200)
12-12-16

Canada

FRIDAY, MAY 15, 2015 ■ THE ENTERPRISE-BULLETIN

COMMUNITY: Collingwood and Lake of Bays' George Daniels recently given award by Governor General in Ottawa ceremony

Daniels honoured with Community Caring Award

Special to the Enterprise-Bulletin

George Daniels of Collingwood and Lake of Bays recently received a prestigious award, along with 49 other Canadians.

The Community Caring Award was presented April 14 by Governor General David Johnston at his home on Sussex Drive in Ottawa. It was given to Daniels for his longtime contributions to the communities in which he lives, including 25 years on the Lake of Bays Association and co-founding the Lake of Bays Heritage Foundation.

The Community Caring award recognizes an individual who volunteers their time to help others and to build a smarter and more caring nation.

In 2009, Daniels was presented with the Betty Day Award which is given annually to a Lake of Bays Association member who has contributed leadership and vision to further the goals of the association and the general welfare of the Lake of Bays.

In 2012, he was recipient of the Queens Diamond Jubilee award which is a medal that symbolizes dedication to their community. In 2013 he receive the Natural Environment Award at the Muskoka Awards which was presented for all his hard work through the Andrew Daniels Fish Stewardship Foundation on their commitment to preserving the Lake of Bays and keeping the lake healthy. In June of 2014, he was the recipient of the Ontario Senior of the Year Award, another provincial recognition that honours one outstanding local Ontarian per community, who after the age of 65 has enriched the social, cultural, or civic life of their community.

MCPL. VINCENT CARBONNEAU, RIDEAU HALL/PHOTO

George Daniels (left) receives the Community Caring Award from Governor General David Johnston.

A valued member of the Lake of Bays community for almost 50 years, he has volunteered with the Lake of Bays Association for 25 years serving two years as its president and was responsible for LOBA's year book being a high quality publication, as well as being co-founder of the Lake of Bays Heritage Foundation. He was instrumental in raising $250,000 to purchase a new fire boat for the Lake of Bays Fire department so that they can respond to inaccessible shoreline fires and do search and rescues on the lake. He is also an active member of St. Johns and St James Anglican parishes at Port Cunnington and Fox Point where he developed a fundraising program for the two parishes.

As a former bush pilot and a member of the Canadian Owners and Pilots Association since 1957, George has donated countless hours of flying time to those in the community that need his help to raise funds through silent auctions and donation-based fundraising.

Although he cares deeply and puts his heart and soul into everything he does, his real passion lays with the Andrew Daniels Fish Foundation. In memory of his late son Andrew, who absolutely loved being on the Lake of Bays, he founded the organization to increase awareness and to help protect fish habitat regeneration and the Lake of Bays Aquatic system. George has worked tirelessly and put forward a lot of time and energy to raise funds to support this foundation.

It has only been a couple weeks since he received word that the Andrew Daniels Fish Foundation has acquired their charitable status, so now any donations towards the foundation will receive an income tax receipt.

George and his wife Ruth came to the lake approximately 50 years ago and now call their place on Lake of Bays their "spiritual home."

The couple has worked hard over the years and live by the words -- "building a dream, putting down roots."

At the age of 80, George hasn't lost his touch on how to motivate people and make things happen. Daniels has made a huge difference in the Lake of Bays area and if there was ever a Canadian who was deserving of Governor General's Caring Canadian Award it would be George Daniels.

-With files from What's Up Muskoka

George Daniels receives the Caring Canadian award from Governor General of Canada His Excellency the Right Honourable David Johnston

June 1992

George E. Daniels
Executive Broadcast Seminar 1971.

The Georgian College of Applied Arts and Technology

One Georgian Drive, Barrie, Ontario

(705) 728-1951 L4M 3X9

Eleanor E. Ley
Chair, Board of Governors

BOARD OF GOVERNORS' AWARD

Presented to
George E. Daniels

Friday, June 12, 1992
10:30 A.M.
Barrie Campus

The Board has created an award for presentation to individuals outside the College who have made a special or noteworthy contribution to education or to the College.

On behalf of the Board of Governors, faculty, staff and students, it gives me great pleasure to present this "Board of Governors' Award" to George E. Daniels, Executive Vice President and Senior Partner of Marketing Plus Inc.

George Daniels' contribution to education at Georgian has spanned the eighteen years that he has served as a member of the Advertising Advisory Committee. This, in itself, deserves recognition, but it is the way in which George has served that prompts this award.

George has been the driving force behind this Committee, since its inception. Serving as Chairperson for many of those years, he has made sure that the Committee consists of members who best represent the many facets of advertising today.

George, through the years, has witnessed many changes in the Advertising Program at Georgian. His energetic leadership has made sure that the Committee has lobbied, both within and outside the School, to keep the advertising program technologically relevant. Most recently, George successfully lobbied for the program to get access to the new "Mac Lab".

George's commitment to education goes beyond his committee work. In his position as Executive Vice-President and Senior Partner of Marketing Plus Inc., an Advertising Agency located in Toronto, George has arranged work experience and co-operative placements for many of our students at his company.

Congratulations George!

Eleanor E. Ley

EEL/dls

Captn.
Brian Hope presents the annual Presidents Award to George

June 18, 2014 www.whatsupmuskoka.com

Province honours Lake of Bays volunteer

By Chris Occhiuzzi

George Daniels may be one of the Ontario Senior of the Year Award recipients but he knows it was the efforts of many which helped him garner this honour.

The 79-year-old from Lake of Bays has been an active member of the community for over 40 years, putting his beliefs into action for a variety of causes.

From volunteering with the Lake of Bays Association for 25 years and even serving two years as its president, to co-founding the Lake of Bays Heritage Foundation, Daniels has long been a valued individual in the township.

Over a number of years Daniels was among those who helped raise the $250,000 necessary to purchase a fireboat for the Lake of Bays volunteer firefighters. He has also put forth tremendous time and effort to raise funds for the Andrew Daniels Fish Foundation, an organization in memory of his son.

The foundation's mandate is to help protect fish habitat regeneration and the Lake of Bays aquatic system including, but not limited to, water quality and shoreline stabilization.

In 2013, $5,500 was directed from the Andrew Daniels Fish Foundation to fish habitat rejuvenation required by a Ten Mile Creek washout.

A humble man, Daniels is more apt to give credit to others and says this award is a result of the collective rather than the individual.

"I'm very proud and honoured," says Daniels. "I have been among many of people in the community who have helped to generate funds which have all gone back into the community. It took a lot of people to generate the funds. Both seasonal and permanent residents have helped make it happen. This award is just icing on the cake."

At a ceremony in the Lake of Bays council chambers on June 17, Daniels was presented the Ontario Senior of the Year Award. The annual award falls under the provincial Ministry of Citizenship and Immigration and the certificates are presented to the recipients by their municipality at a local event during the month of June, which is Seniors' Month.

According to the Ministry, the Ontario Senior of the Year Award gives each municipality in the province the opportunity to honour one outstanding local Ontarian who after the age of 65 has enriched the social, cultural or civic life of his or her community.

Daniels' activities in Lake of Bays span pretty much all the criteria necessary for being named a recipient of this award. He and wife Ruth are active members of the Anglican Church and Daniels has served for 10 years as commodore of the Anglican Mission's annual fundraising regatta.

Last winter, Daniels' began the first ever local ice fishing survey to provide government marine biologists with previously unknown information about the type and size of fish caught during Lake of Bays winter conditions.

Still a licensed pilot and a member of the Canadian

George Daniels has been with many organizations in Lake of Bays, and now he's being honoured by the province.

Owners and Pilots Association since 1957, Daniels flies conventional and float aircraft. He has used his own plane to fly a marine biologist over Lake of Bays to get a different view of the territory as part of the Take Care of Your Lake program.

Daniels also donates flying time to support Lake of Bays fundraising causes and he says the flights are quite popular at silent auctions.

But what he's most proud of is being able to give back to an area and a community he loves.

"I'm very honoured and flattered by the whole situation," says Daniels. "I really think it's a recognition of all the people and organizations that I've been associated with over the years. It's a confirmation that you get out of life what you put in, and I'm a firm believer of that."

Queen Elizabeth II
Diamond Jubilee Medal

Médaille du jubilé de
de la reine Elizabeth II

George Daniels

By Command of Her Majesty The Queen,
the Diamond Jubilee Medal is presented to you
in commemoration of the sixtieth anniversary
of Her Majesty's Accession to the Throne
and in recognition of your contributions to Canada.

Par ordre de Sa Majesté la Reine,
la Médaille du jubilé de diamant vous est présentée
en commémoration du soixantième anniversaire
de l'accession de Sa Majesté au Trône et en reconnaissance
de votre contribution au service du Canada.

Governor General of Canada — *Gouverneur général du Canada*

1952 - 2012

THE GOVERNOR GENERAL · LE GOUVERNEUR GÉNÉRAL

Dear Mr. Daniels:

On April 12, 2016, the Governor General's Caring Canadian Award was replaced by the Sovereign's Medal for Volunteers. This change represents an elevation of the recognition into the Canadian Honours System while carrying on with the same values and legacy of this established honour.

As a recipient of the Caring Canadian Award, it is my pleasure to award you the Sovereign's Medal for Volunteers to complement your existing award.

Throughout my visits across Canada, I have had the pleasure of meeting individuals like yourself, who care about the well-being of others and who share a desire to make our communities kinder and healthier places in which to live. It is my hope that in receiving this Medal, it will encourage you to continue your good work and affirm your commitment to giving.

Thank you for helping make Canada smarter and more caring.

Warmest regards,

David Johnston

Mr. George E. Daniels
Dwight, Ontario

25 YEARS
THE CANADIAN
HERALDIC AUTHORITY

25 ANS
L'AUTORITÉ HÉRALDIQUE
DU CANADA

1 PROMENADE SUSSEX DRIVE OTTAWA · CANADA · K1A 0A1 · WWW.GG.CA

Federal Aviation Administration

NOMINATION. FAA Wright Brothers Master Pilot Award .. Recognizes pilots who have conducted 50 or more consecutive years of safe flight operations.

Letters of recommendation from; 2015

EAA, Naples Air Centre (Fl.) The Pilot Shop (Fl)

Dear Sirs:

RE: George E. Daniels Wright Brothers Master Pilot Award
FAA US Private # 349600
Based on CDN CPL CA22467

I have known George Daniels for twelve years and highly recommend him for the Wright Brothers Master Pilot Award. I have known him to always operate aircraft in a safe and professional manner.

Respectfully submitted,

Zachary Baughman
EAA AirVenture Museum

This memorandum is to inform you that I will not be able to award you the Wright Brothers Master Pilot Award. I find that one of the requirements is to be a US Citizen.

Barry G. Byrd Sr
FAASTeam Program Manager
Avionics/Airworthiness

CANADIAN OWNERS AND PILOTS ASSOCIATION

AIR CREW

Member # 232379
Year Joined 1956
Expires 30 APR 13
2019

GEORGE E. DANIELS
47 FOURTH ST E
COLLINGWOOD ON
CANADA L9Y 1T2

Tencennial 2004 - 2014

Is Pleased to Recognize

George E. Daniels

COPA #: 233379

For His Vision and Foresight

as a

Founding/Charter Member

of

COPA Flight 85

Collingwood's Community Chapter

Flying Youth for Tomorrow

at CNY3 Collingwood's Regional Airport

2013 Muskoka Awards
Natural Environment
George E. Daniels
Trophy Sponsor: Lake of Bays Brewing Company

PART XIV

Acknowledgements and Appendices

Part XIV

Acknowledgements And Appendices

I would like to thank friends and various organizations such as the Ad & Sales Clubs, Scouts Canada, Industry Associations, EAA and the Canadian Owners & Pilots Association, Governor General David Johnstone, and my family who all contributed in putting this book together. Some notables are:

Glenys Stow, who helped me get started several years ago with her "Saving your life and writing your story" workshop.

Larry Schachter, my Signature Advertising partner, for his unique collaboration and management of our creative business.

My editor, life-long partner and wife Ruth, who scrutinized the manuscript, with adjustments for best authorship.

Paul Dulmage, long-time friend and editor, to whom I am indebted for making this book better.

Craig Thornton, Apple Mac specialist, who was always available for copywriting, format and illustration display on my MacBook Pro. Paris Bosstock and Andrew Heidmann of the Collingwood Copy Centre for desktop digital assembly of the manuscript.

My UK cousins Norman and June Daniels, Toni and Harold Batcheldor, Canon Paul Nener, Ms Lindsay Gibson for genealogical research.

Richard & Jeanette Moody, President of Standard Broadcast Sales, who championed my nominations for the Governor General's volunteer Sovereign Medal and Ontario Senior of the Year award, presented to me by Governor General David Johnstone at Rideau Hall in 2016.

Ben Boivin, Muskoka District Councillor, who steered my Queen's Diamond Jubilee citation, presented to me by Tony Clement (MP Muskoka-Parry Sound) in 2012 at the Algonquin Theatre Huntsville Awards Ceremony.

Zack Beaumister, curator of the EAA Oshkosh Wisconsin Aviation Museum, who has me featured in their Timeless Voices of Aviation memorable gallery that is also linked to the USA Library of Congress.

Bruce Gowan CA, (now Magellan Aerospace Director) and fellow comptroller when I worked in automotive manufacturing at Galtaco Transit Seating and Ductile Iron Castings, for his verification of Part 1X.

Lieutenant General Richard Rohmer, OC, DFC, QC, a fellow broadcast executive from CFRB days and aviation author, for his encouragement on this project.

My sister Fay for a Muskoka nomination award and my brother Bill for filling in the blanks.

There are many more and to all, I am deeply grateful.

SPECIAL FEATURE

HIDDEN HABITAT

Few people understand what goes on under the surface of the water in Muskoka better than George Daniels. In 2004, George established the Andrew Daniels Fish Stewardship Foundation in memory of his son. The organization's goal is to help protect fish habitat and fish regeneration in Lake of Bays and the entire Muskoka aquatic system.

"Fish are really the canaries in the coal mine," says Daniels. "If you have no fish, that means you don't have quality lakes."

Daniels says the most common guests found around Muskoka's docks are bass and other fish that enjoy warm water. Cold-water fish, like trout, typically stick to the deeper water for the majority of the year.

Fish are drawn to docks in Muskoka because of the type of structure, says Daniels, but they also sometimes come because of what they're made of.

"Acid rain was a massive problem here in Muskoka during the 1980s," he says. "There was a big push on to use limestone in crib beds to counteract the acidity."

The limestone was great for the lakes, but not always ideal for the docks – in the acidic waters, it began to break down quickly, prompting many builders to switch to using granite or other more durable stone. However, it did have a secondary effect of increasing the nutrients available for both fish and plants.

Having a dock that promotes the fish population isn't just good for the lake: it can also have an effect on your bottom line, says Daniels.

"I've talked to a lot of real estate agents and the one question they always get asked is: 'are there fish near my property?" he says. "It might seem like an inconsequential question, but everything is interrelated. A thriving fish population at the end of your dock increases the value of your property."

Daniels points out that docks are also an ideal place to introduce young anglers to their first fishing experience. It's a much safer and easier way to try out fishing than getting into a boat, he says, and it can help spark a lifelong interest in conservation and aquatic health.

As FOCA's Terry Rees puts it, the Muskoka lakes and forests that have drawn people to the region for more than century are the same environments that provide a crucial habitat for a multitude of different species.

"We need to find ways to learn to enjoy wildlife without harming it or creating unnecessary tensions," he says. "We're at the lake to enjoy nature and to do our best to ensure our time there doesn't cause negative impacts to the very things that we treasure so much. Instead of working against wildlife, why not weave their needs with our own needs?" L

HABITAT PROTECTOR
George Daniels leads the Andrew Daniels Fish Stewardship Foundation, an organization dedicated to enhancing fish habitat in Lake of Bays and throughout Muskoka.

Muskoka Moments

Family and community - Lake of Bays blessings

By George Daniels

The lure of Muskoka's Lake of Bays was fueled by my McMaster University buddy Bob McCullagh in 1955. He drove with me in an old ragtop Jeep to meet Percy Cunnington who had sold him a large stretch of shoreline near Dwight.

Bob bought a do-it-yourself cabin kit and then cajoled his school chums to help him build it.

Our pay? A few cases of beer, swimming, fishing and sunburns. Further fun was available at the Bigwin Inn bar.

The following summer of 1956, I flew to Muskoka. Owen Boris and I rented a two-seat Piper PA11 on floats and our plan was travel to some well-known Muskoka lodges. One guy would fly the aircraft, the other would drive the car and we'd rendezvous, often at Milford Manor. This lodge was a roaring party scene and we junior aviators charged resort guests $3.00 for a 15-minute Muskoka flight.

I then partnered with Bob McCullagh and bought Muskoka Air Trails, Charters and Flight School on Lake Vernon. With an aircraft strapped to my behind, I had the luxury of experiencing the majesty of many corners of Muskoka from the air.

Limberlost Lodge on Lake Solitaire had a modest ski hill. This is where I met Ruth, my wife-to-be . . . truly a monumental Muskoka Moment. We were married in 1961 and returned to Lake of Bays in 1965. Engaging with the north Lake of Bays community was the foundation for many friendships.

Our first boat was a mahogany Shepherd but after one expensive season, we sold it. A series of cedar runabouts gave way to our easier-to-handle aluminum fishing boats.

Meeting Dr. Royal Montgomery, our neighbour, was propitious. Doc was a director of Lake of Bays Association. His father had bought Montgomery Point in 1919 and in February 1968, he invited me to stay at Port Cunnington Lodge to experience winter. We rented a snowmobile and skimmed across the frozen lake, checking out fish huts.

Photograph: Kelly Holinshead

George Daniels feels blessed by his unique Muskoka lifestyle.

A spectacular on-ice bonfire with hot dogs and beer introduced us to many locals who are friends to this day. Before heading back to New York, Doc said, "George, you are going to replace me as the director of the Lake of Bays Association."

I became actively involved with LOBA and was president from 1988-1990. With Robin Cummine's help, we founded the Lake of Bays Heritage Foundation in 1986. I am continually working with the Andrew Daniels Fish Stewardship Foundation, which is in memory of our son who died at 37 in 2004.

Regattas are the venue for the Muskoka community coming together. Our family would dive right in with paddles, swimming trunks, donations and bake sales at these events. With my public speaking skills, I have often been the commodore/announcer. Our boys, Andrew, Tiff and Chris competed at these events. Our cottage trophy wall is festooned with pins, metals and pictures of their trophies.

May 24 marks Sweat Equity Weekend, when we all pitch in to open cottages, take down shutters, launch boats and help each other. The camaraderie has no cost but it's priceless.

I was proud to be part of a volunteer fireboat fundraising group. Over a two-year period, we raised several hundred thousand dollars to purchase a new state-of-the-art Stanley fireboat. The fire department first responders do a super job with this equipment.

A cottage is not a building but rather a unique Muskoka lifestyle. It is our spiritual home. Surrounded by the majesty of nature on land and helping protect fish habitat and species at risk underwater, in streams and shorelines, we feel blessed. I feel a special bond in helping grow this significant world biodiversity site for future generations.

George and Ruth Daniels and family are residents at Montgomery Point, Lake of Bays. George is a recipient of the Sovereign Medal for Volunteers awarded by Governor General David Johnston in 2016, acknowledging his Muskoka leadership of LOBA and the Heritage and Andrew Daniels Fish Stewardship Foundations. His memoir, George Works, will be self-published this summer. Enquiries: e-mail geofoof2017@gmail.com

76 **UNIQUE MUSKOKA** July 2018

Links on YouTube to George E. Daniels videos.
Search: **George E. Daniels**

https://youtu.be/sb_OBqRHAcw

- Speech to Kiwanis Club PMA 1979
- Interview for Timeless Voices of Aviation video at EAA Oshkosh 2003
- Presentation to Muskoka Conservation Seminar 2012 re the Andrew Daniels Fish Foundation stewardship
- Presentation to the Collingwood Historical Society in 2016: Adventures of a Bush Pilot
- Presentation to Lake of Bays Heritage Foundation in 2014: Memories of The Early Years
- Interview on Cottage Life TV in 2000 as Regatta Commodore
- Video: Blitz on the North (historical documentary)
- Video: Eulogy delivered at funeral service for long-time friend and cable TV pioneer Boris Owen

CPSIA information can be obtained
at www.ICGtesting.com
Printed in the USA
LVHW022351300119
605857LV00002B/2

9 781525 537745